CLASSIC FLASH

IN 5 BOLD COLORS

Jeromey "Tilt" McCulloch

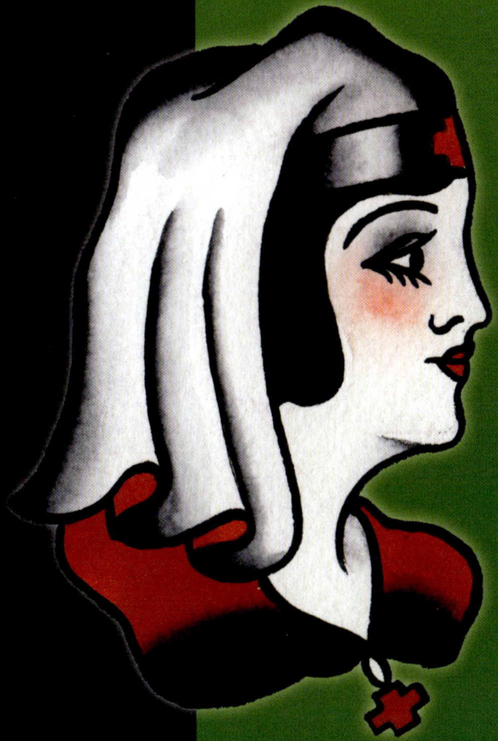

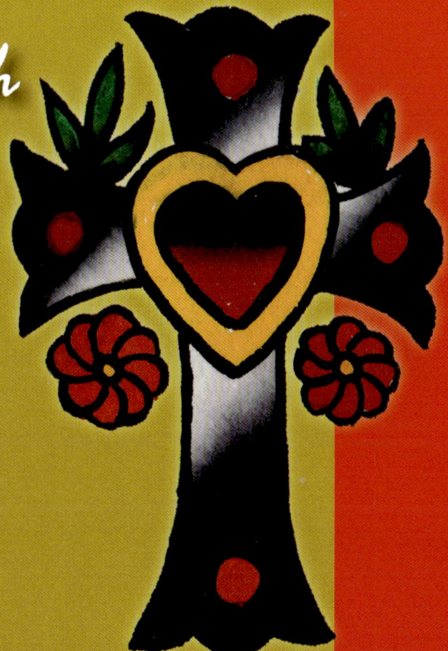

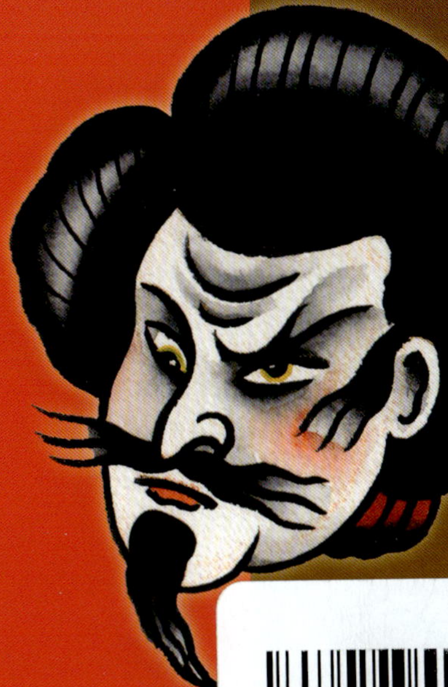

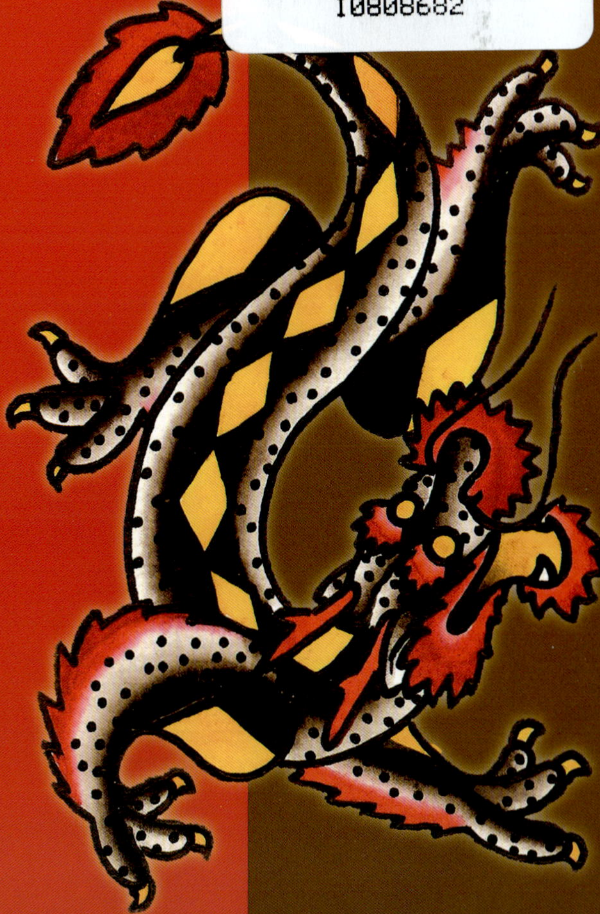

Schiffer Publishing Ltd
4880 Lower Valley Road Atglen, Pennsylvania 19310

MIX
Paper | Supporting responsible forestry
FSC® C104723

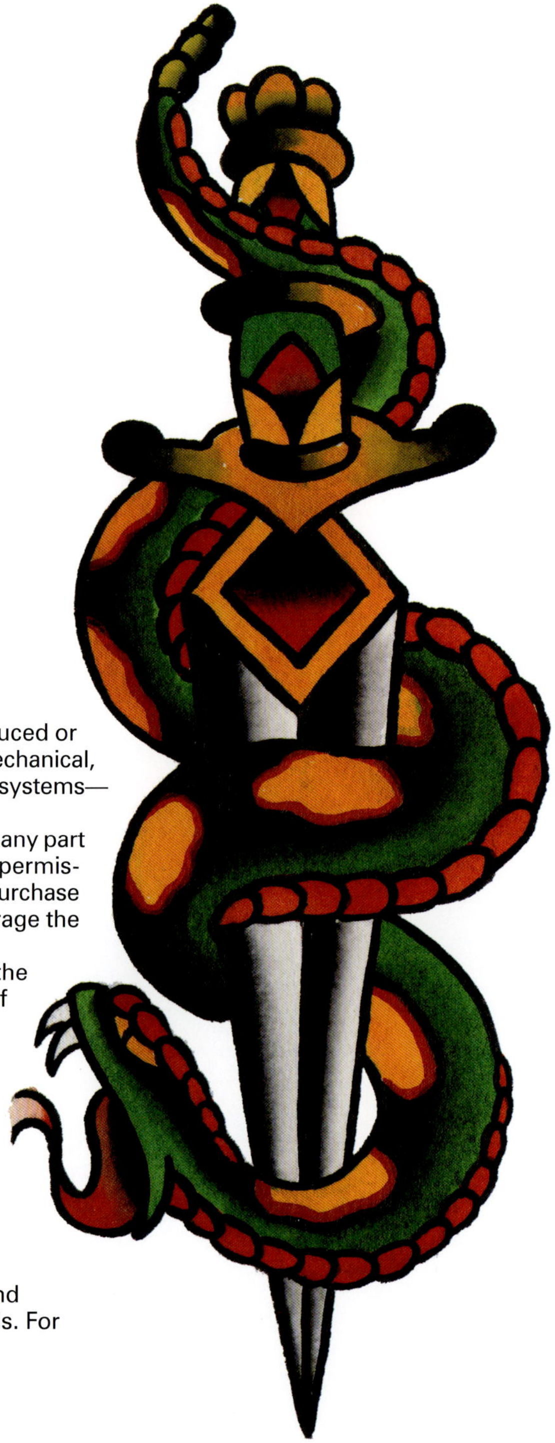

Library of Congress Control Number: 2008939042

Type set in Rage Italic/Zurich BT

ISBN: 978-0-7643-3165-7
Printed in China
8 7 6 5

Schiffer Books are available at special discounts for bulk purchases for sales promotions or premiums. Special editions, including personalized covers, corporate imprints, and excerpts can be created in large quantities for special needs. For more information contact the publisher:

Published by Schiffer Publishing Ltd.
4880 Lower Valley Road
Atglen, PA 19310
Phone: (610) 593-1777; Fax: (610) 593-2002
E-mail: Info@schifferbooks.com

For the largest selection of fine reference books on this and related subjects, please visit our web site at
www.schifferbooks.com
We are always looking for people to write books on new and related subjects. If you have an idea for a book please contact us at the above address.

This book may be purchased from the publisher.
Include $5.00 for shipping.
Please try your bookstore first.
You may write for a free catalog.

In Europe, Schiffer books are distributed by
Bushwood Books
6 Marksbury Ave.
Kew Gardens
Surrey TW9 4JF England
Phone: 44 (0) 20 8392-8585; Fax: 44 (0) 20 8392-9876
E-mail: info@bushwoodbooks.co.uk
Website: www.bushwoodbooks.co.uk
Free postage in the U.K., Europe; air mail at cost.

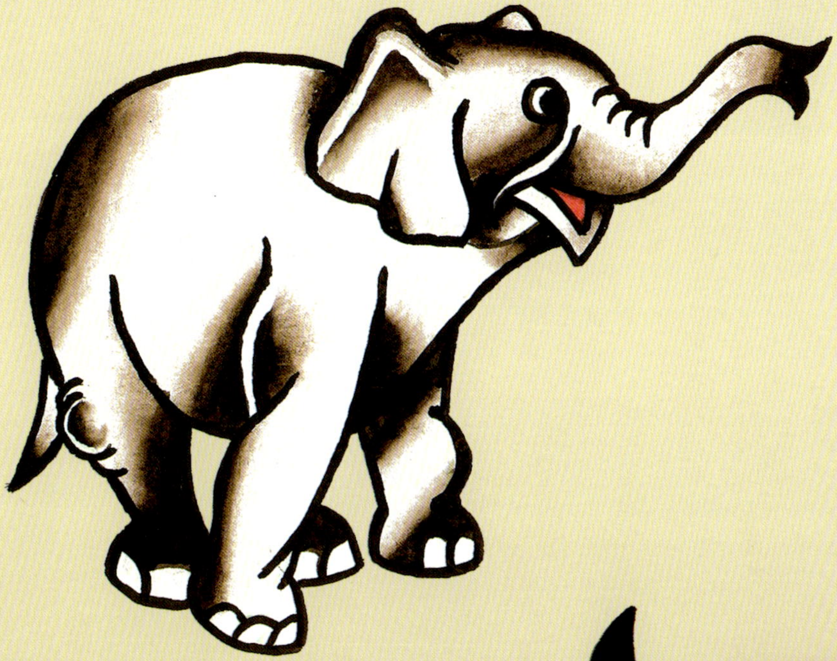

Contents

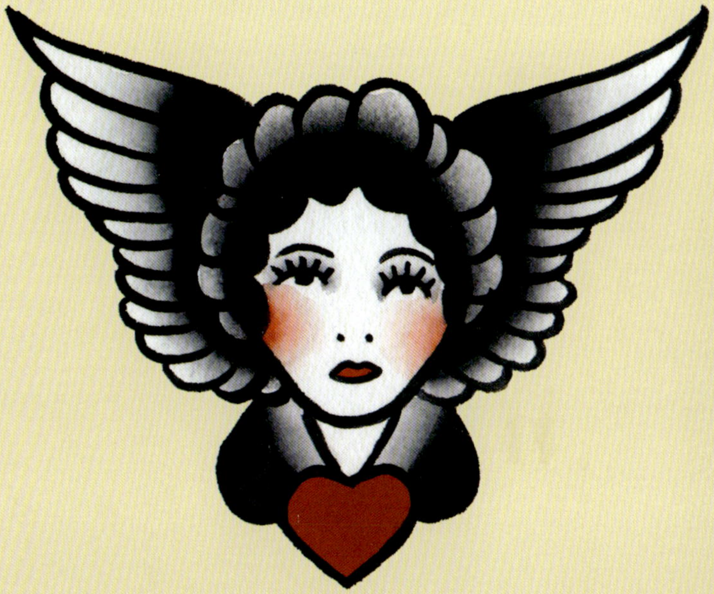

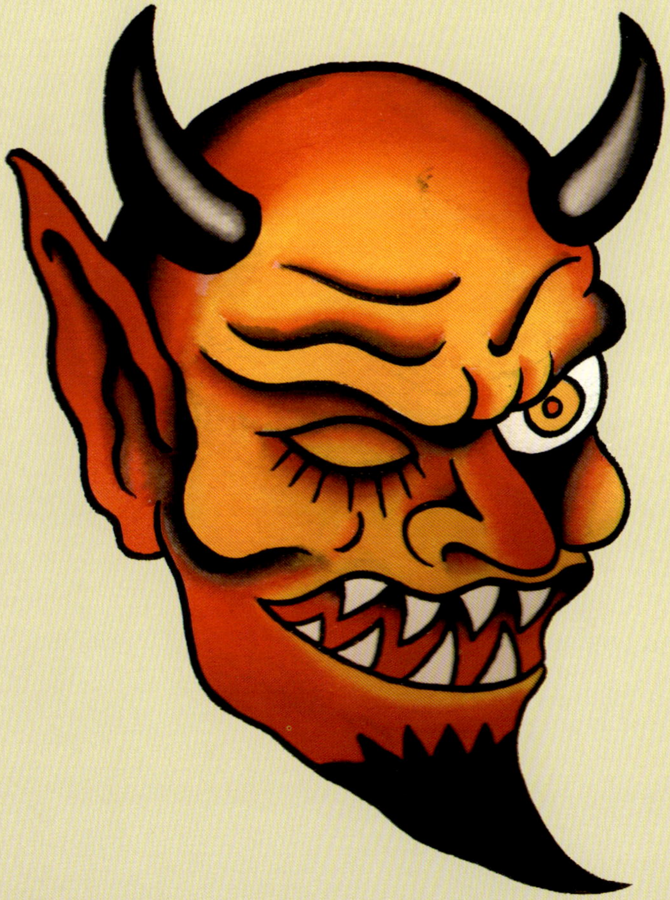

Forewords

I.

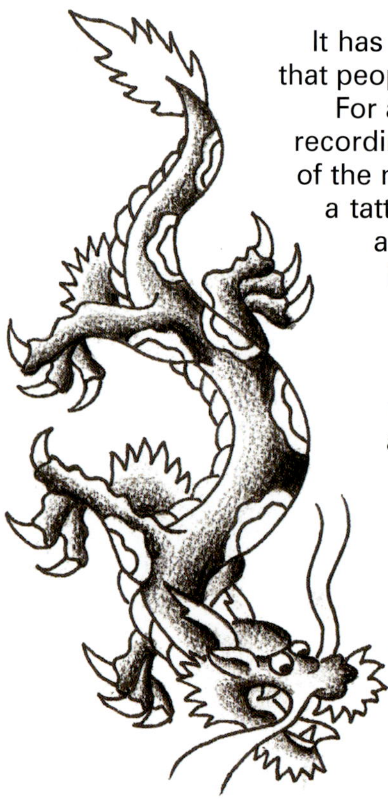

It has been said that people paint to build walls against their death; if that's true, then I say that people tattoo themselves as a reflection of their immortality.

For a professional in any field it is beneficial to know the history of one's chosen craft. The recording of tattoo history is a relatively new practice, but there is much to learn from it. One of the most fruitful ways of studying it is through the repainting of antique tattoo flash. When a tattooer endeavors to do this, not only does he revitalize the old images, adding personal touches or updating the imagery to fit the times, he also finds himself immersed in the established vocabulary of tattoo imagery. As he becomes more acquainted with the canon or library of ideas, it becomes easier to deviate from the standard archetypes while staying true to the foundations of the art, literally allowing them to become part of a living tradition.

Five Bold Colors is the culmination of a year-long study of traditional American tattoo flash. Over the past year I have been fortunate to witness and study alongside Jeromey "Tilt" McCulloch as he explored this great passion that so many of us share. Tilt has not only been a friend and a teacher, he has also been an inspiration, with an ever-present desire to move creatively into the future with a greater understanding of the past.

A.P. Shrewsbury
Champaign, Illinois
March 2008

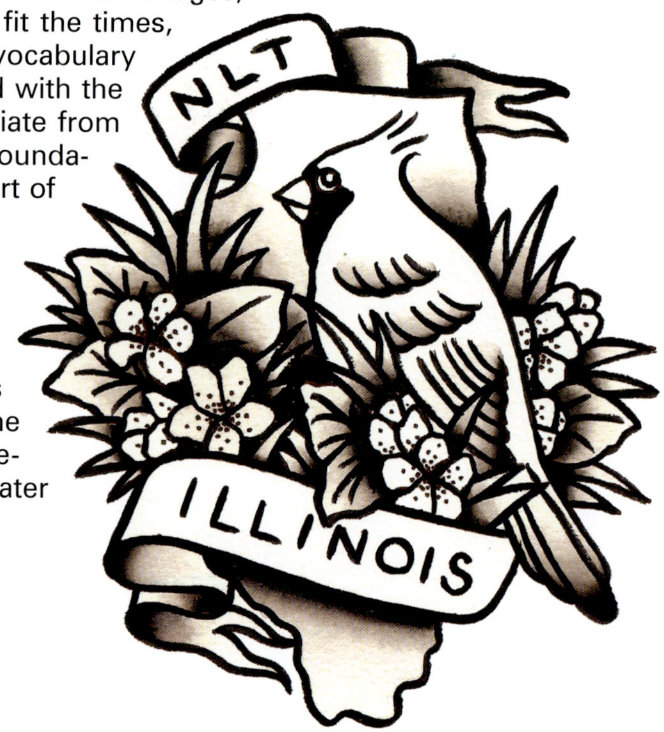

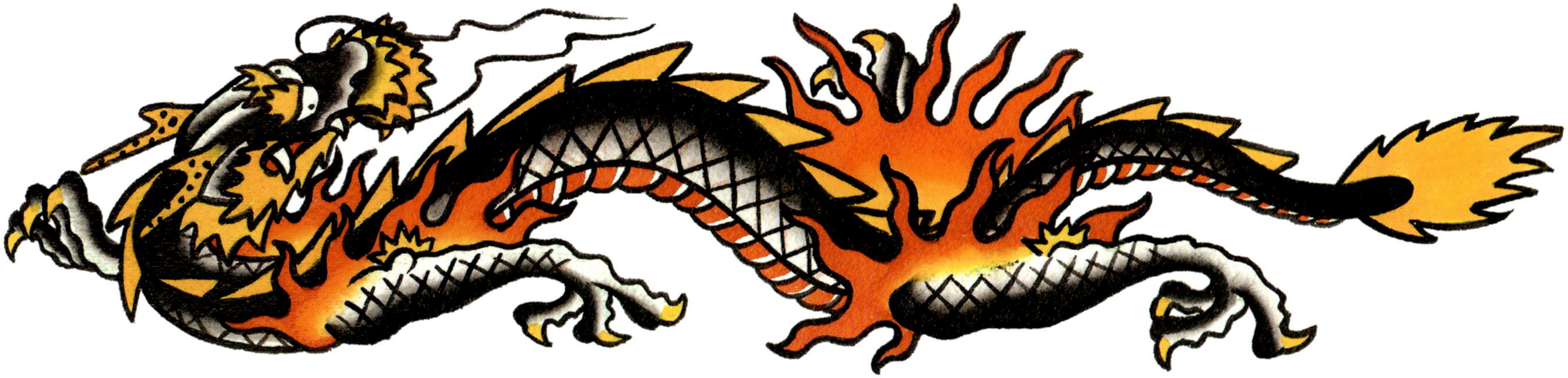

2.

Tilt is one of the most dedicated young artists I know. This book is a collection of a year's worth of work in pursuit of styles and subtleties of past tattooists, an effort to tap into the essence of past tattoo symbolism. During such a process, one is forced to slow down and dissect designs that appear to be similar on the surface, only to find unique shading and line quality as individual as the artists themselves.

Despite trying to duplicate these designs, Tilt's own style has emerged. Certain aspects of different artists appear in his present work and no doubt will be stored away to be developed in future designs. I think many new school artists dismiss the validity of reproducing old designs, ego replacing an appreciation for the past. It took years for me to appreciate the naive folk art style of the designs that I now embrace. As an artist, I've found that an image can be duplicated differently but not necessarily improved. Early tattoo designs have their own charm in their basic execution, as does most folk art. The art hasn't changed; however, some of society's aesthetics have developed enough to appreciate it. Tilt is a prolific artist preserving past designs and tattoo techniques for the future, as well as providing his services for those already enlightened to our past.

Dana Brunson, Tattooist

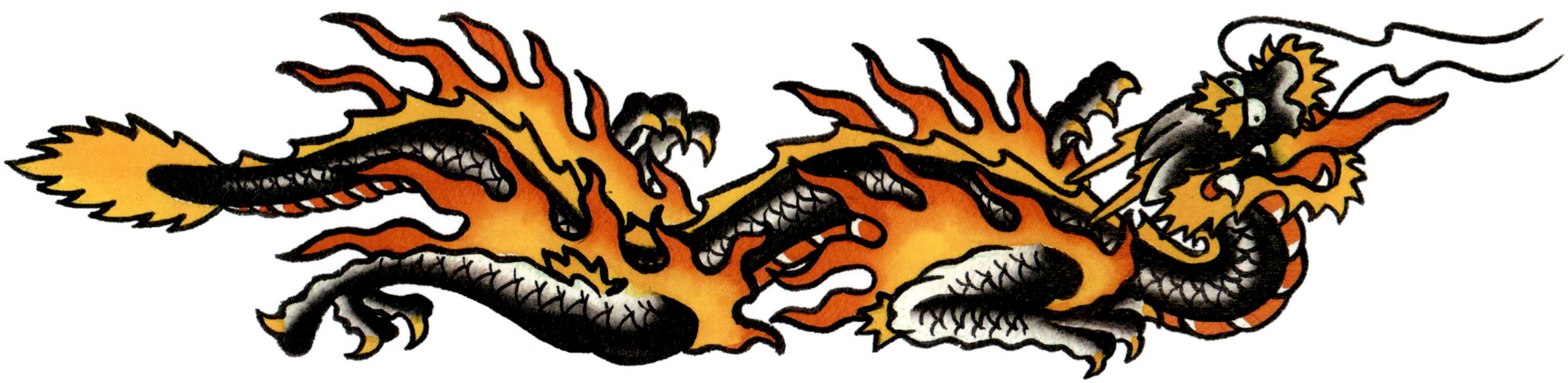

Introduction

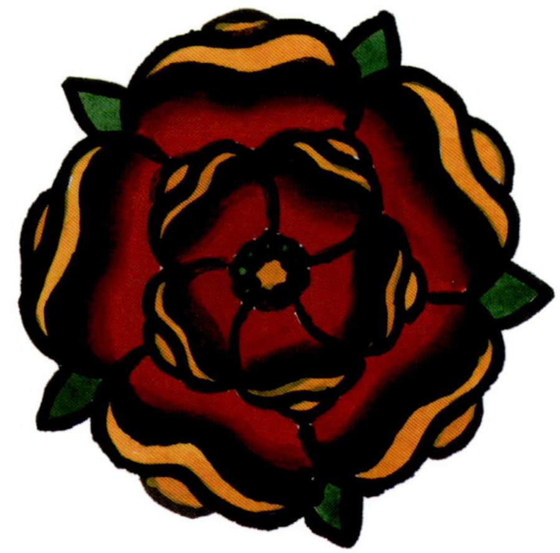

This book represents a year's worth of painting and studying. In 2006 I started looking at early American tattooing. Around the same time, I met a dedicated tattooer named Timmy Tatts. We sat together for hours, discussing designing traditional imagery. When asked about the key to traditional design he said, "You have to take your ego out of it."

Sometime after speaking with Timmy I came across the Don Ed Hardy interview of Dan Higgs. Dan's and Timmy's thoughts on traditional tattooing inspired me. At the end of 2006, I decided the only way to learn was to immerse myself into traditional design. I boxed up all my paint and pigment that was not black, red, yellow, green or brown. I thought working with the main colors of the era would teach me about the designs. I also tried not to create any new designs. Keeping the imagery alive was important to me.

This book is the result of that endeavor. Enjoy. I hope there is something you can take from this collection.

Jeromey "Tilt" McCulloch

Acknowledgments

Special thanks to Lebobski, Lunchbox, Matt, Adam, Joel, Timmy Tatts, Jeff Shea, Jason Kelly, Coopr, Stickler, Ben Cheése, Prof. Wizzo, Skunkshaw, Jef Wright, Minnie and the unknown legend Dana Brunson.

A special thanks also to Chuck Eldridge and The Tattoo Archive, www.tattooarchive.com.

Contributing Artists:

In the process of developing this book I had the opportunity to work with some talent tattoo artists. There contributions are noted in the captions.

A.P. Shrewsbury
Name Brand Tattoo
209 South State Street
Ann Arbor, MI 48014
Phone: 734-623-0553
www.apsrewsbury.com

Andrew Stickler
Odds N Ends Tattoo Studio
1349 South Alpine Road
Rockford, IL 61108
Phone: 815-229-7273
www.sticklertattoo.com

Cooper
Cow Pok Tattoo
177 Elmwood Avenue
Buffalo, NY 14201
Phone: 716-885-0252
www.cowpok.com

Ben Cheése
Faith Tattoo
608 Mendocino Avenue
Santa Rosa, CA 95401
Phone: 707-566-9955
www.faithtattoo.com

Jason Kelly
Ink and Dagger Tattoo Parlour
1036 West College Avenue
Decatur, GA 30030
Phone: 404-373-6655
www.jasonkellytattoo.com

Joel Molina
NewLife Tattoos
404 East Green Street
Champaign, IL 61820
Phone: 217-367-5320
www.myspace.com/joeljmolina

Jef Wright
Love Tattoo
7450 Union Avenue
Jenison, MI 49428
Phone: 616-457-5683
www.lovetattoo.net

Inspirations

Behind this book there is a long history and rich culture of tattoo. From its prehistoric roots to its present practitioners, there are thousands of artists, most of them unrecognized and uncelebrated, who have contributed to the world of tattoo. But there are a few who have shown above the others, at least in my life and work. And they have had a profound influence on the tattoos in this book.

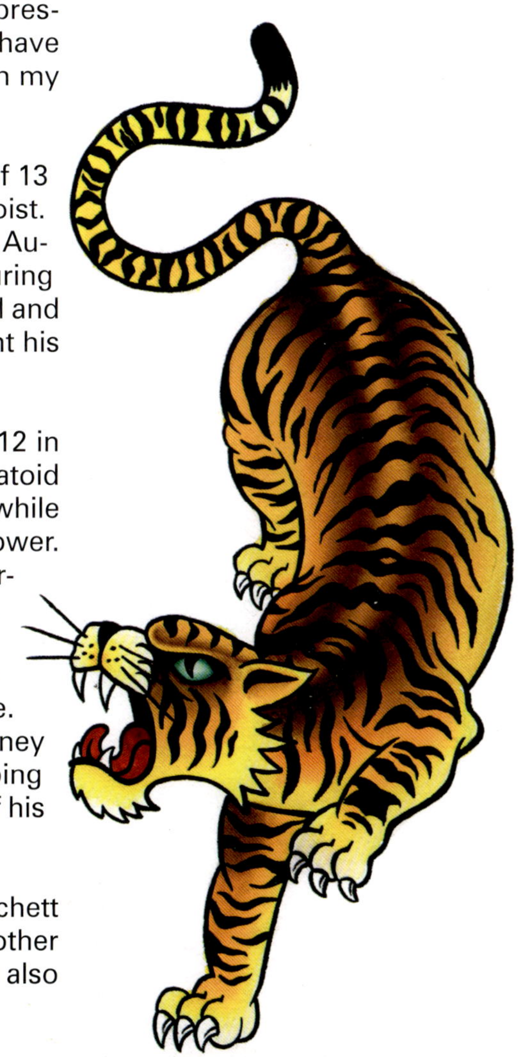

Paul Rogers was one of the most respected tattooers in the industry. Born in 1905, by the age of 13 he was working in the cottonmill. In 1932 he started working with the circus as an acrobat and tattooist. After the circus, he worked in Charleston and Spartanburg until he got the opportunity to work with August "Cap" Coleman in 1945. He stayed with Coleman until tattooing was made illegal in Norfolk. During his time with Coleman, Paul began building and tuning tattoo machines. When he left Coleman, Paul and Huck Spaulding started one of the most well respected supply companies in the industry. Paul spent his later life in Florida building machines and teaching those who would visit him. He died in 1990.

One of my favorite stories in tattooing is **Leonard "Stoney" St. Claire.** Stoney was born in 1912 in West Virginia. He was a sickly child. At a young age Stoney's tonsils burst and he contracted rheumatoid arthritis. At the age of four, Stoney could only partly move and open his hands. He learned to draw while spending time in the hospital. In 1927, the circus life called for Stoney to perform as a sword swallower. On a stop in Norfolk, Virginia, Stoney stopped into Cap Coleman's shop and his life was changed forever. Stoney thought he could draw a better eagle than Cap. He showed Cap one of his drawings, and Cap told him to give up sword swallowing to learn tattooing.But after only a couple of days learning from Cap, Stoney was back on the road with the circus. Coleman told him to practice on grapefruits in the mean time. A couple of months and several grapefruits later, Stoney began to tattoo people. Stoney continued traveling and tattooing with the circus for twenty years. Throughout his career, Stoney operated several shops in different towns. Like he did with life in general, Stoney approached tattooing with a sense of humor. As a designer, his work was simple, solid, and light-hearted. The last years of his life were spent in Ohio. Stoney died in 1980.

English born tattooer, **George Burchett**, live from 1872-1953. His given name was George Burchett Davis, but he dropped the Davis after going AWOL from the Royal Navy. George worked with his brother Charles Davis for a short time. George's designs were elegant and refined. His English heritage was also visible in his designs.

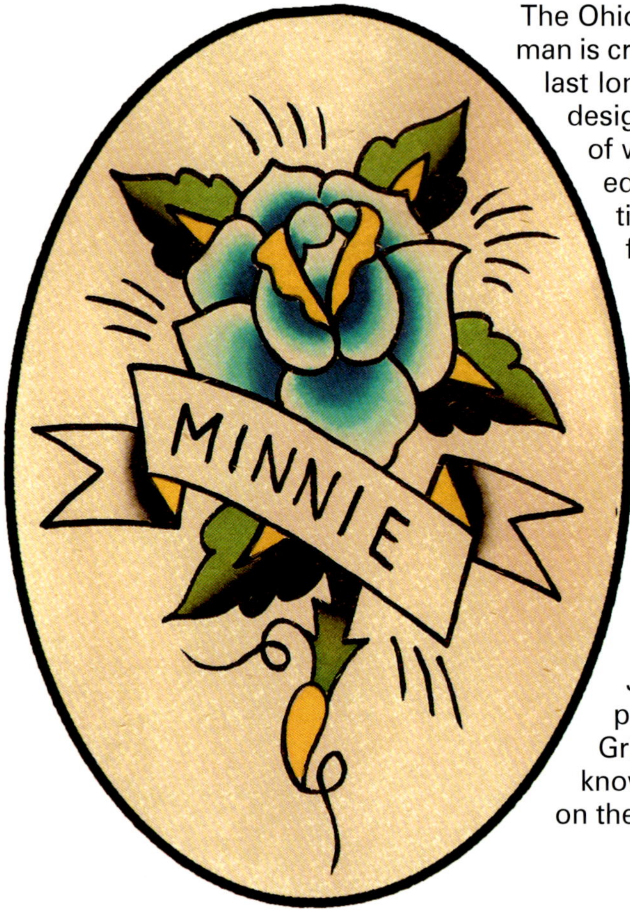

The Ohio-born **August "Cap" Coleman** was one of the industry's most influential characters. Coleman is credited to developing the "bold will hold" philosophy, which basically means that tattoos will last longer and look better based on the amount of black put into the design. He also simplified designs so when they aged, details would not be lost. Coleman is known as much for the quality of work he did as for his character. He was a hard working tattooer that had extensive knowledge about machines, tattooing, and painting. Before settling in Norfolk, Virginia, Cap spent time painting signs up and down the river via a homemade raft. Coleman worked in Norfolk from 1918-1950. August Coleman lived from 1884-1973.

Percy Waters was born in Alabama in 1888. He spent his early years as a foundry worker and was a tattoo enthusiast before he began tattooing. He spent time traveling and getting tattooed while working in the foundry. After he began tattooing himself, Percy was told to leave the area after tattooing the wrong person, so Percy moved to Detroit. He's known for having a supply business and for his tattoo machine patent in 1929. At one point, Percy sold blue prints of tattoo flash through his supply business. Percy advertised himself as "Just a Good Tattooer." Percy Waters died in 1952.

Owen Jensen was a traveling tattooer. Jensen saw his first tattooed man and got his first tattoo at the circus. Traveling was in his blood after that first encounter. He tattooed part-time while being enlisted in in the military during World War One. After the service, Jensen tattooed on the circus circuit. The list of towns he worked in is as long as the list of people he worked with. It included Jack Julian, Charlie Barr, Harry Lawson, "Cap" Coleman, Bert Grimm, Edwin Brown, and he was working with Lee Roy Minugh just before he died. Jensen is known for his simple and elegant painting style. He also owned the first quality supply business on the west coast. Owen Jensen lived from 1891-1976.

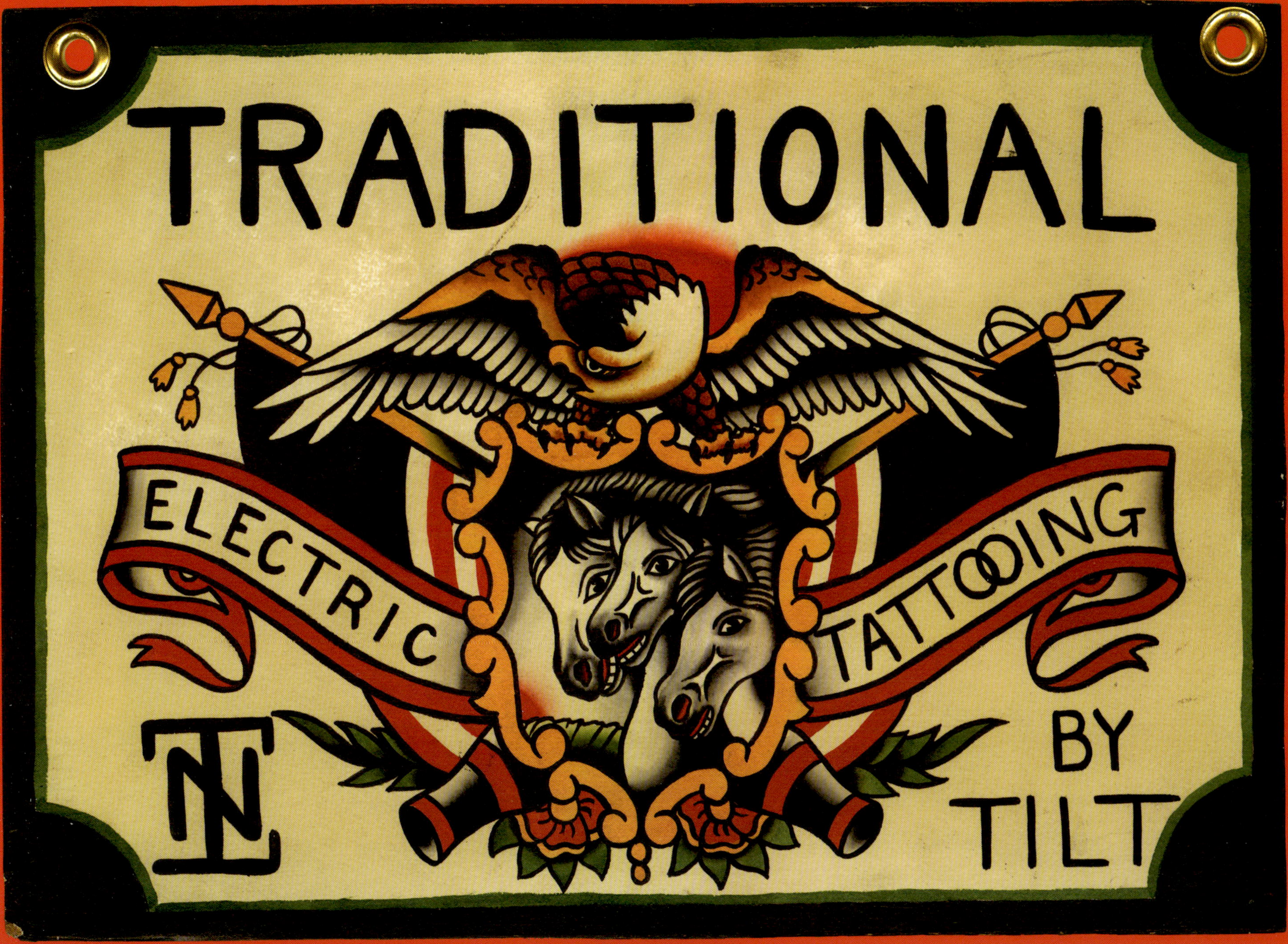
TRADITIONAL
ELECTRIC
TATTOOING
BY
TILT

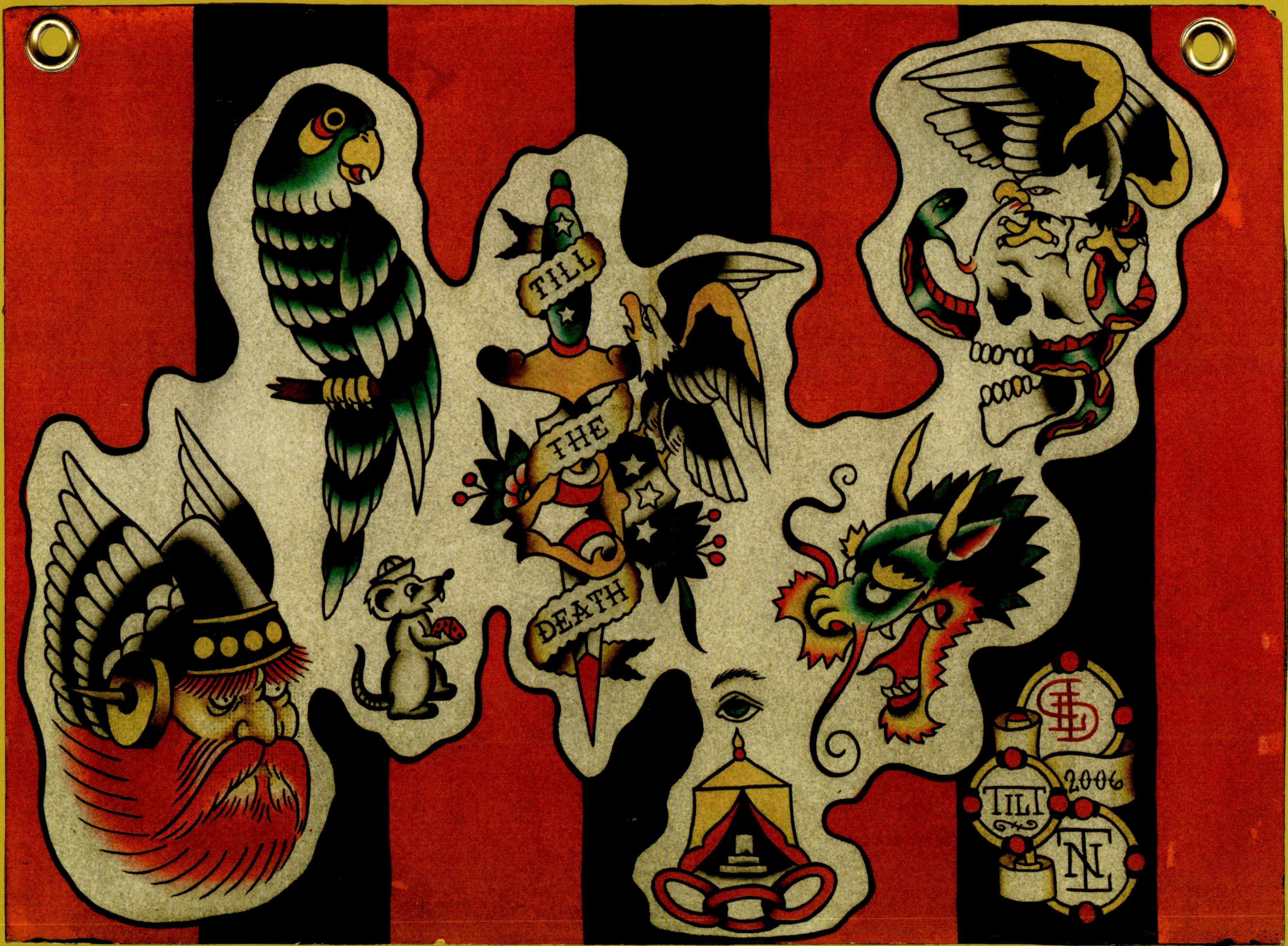
TILL
THE
DEATH
2006
TILL

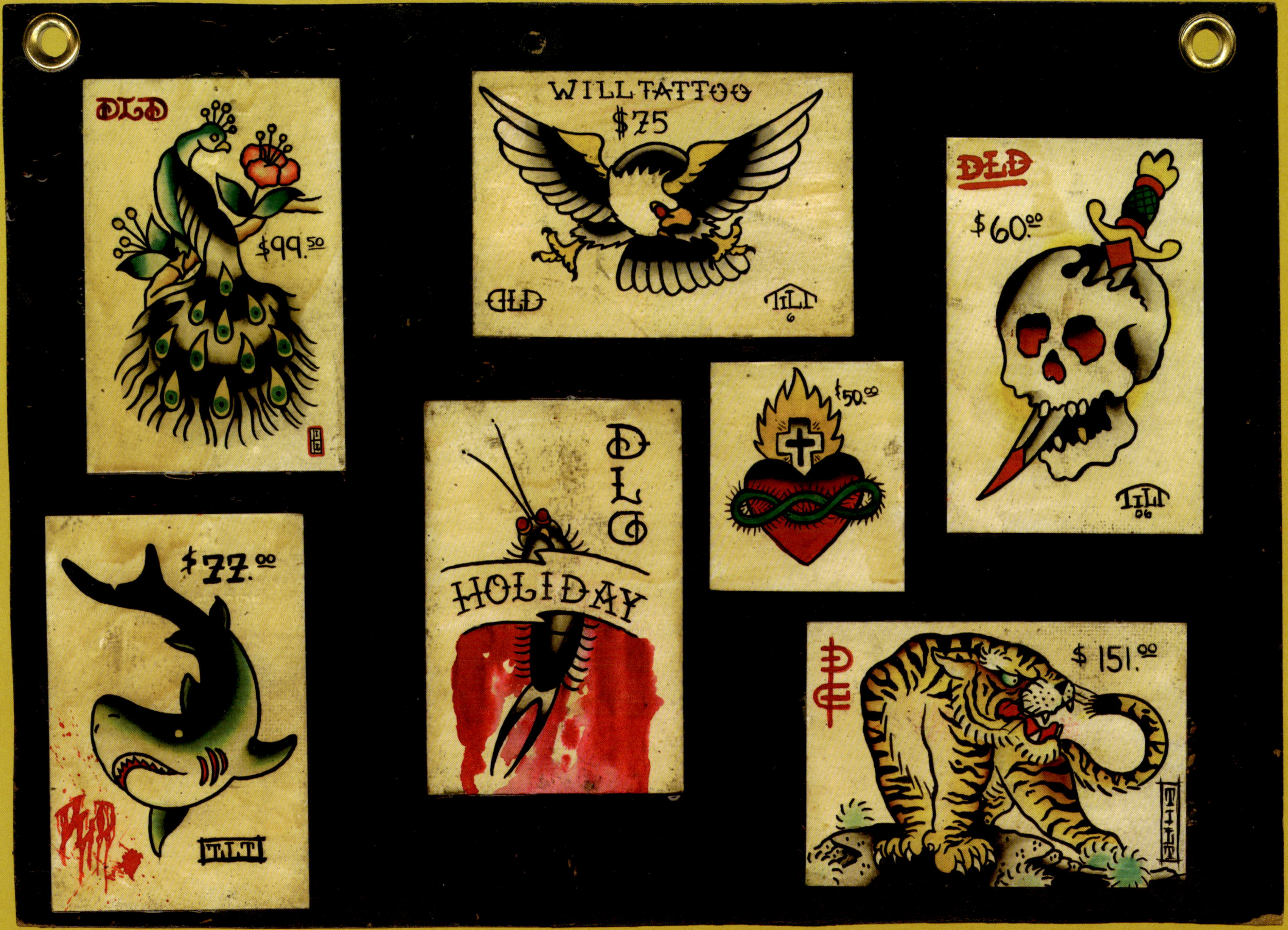
DLD
$99.50
WILL TATTOO
$75
DLD
$60.00
$50.00
$77.00
HOLIDAY
$151.00

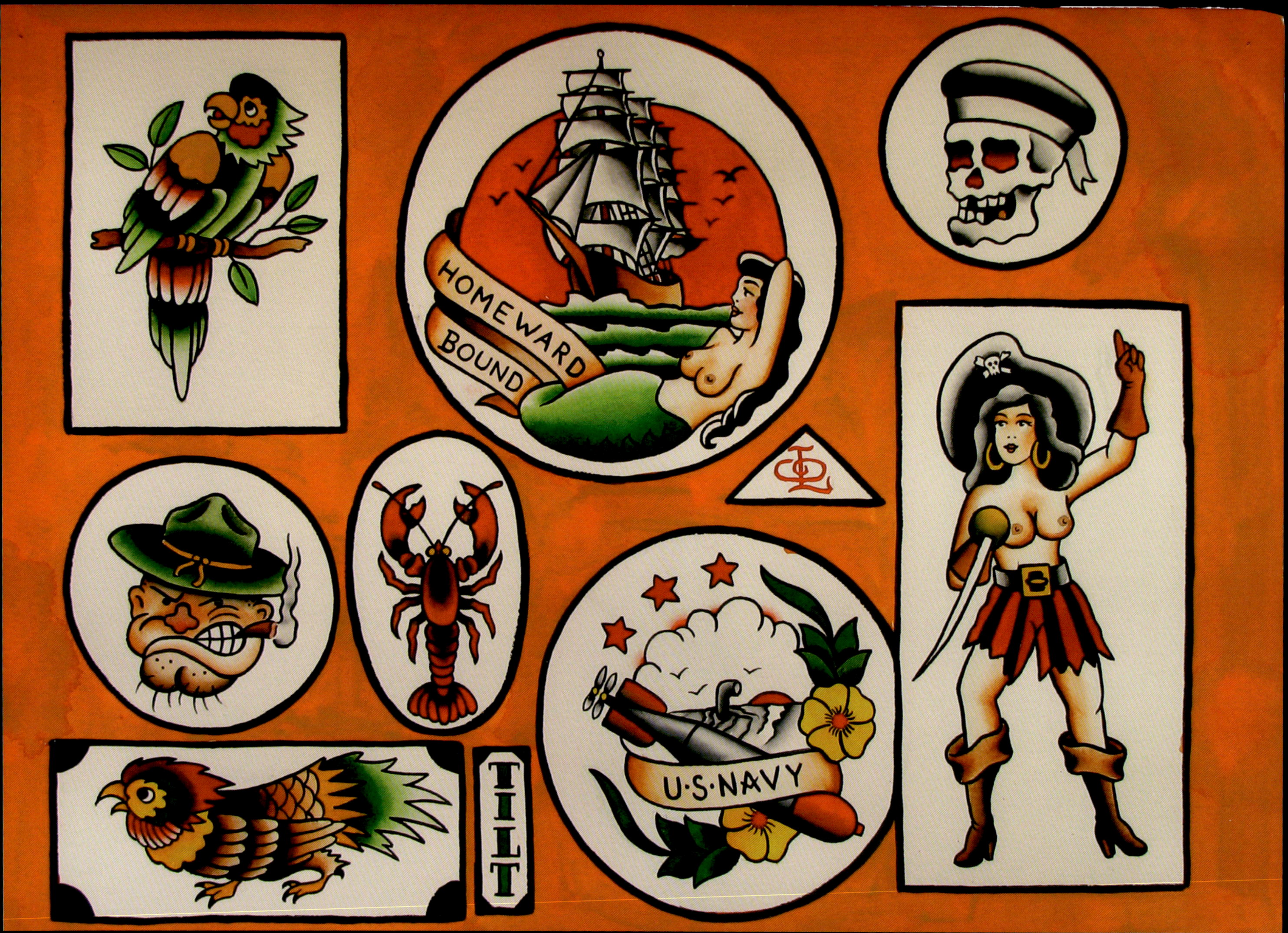
HOMEWARD
BOUND
U·S·NAVY
TILT

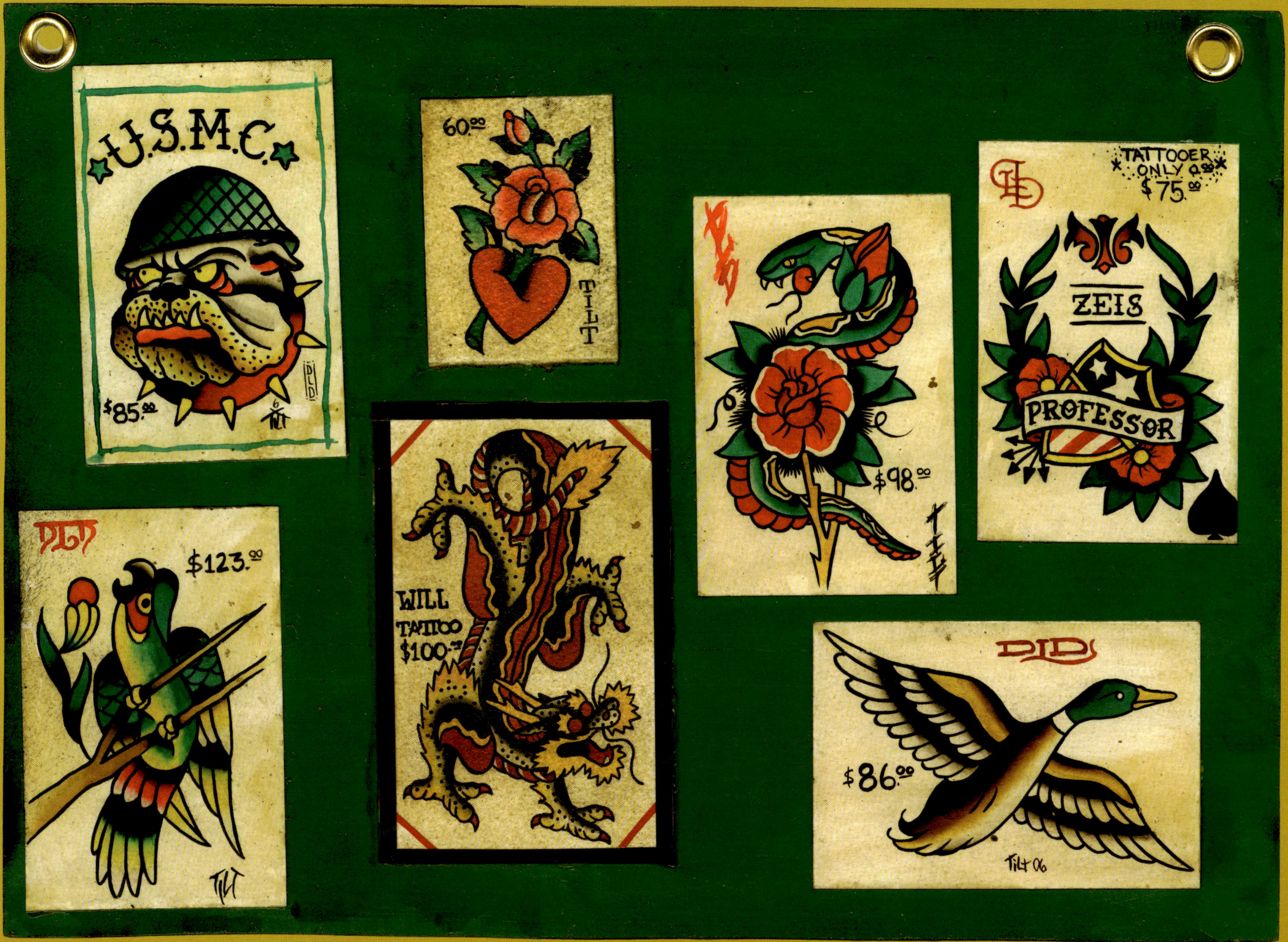

U.S.M.C.
$85.00
60.00
TILT
TATTOOER
ONLY
$75.00
ZEIS
PROFESSOR
$98.00
$123.00
WILL
TATTOO
$100.00
$86.00
TILT 06

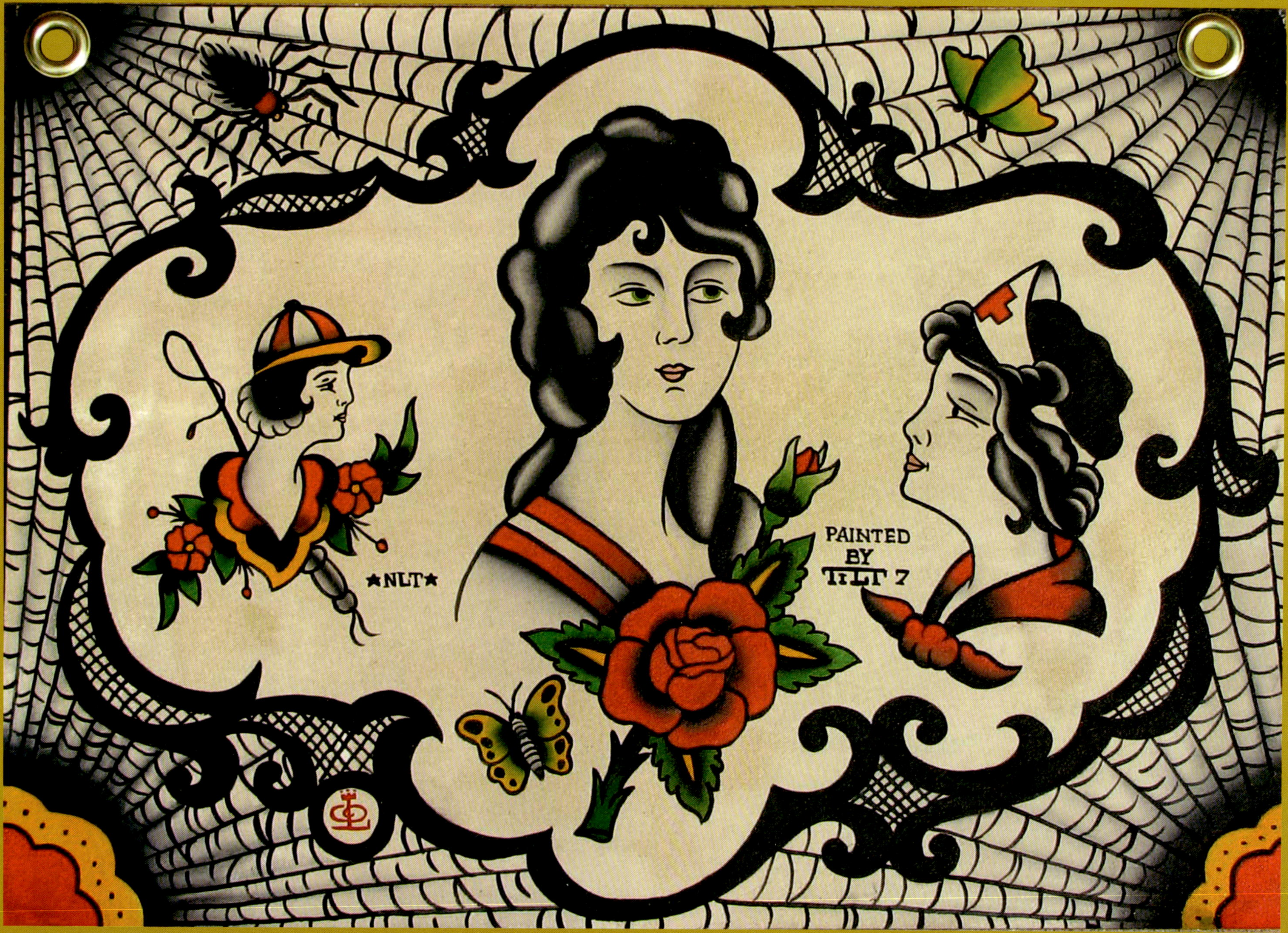
★NLT★
PAINTED
BY
TiLT 7

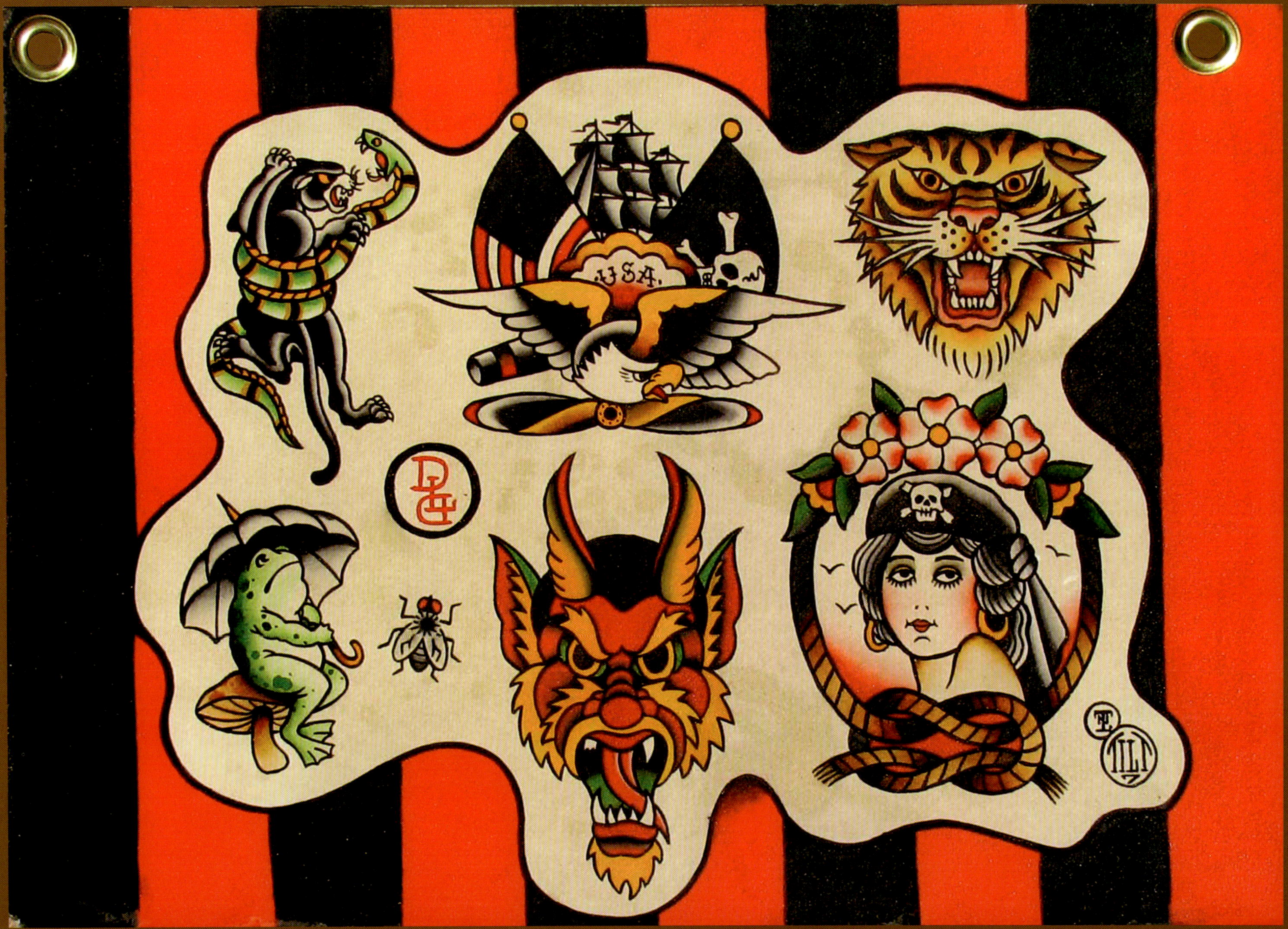
USA

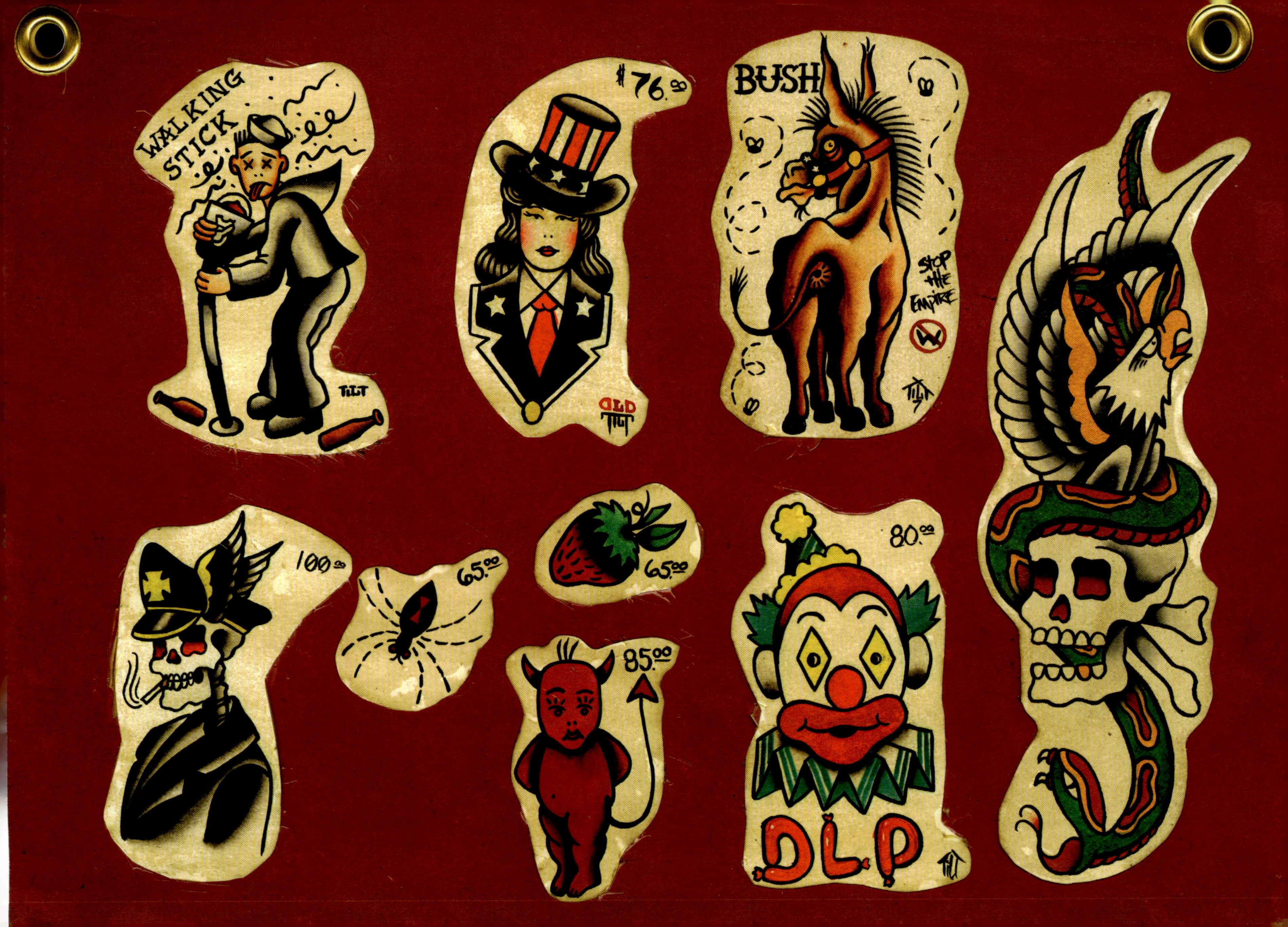

WALKING STICK
TILT
$76.00
OLD
TILT
BUSH
STOP the EMPIRE
TILT
100.00
65.00
65.00
85.00
80.00
DLP
TILT

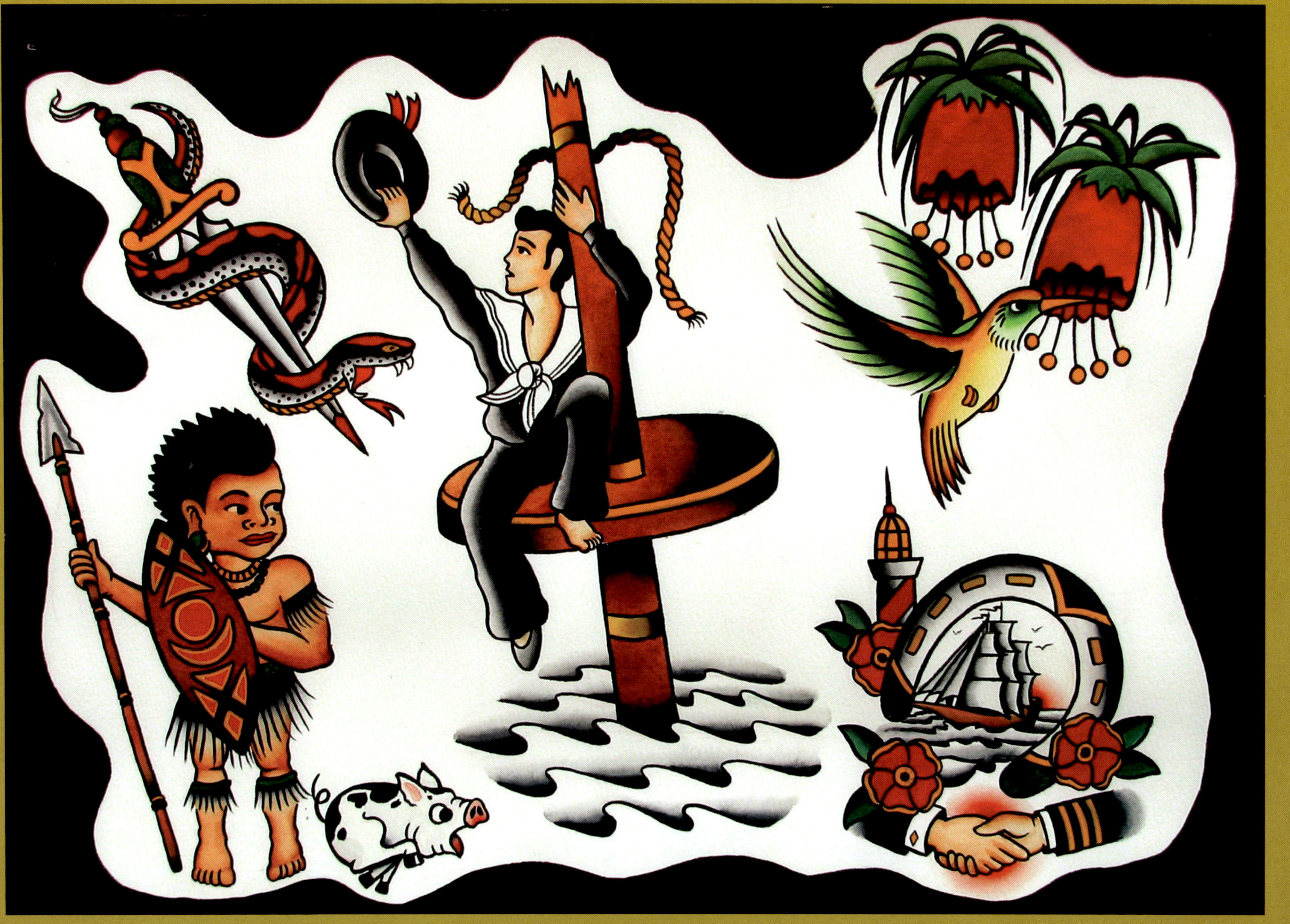

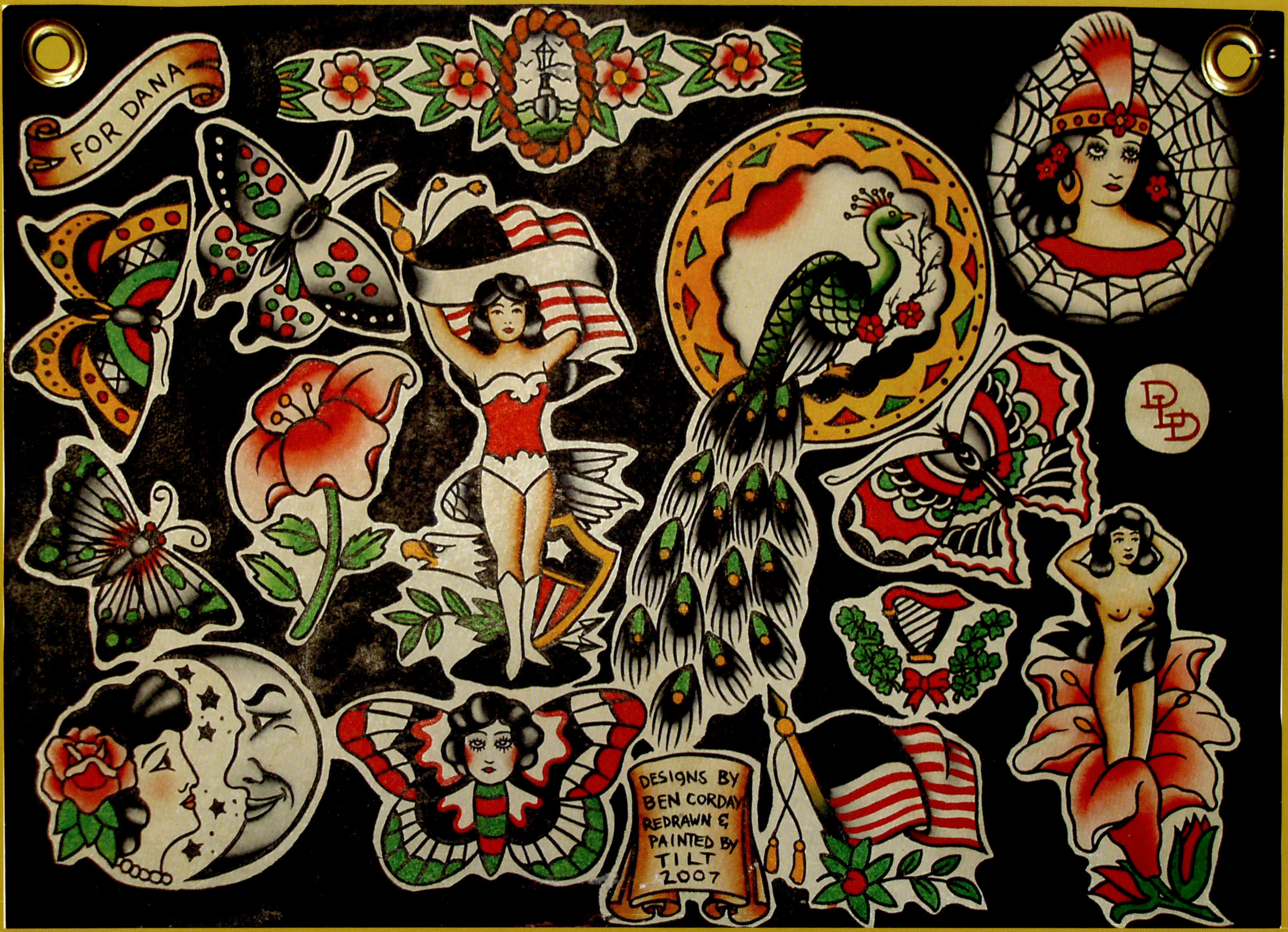
FOR DANA
DLD
DESIGNS BY
BEN CORDAY
REDRAWN &
PAINTED BY
TILT
2007

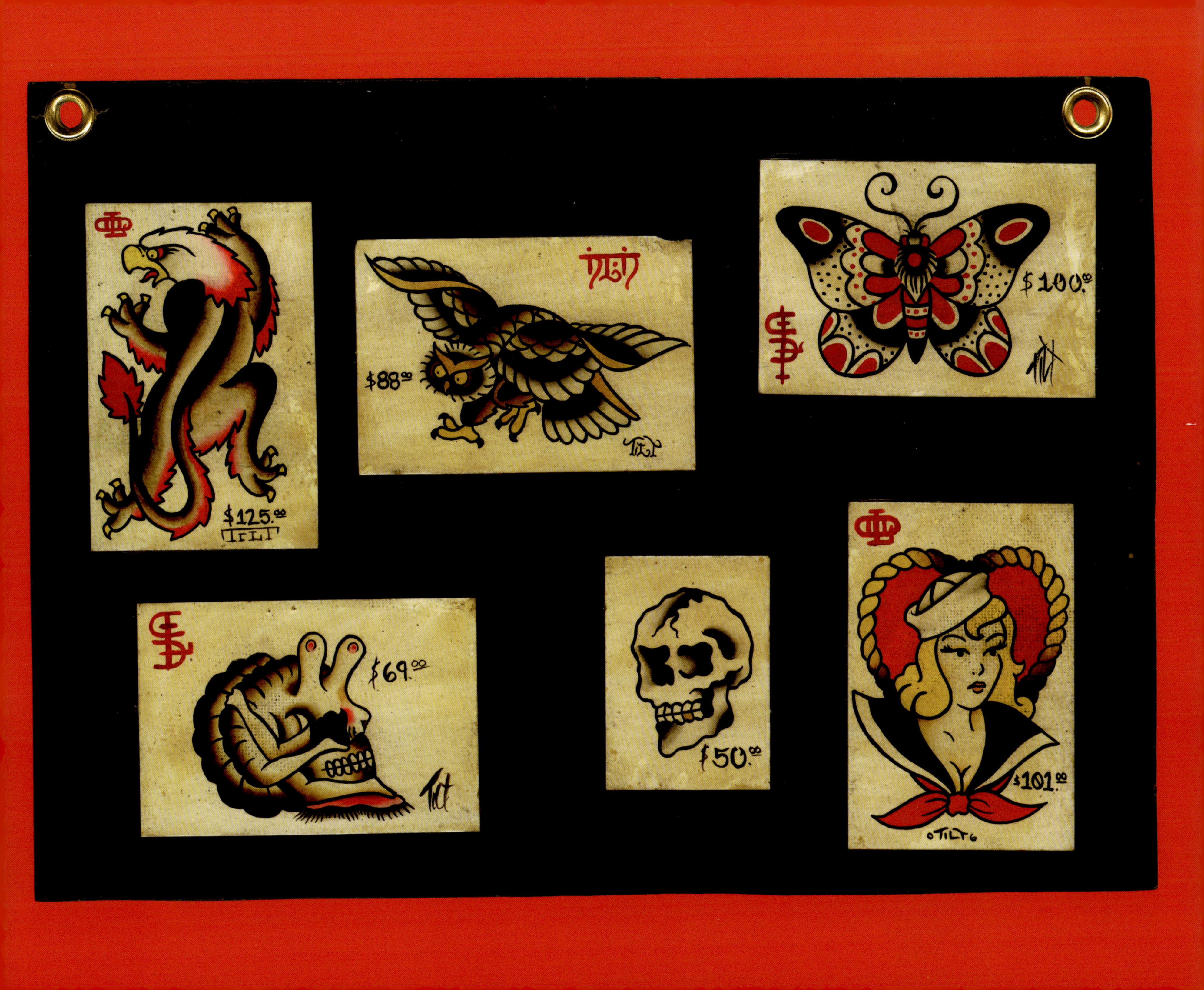
$125.00
$88.00
$100.00
$69.00
$50.00
$101.00
TILT

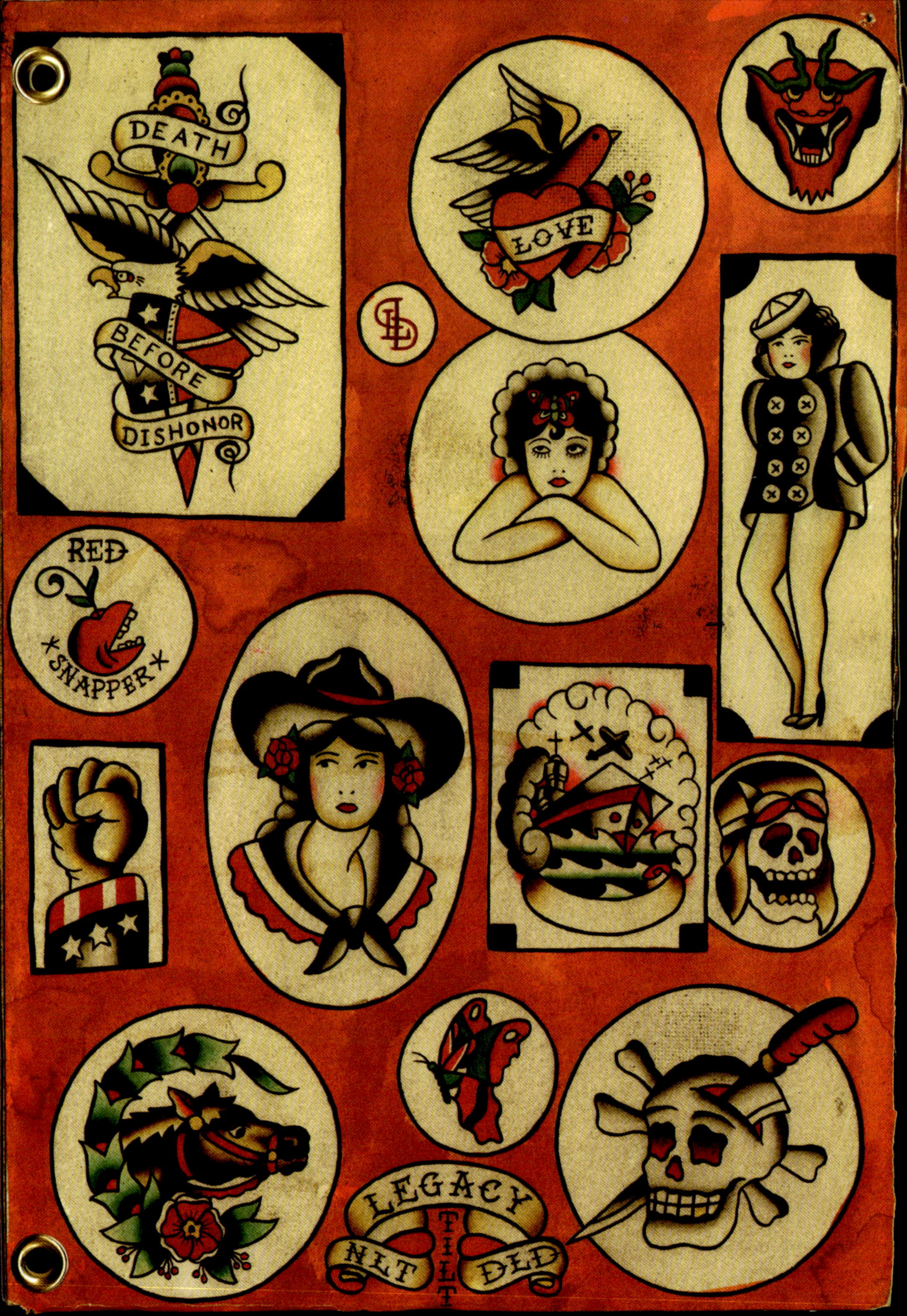
DEATH
BEFORE
DISHONOR
LOVE
RED
SNAPPER
LEGACY
TILT
NLT
DLD

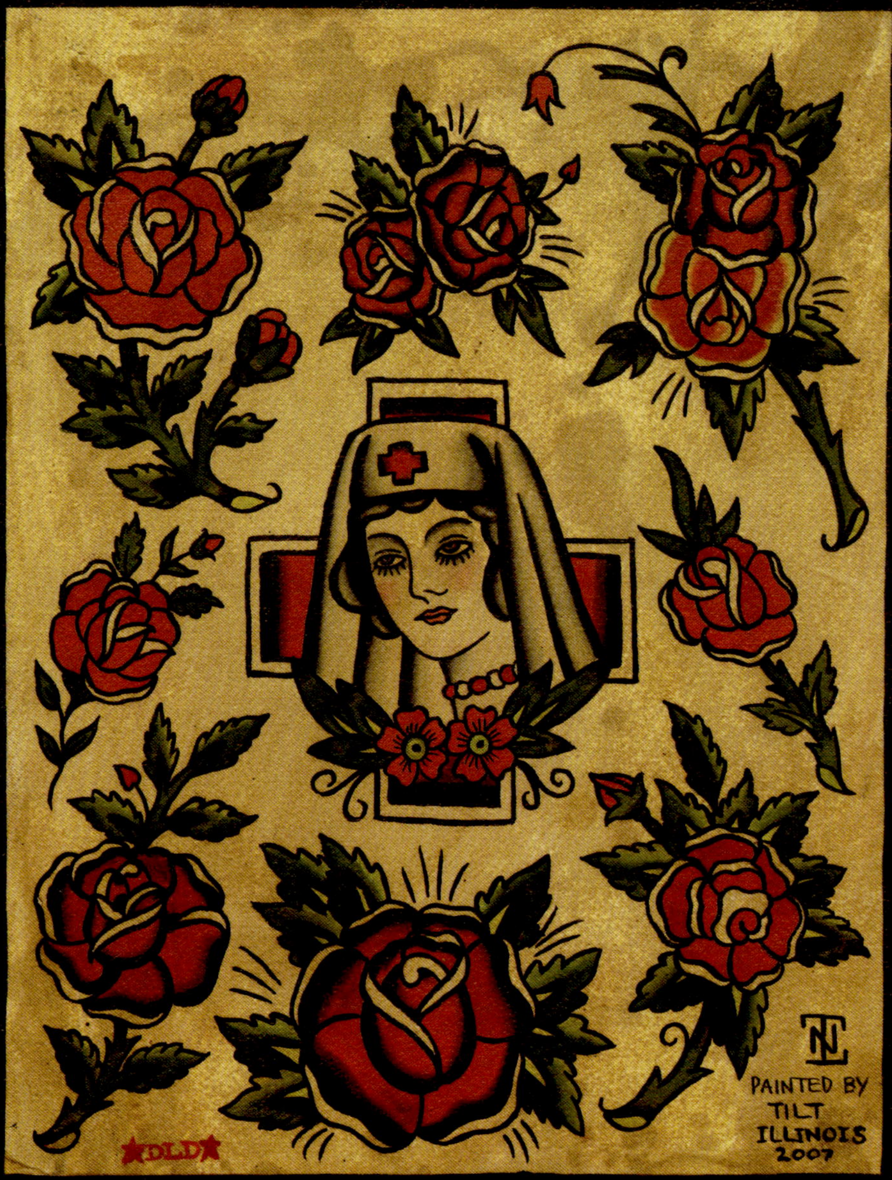
PAINTED BY
TILT
ILLINOIS
2007
DLD

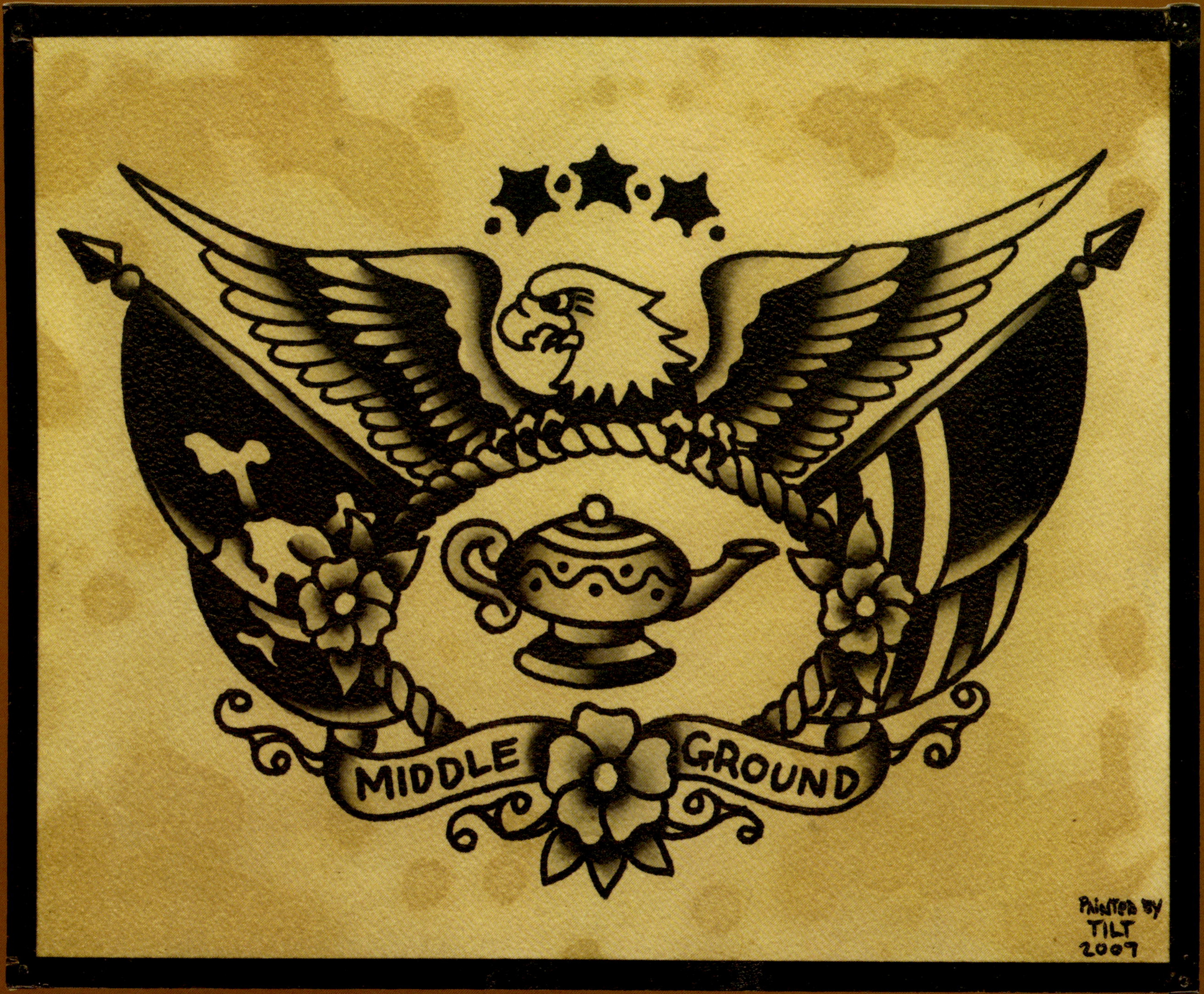
MIDDLE
GROUND
PAINTED BY
TILT
2009

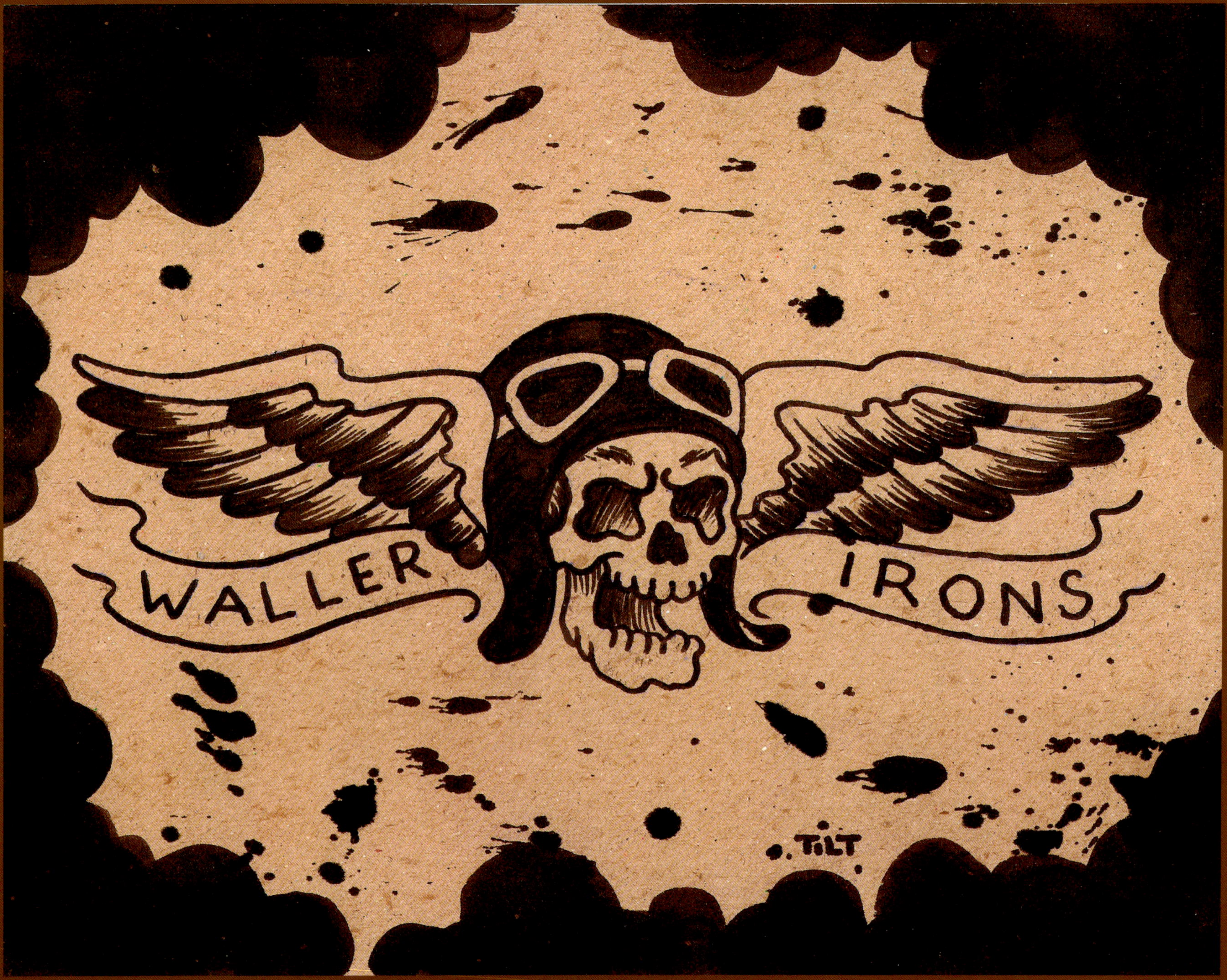
WALLER
IRONS
TILT

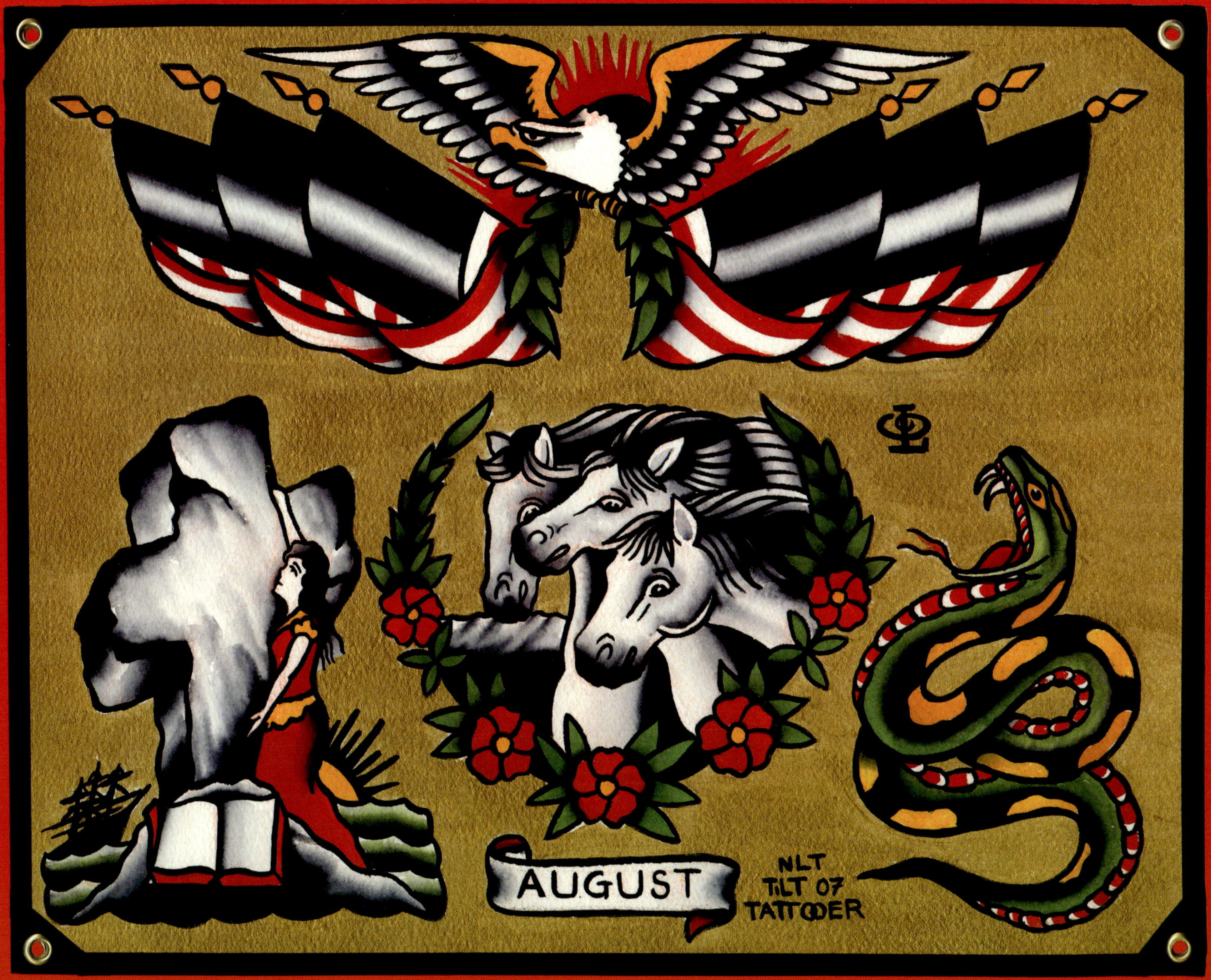
AUGUST
NLT
TILT 07
TATTOOER

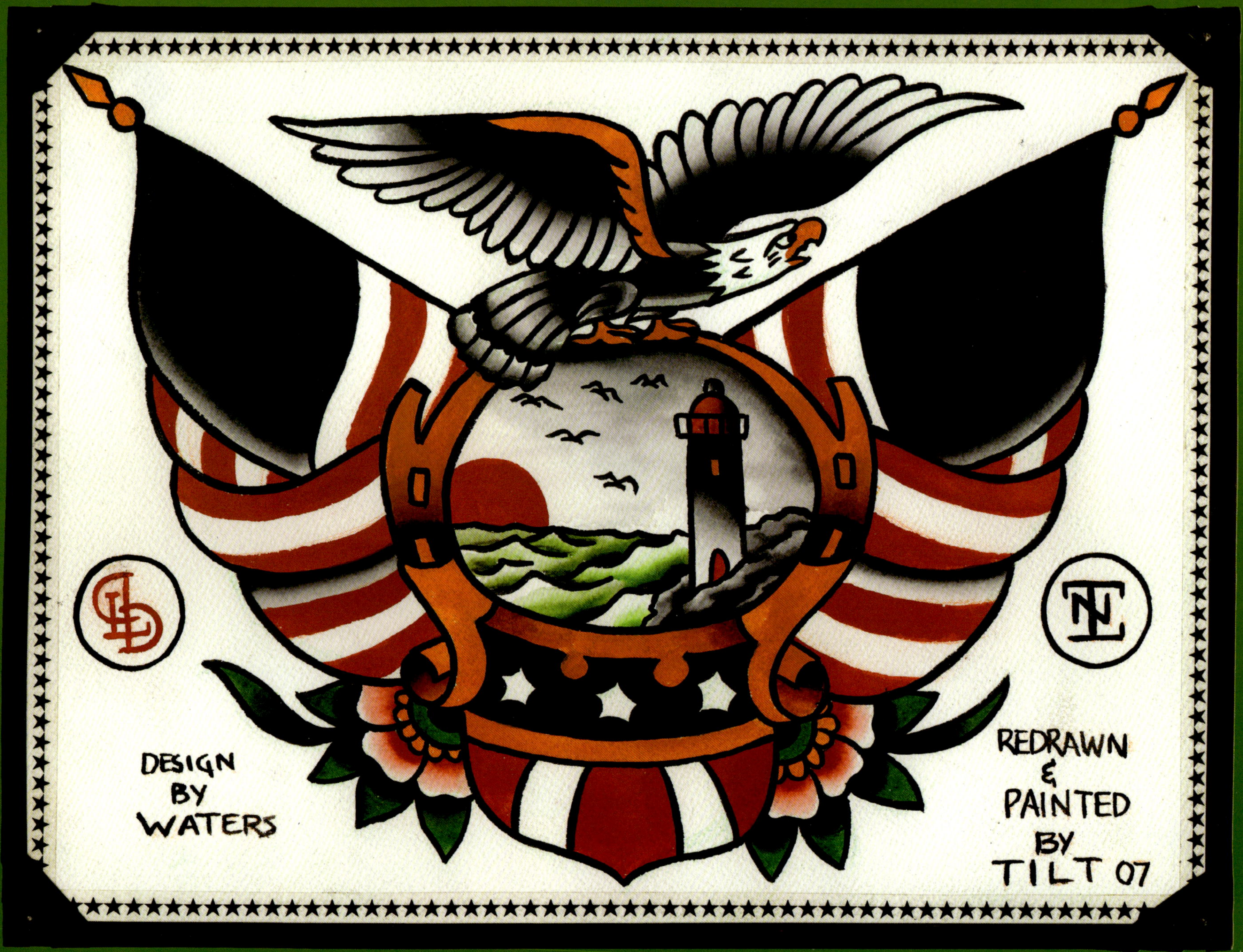
DESIGN
BY
WATERS
REDRAWN
&
PAINTED
BY
TILT 07

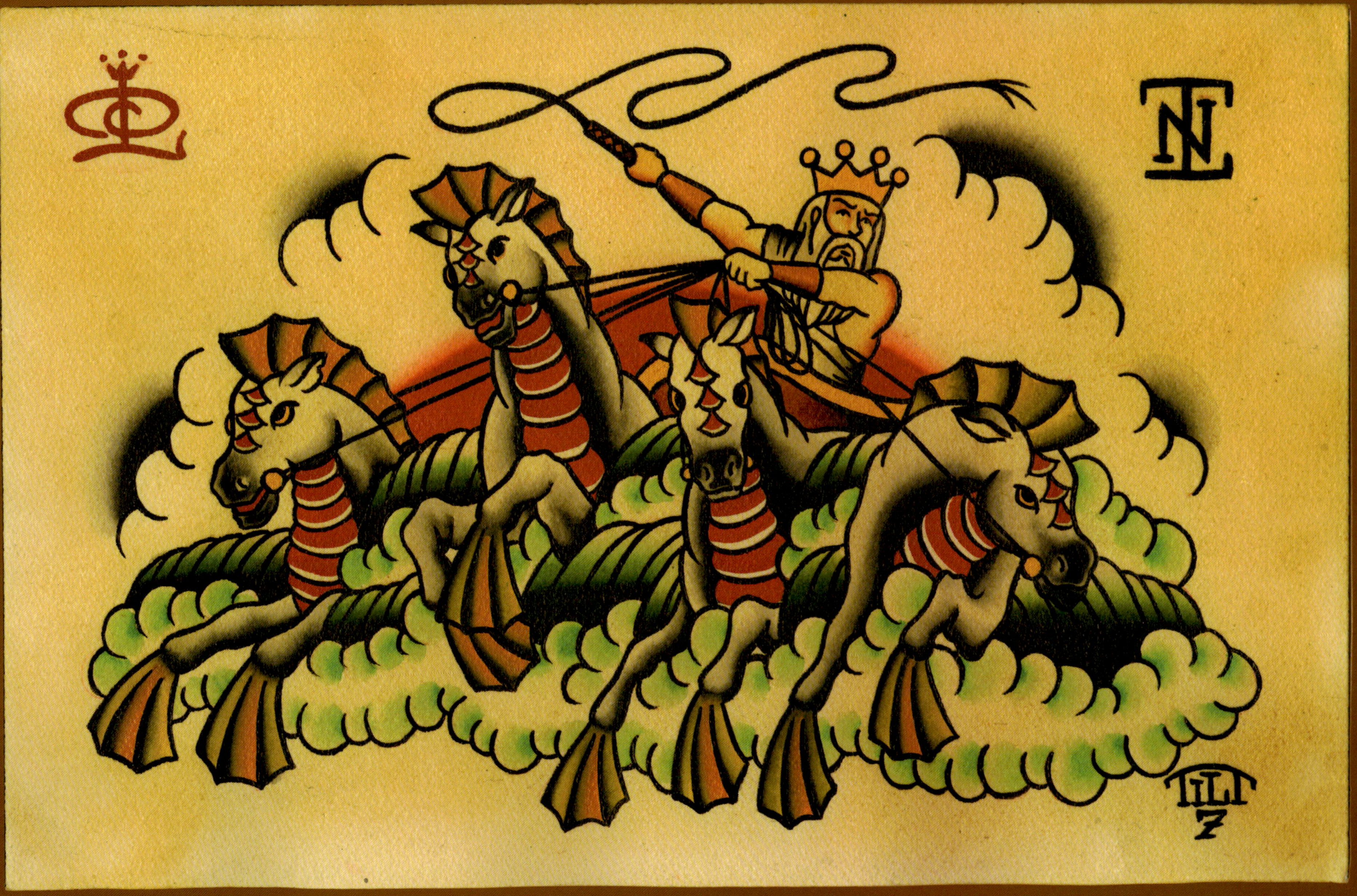

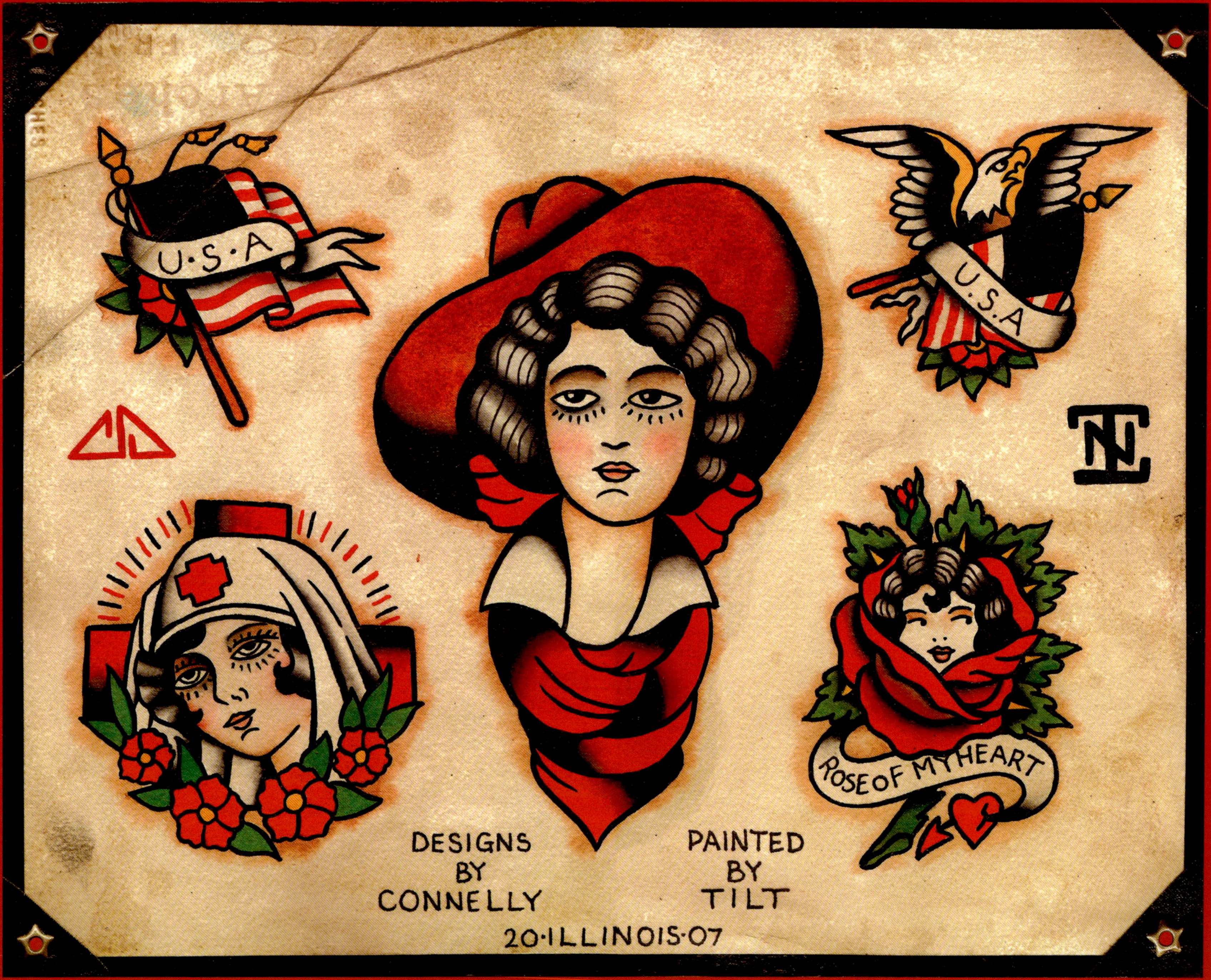
U·S·A
U.S.A
ROSE OF MY HEART
DESIGNS BY CONNELLY
PAINTED BY TILT
20·ILLINOIS·07

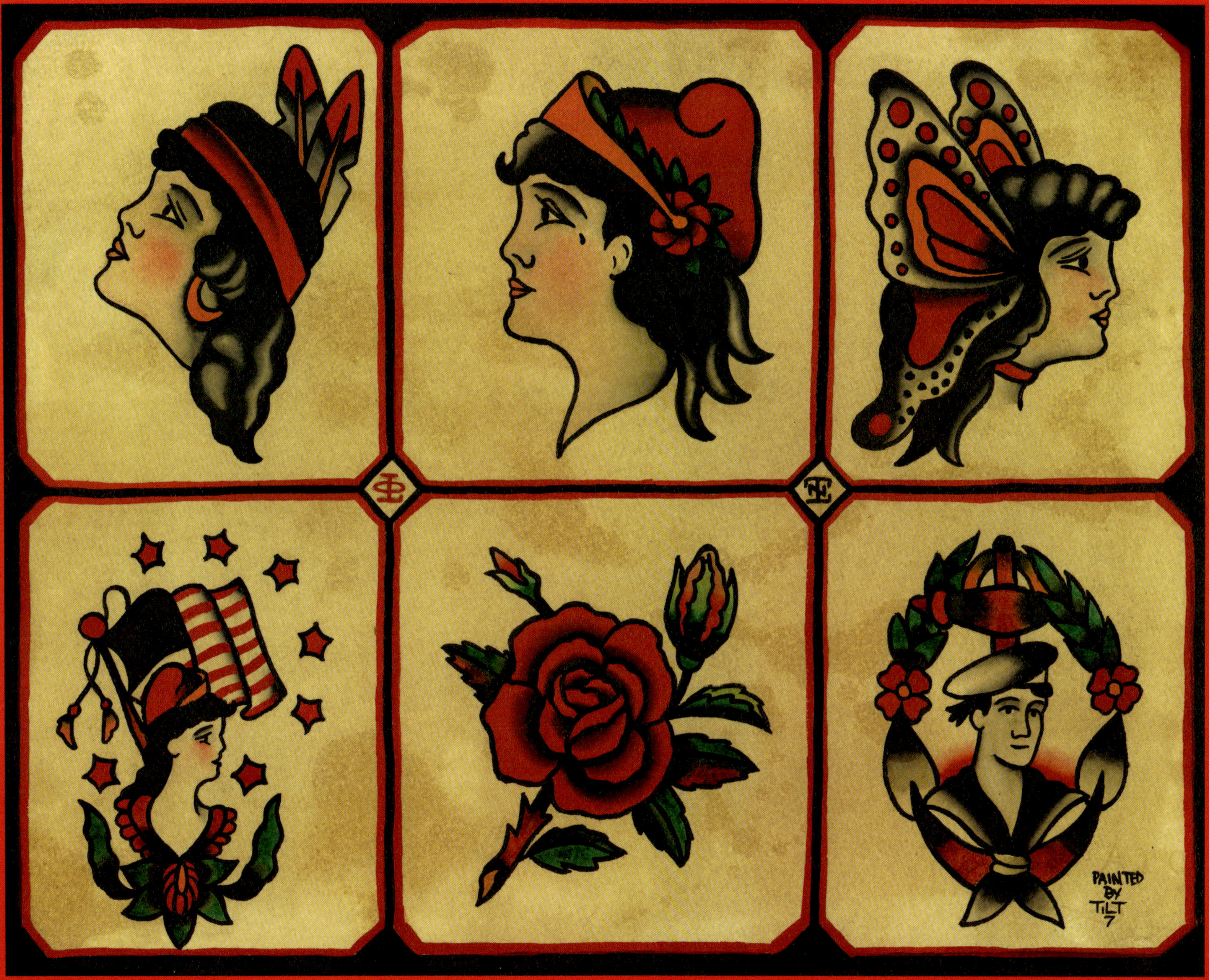
PAINTED
BY
TILT
7

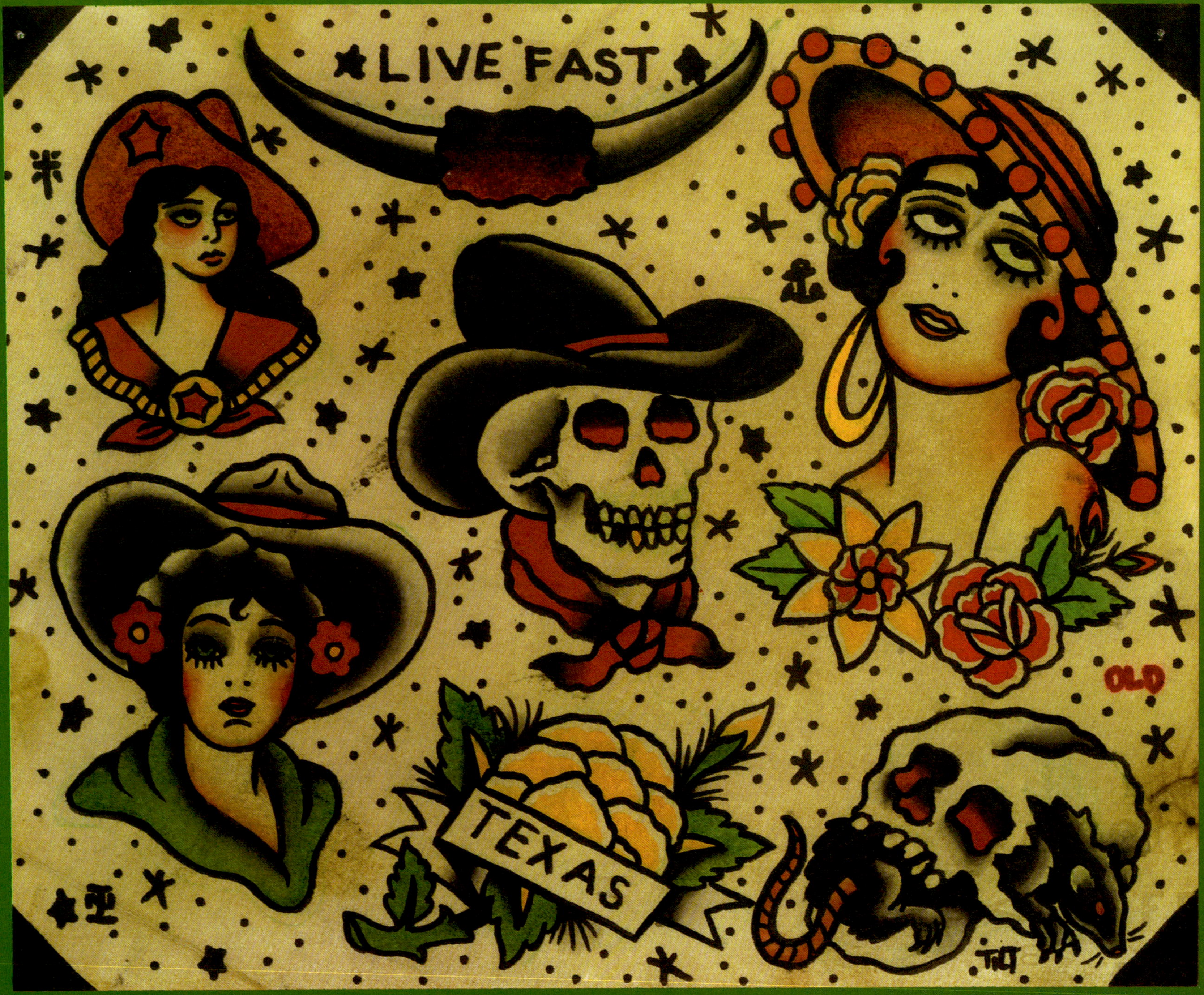
LIVE FAST
OLD
TEXAS

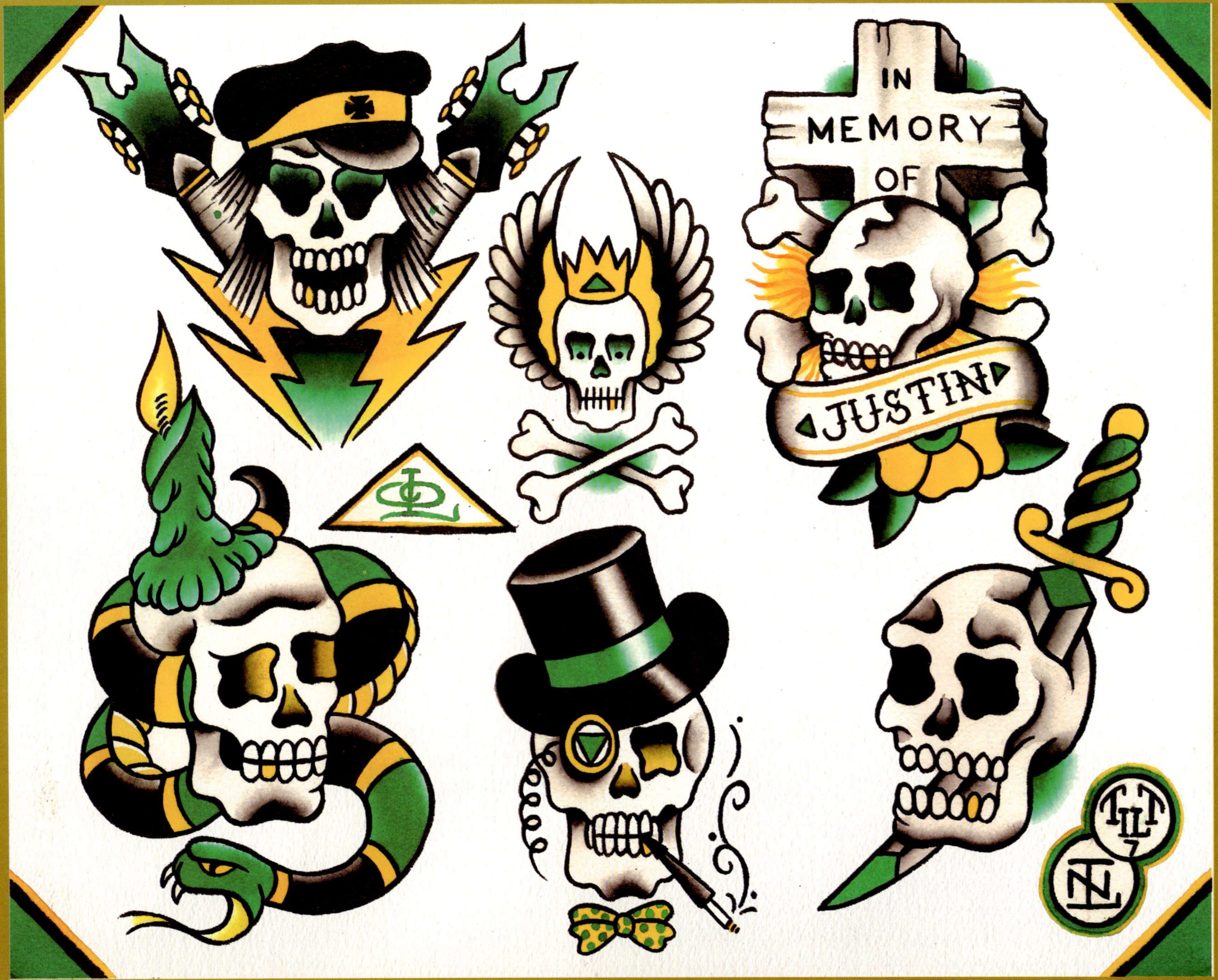
IN
MEMORY
OF
JUSTIN

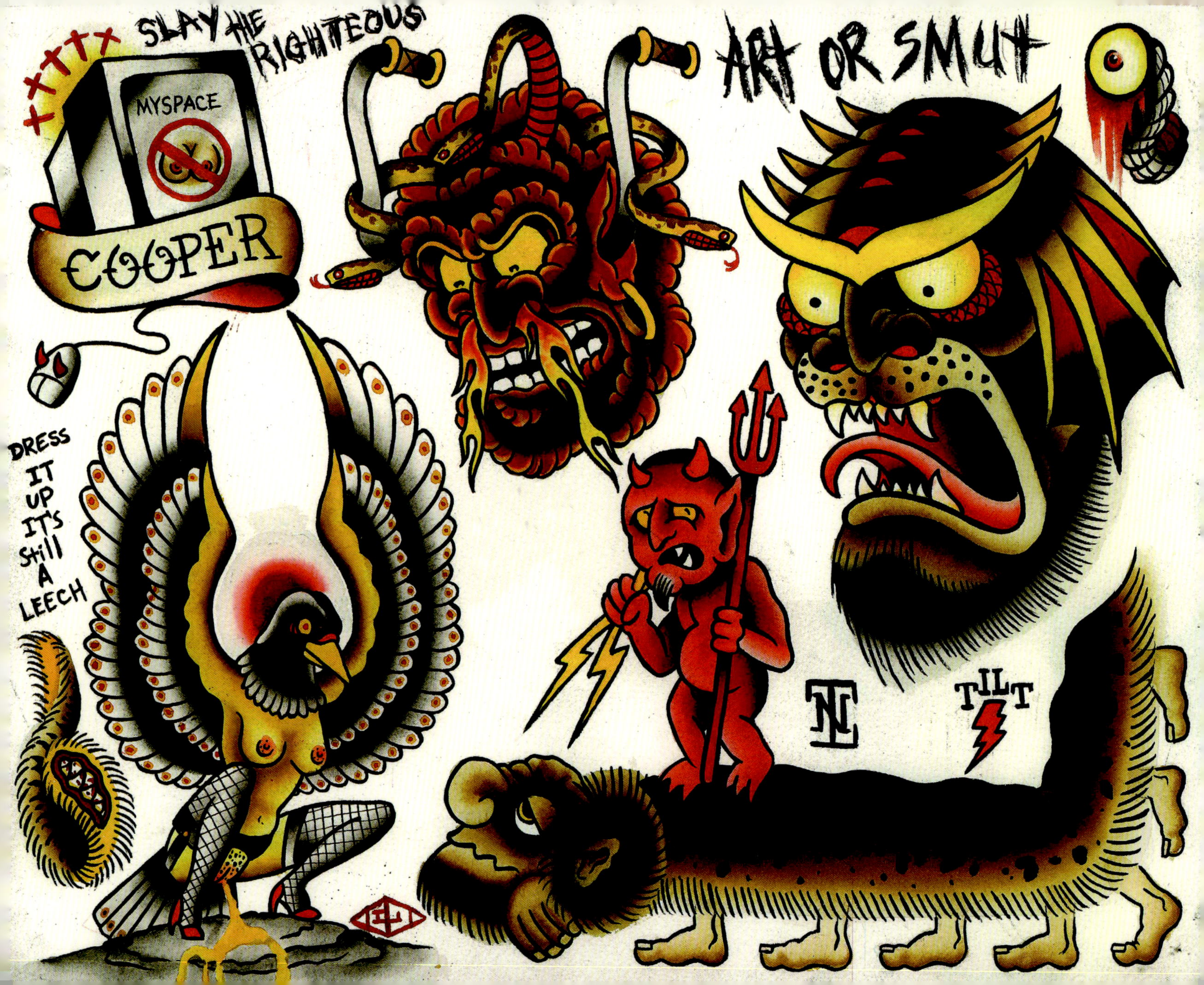

SLAY THE RIGHTEOUS
MYSPACE
COOPER
ART OR SMUT
DRESS IT UP IT'S Still A LEECH
TILT

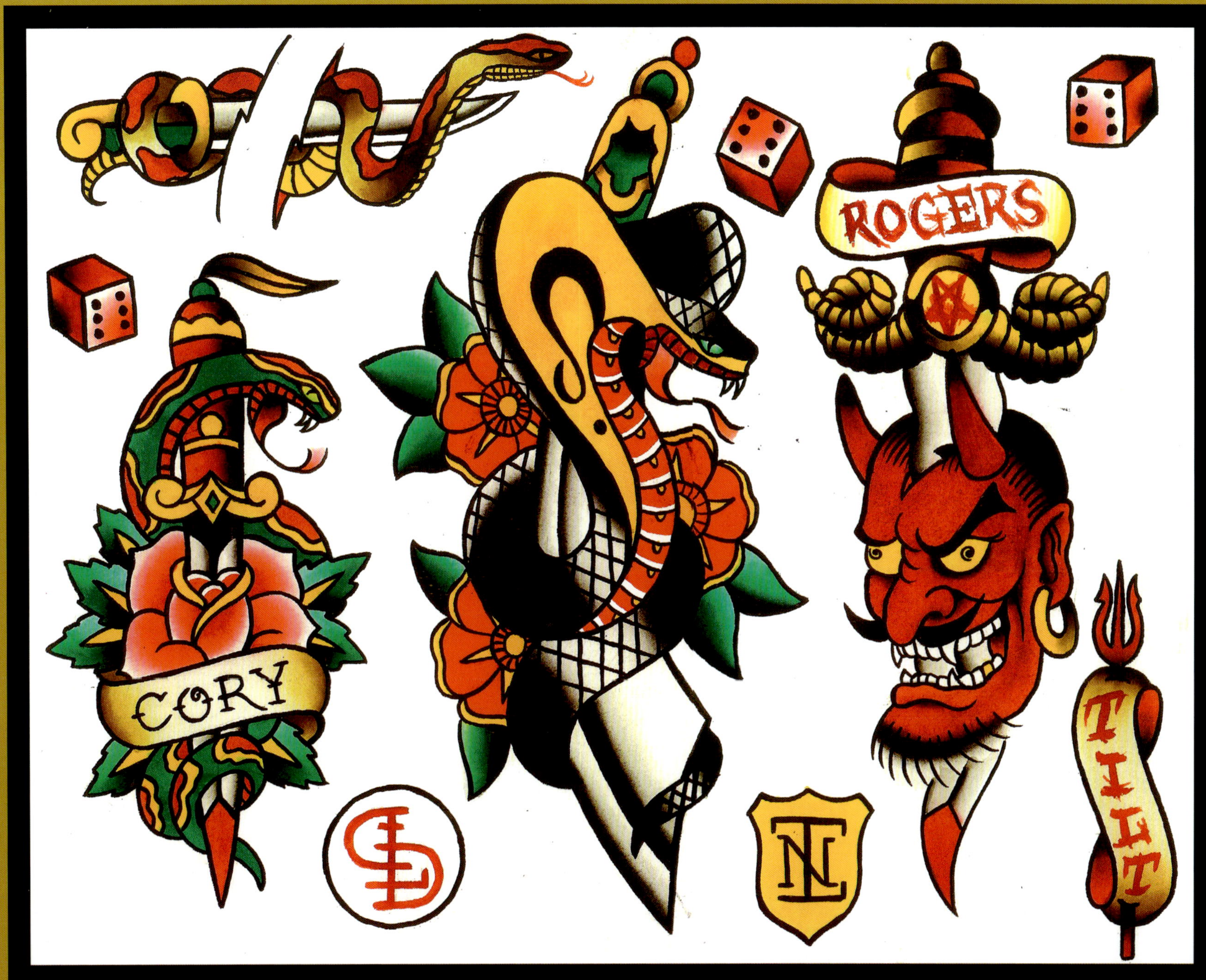
ROGERS
CORY
TILT

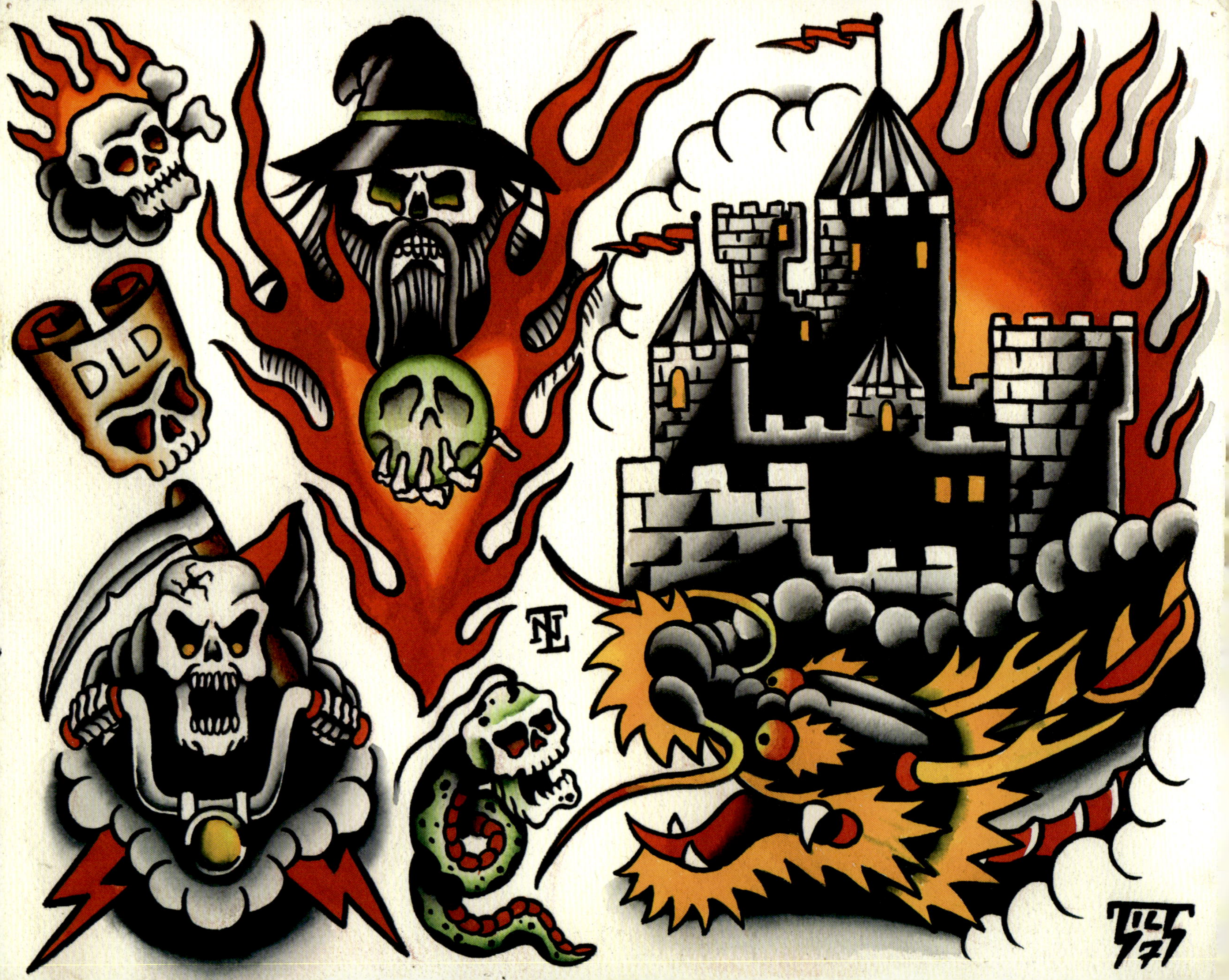
DLD

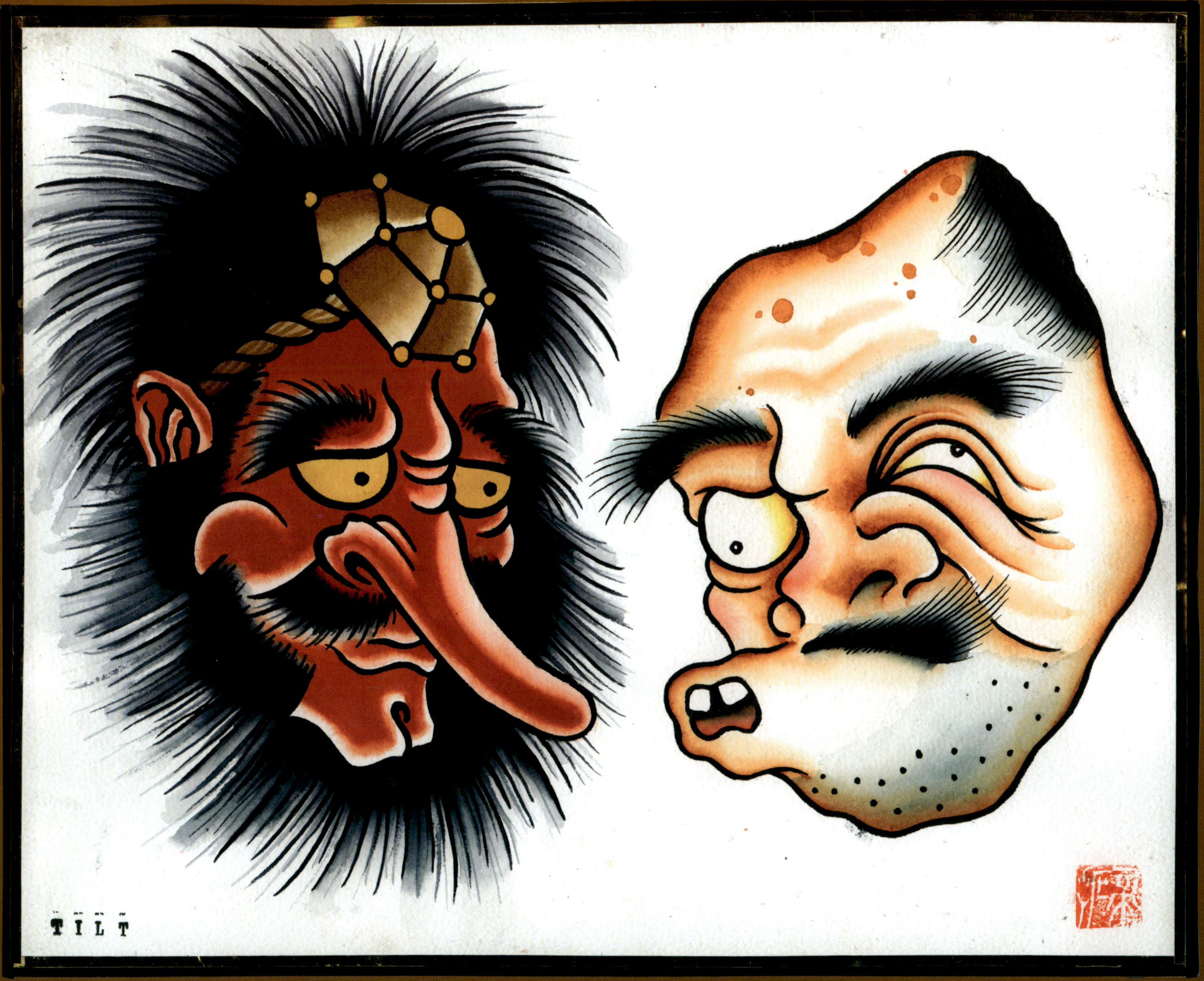
TILT

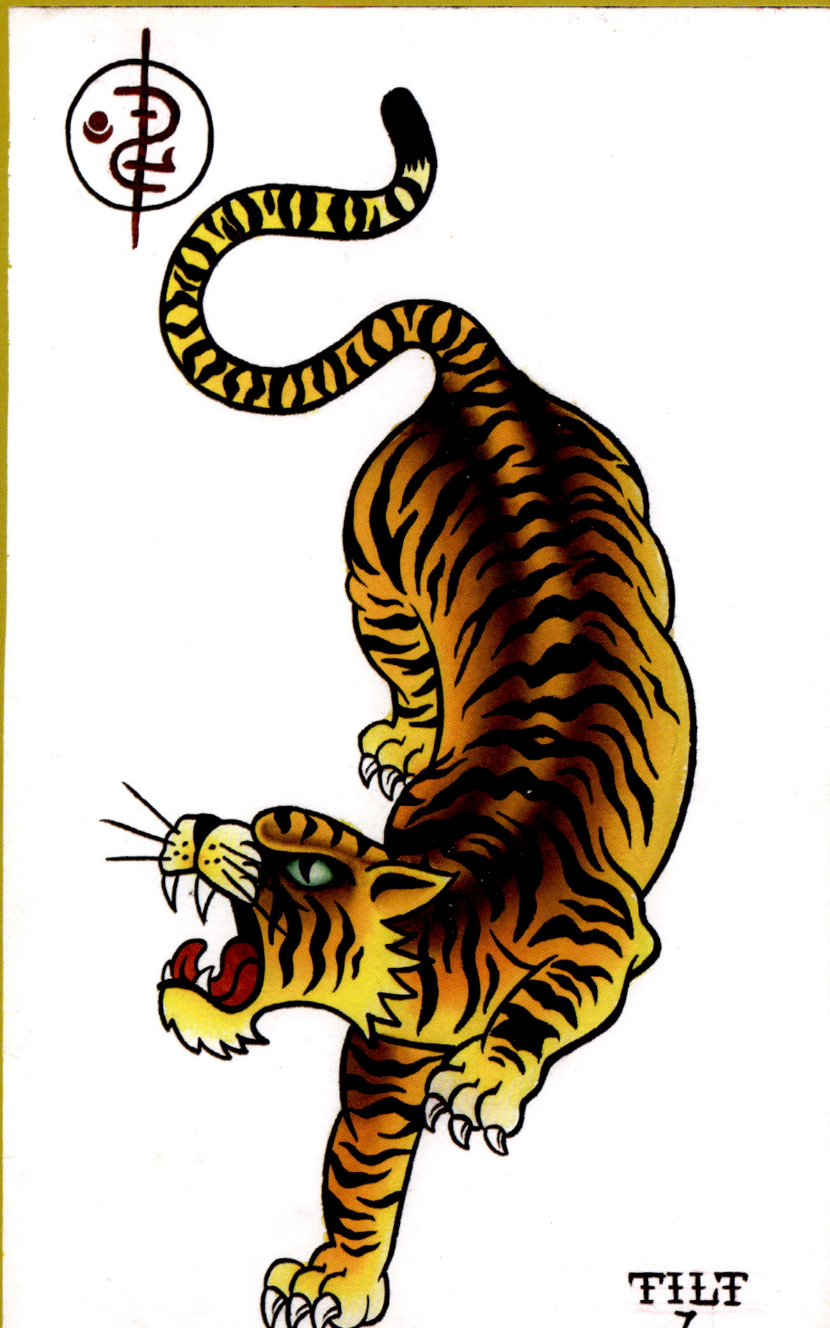
TILT

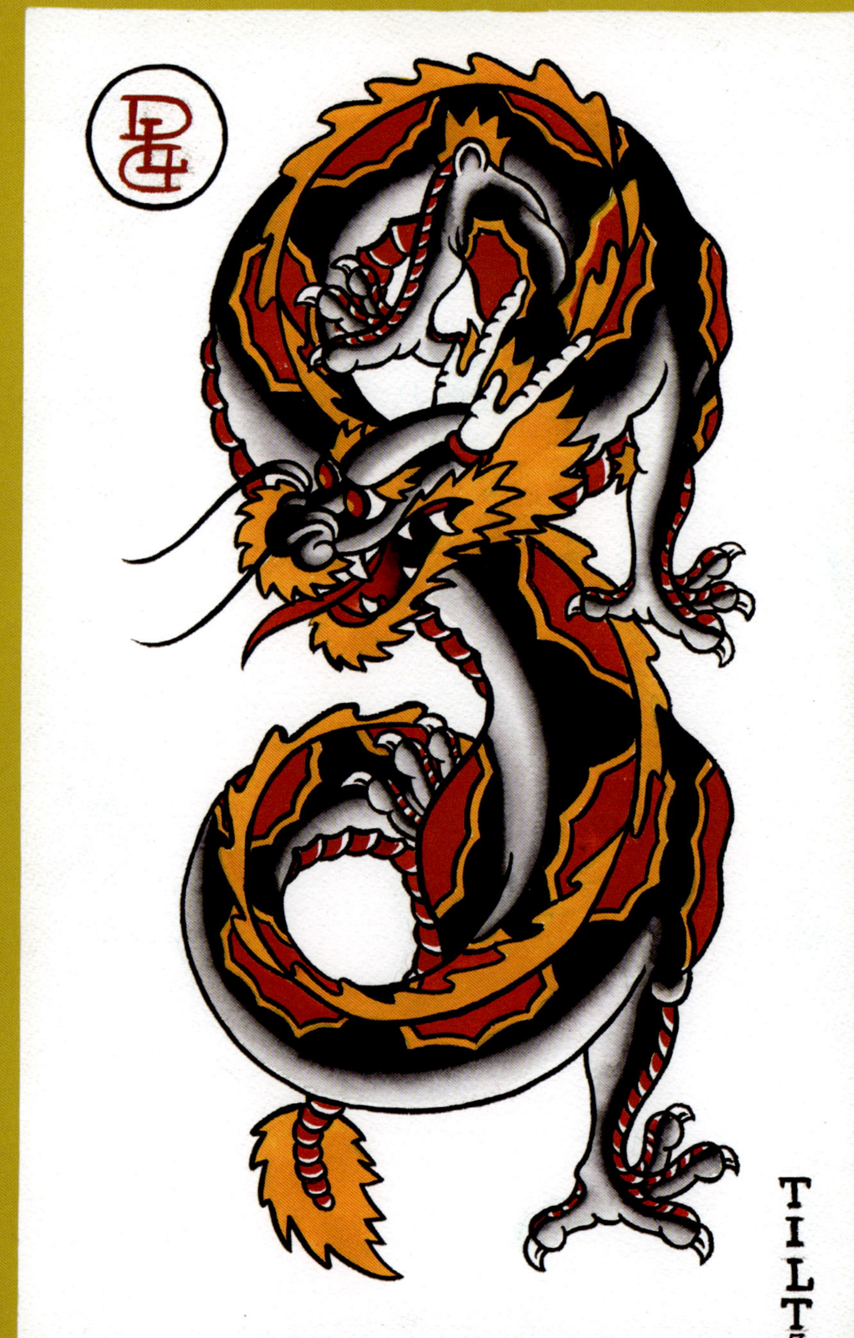
TILT

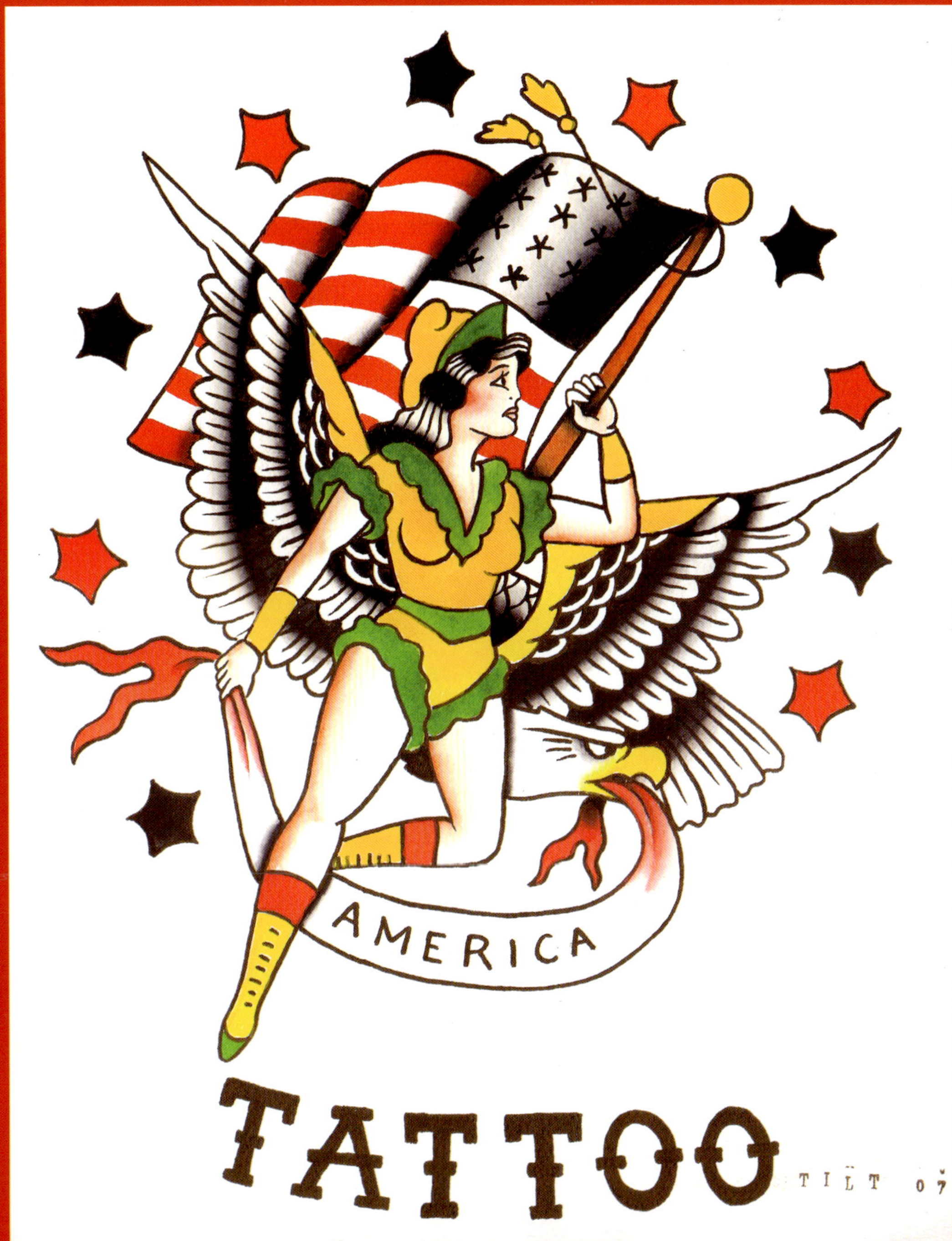
AMERICA
TATTOO
TILT 07

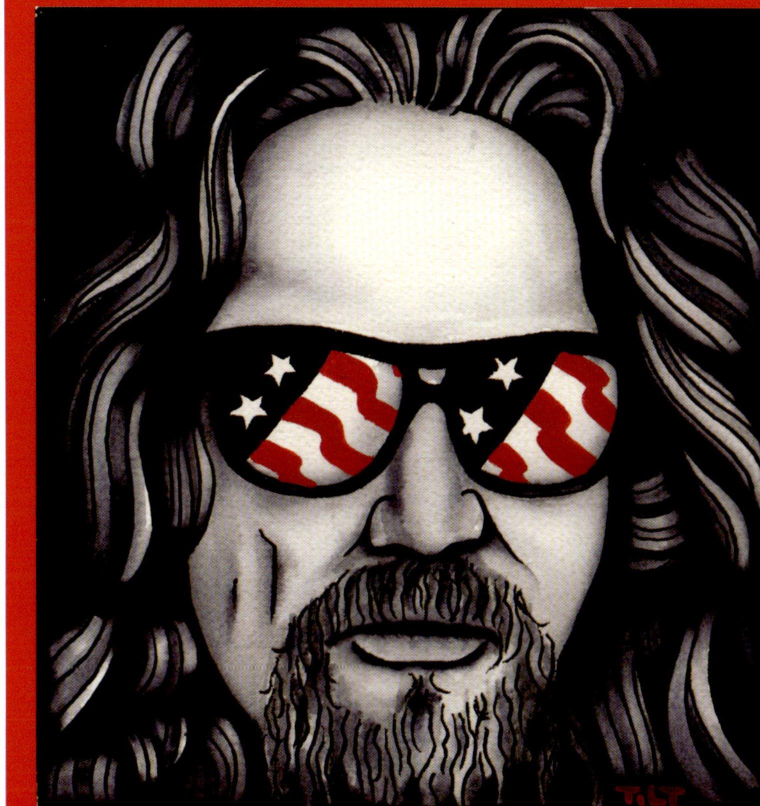
TILT

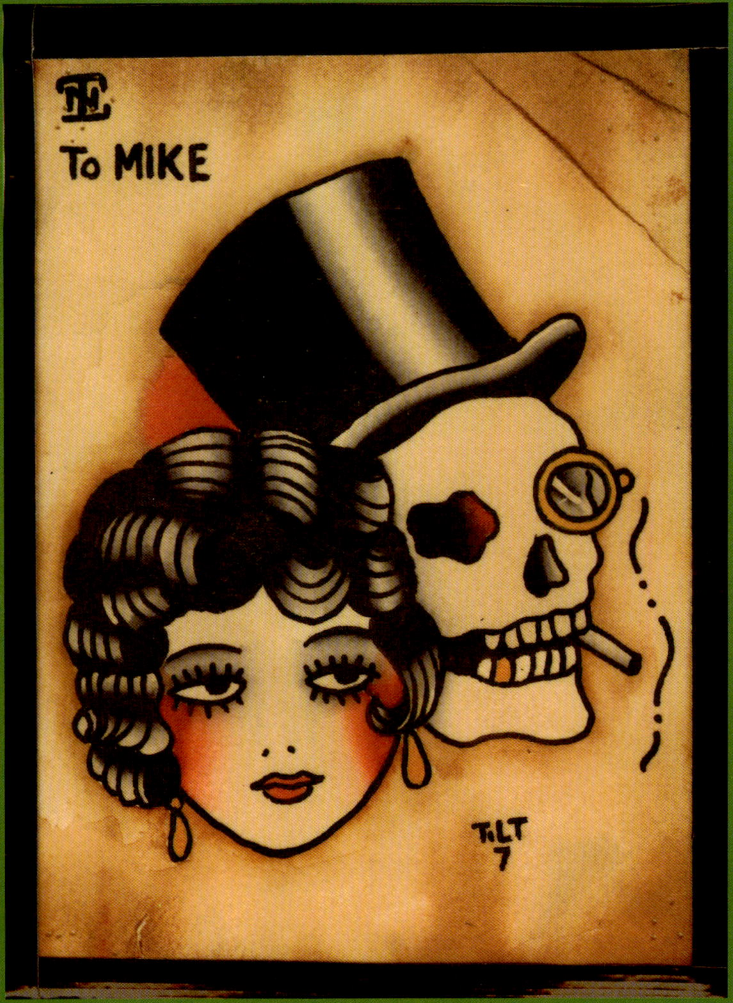
To MIKE
TiLT
7

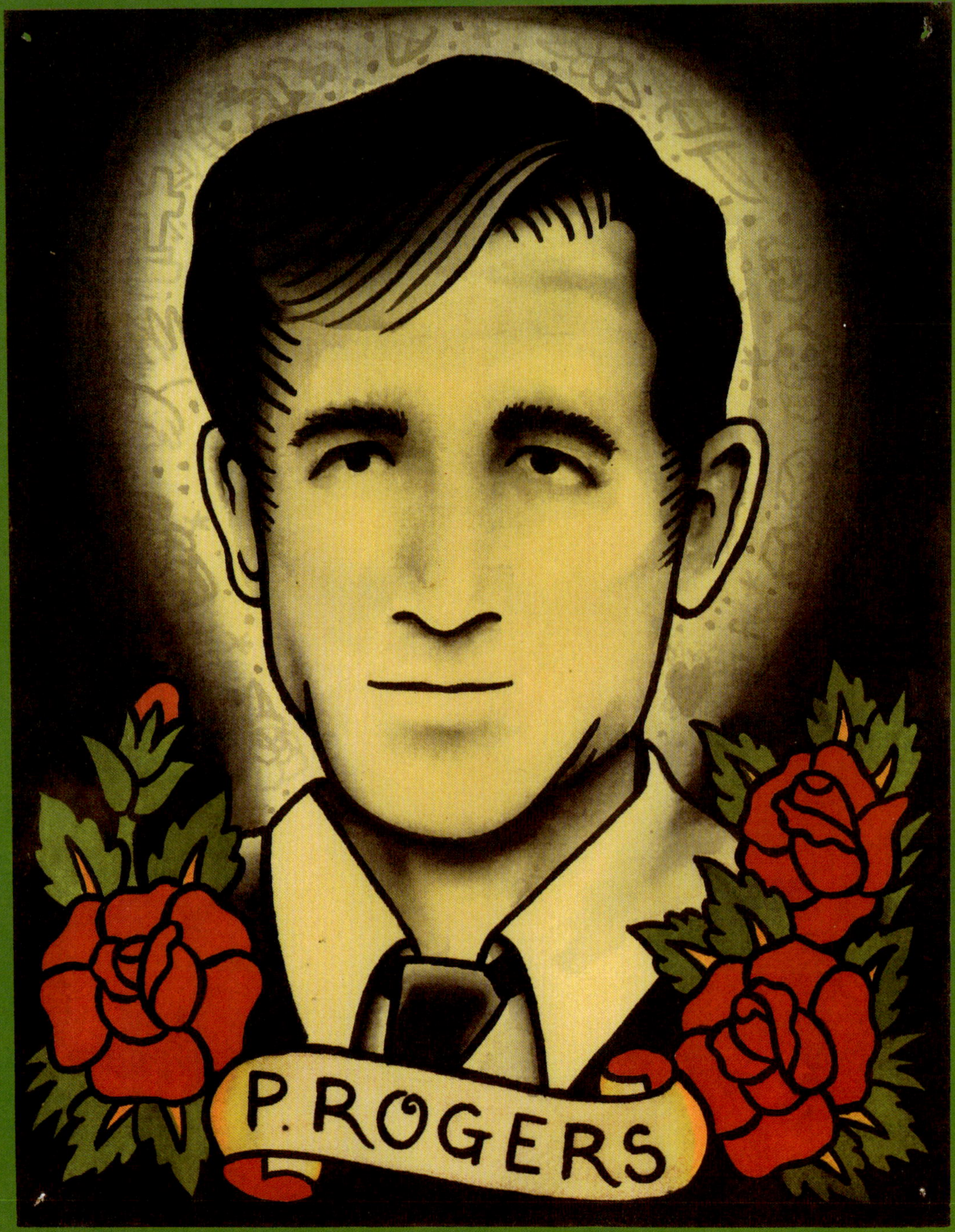
P. ROGERS

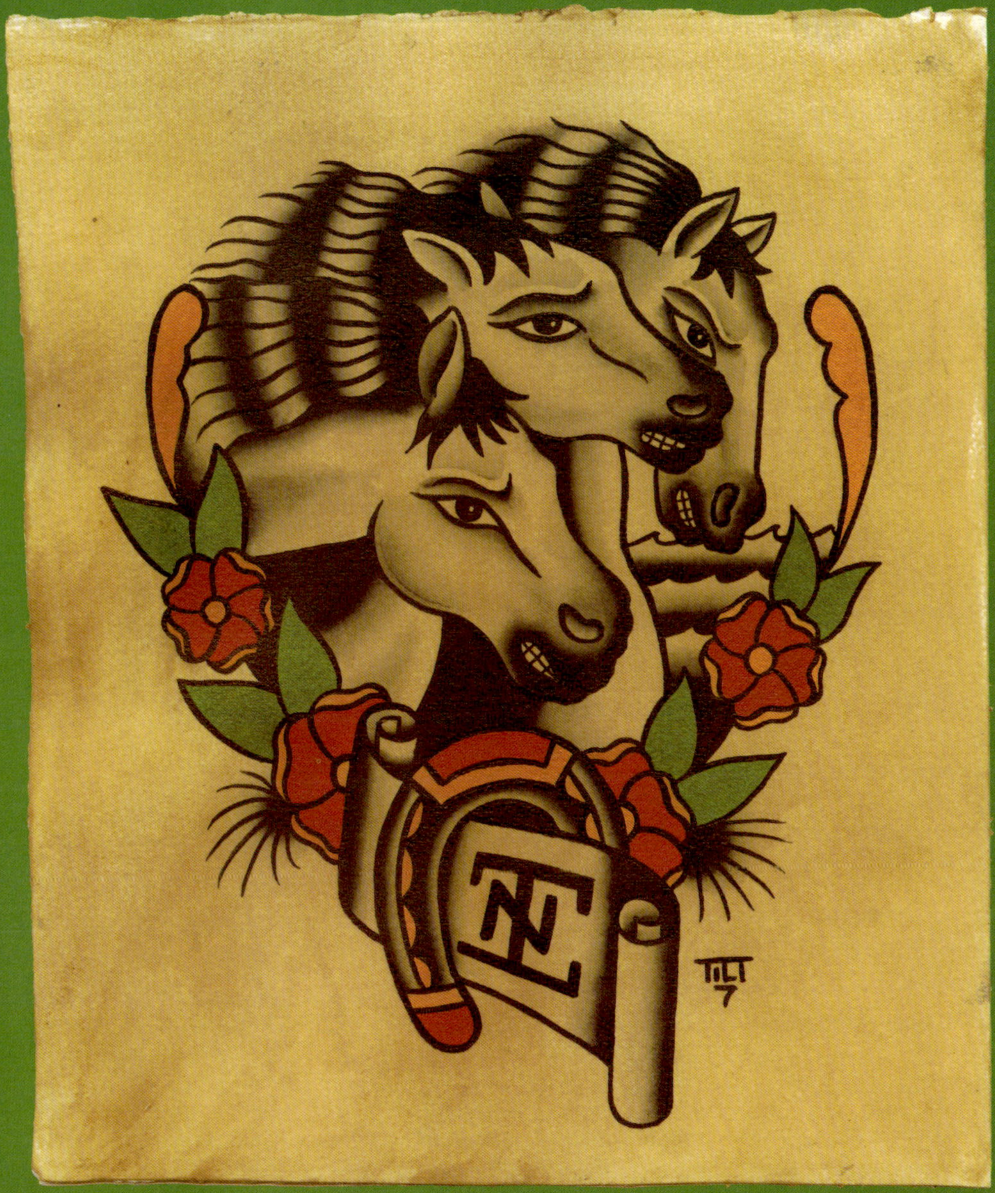

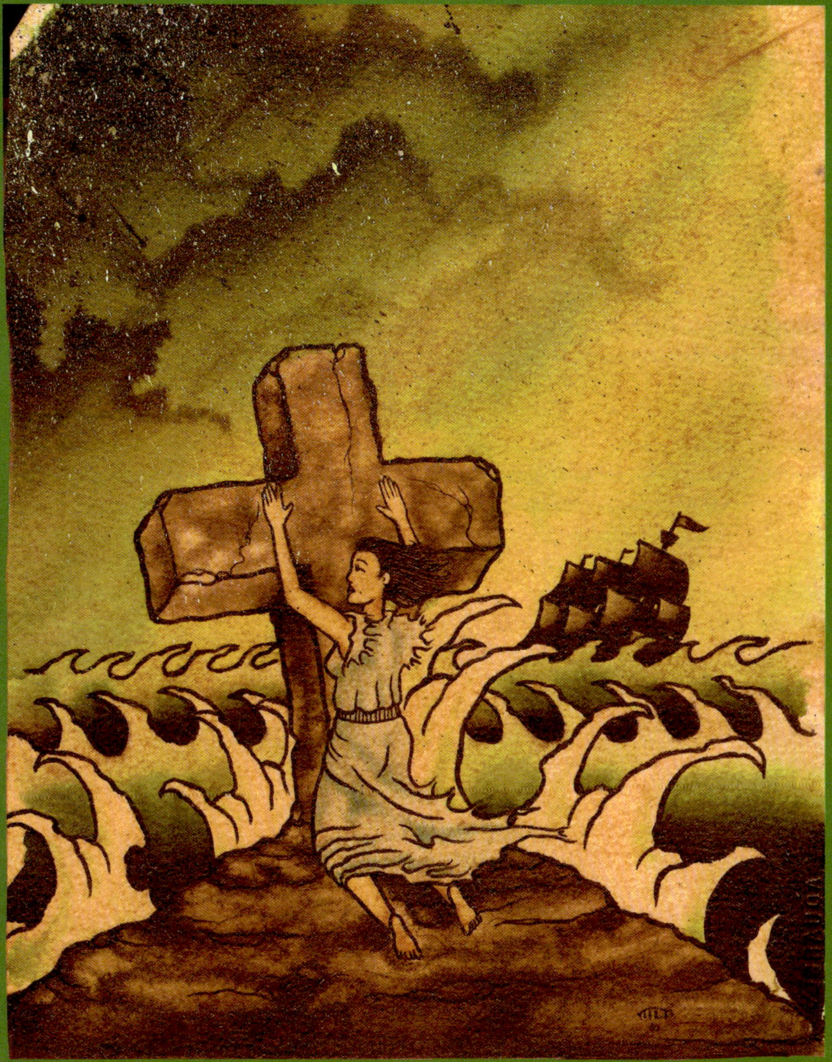

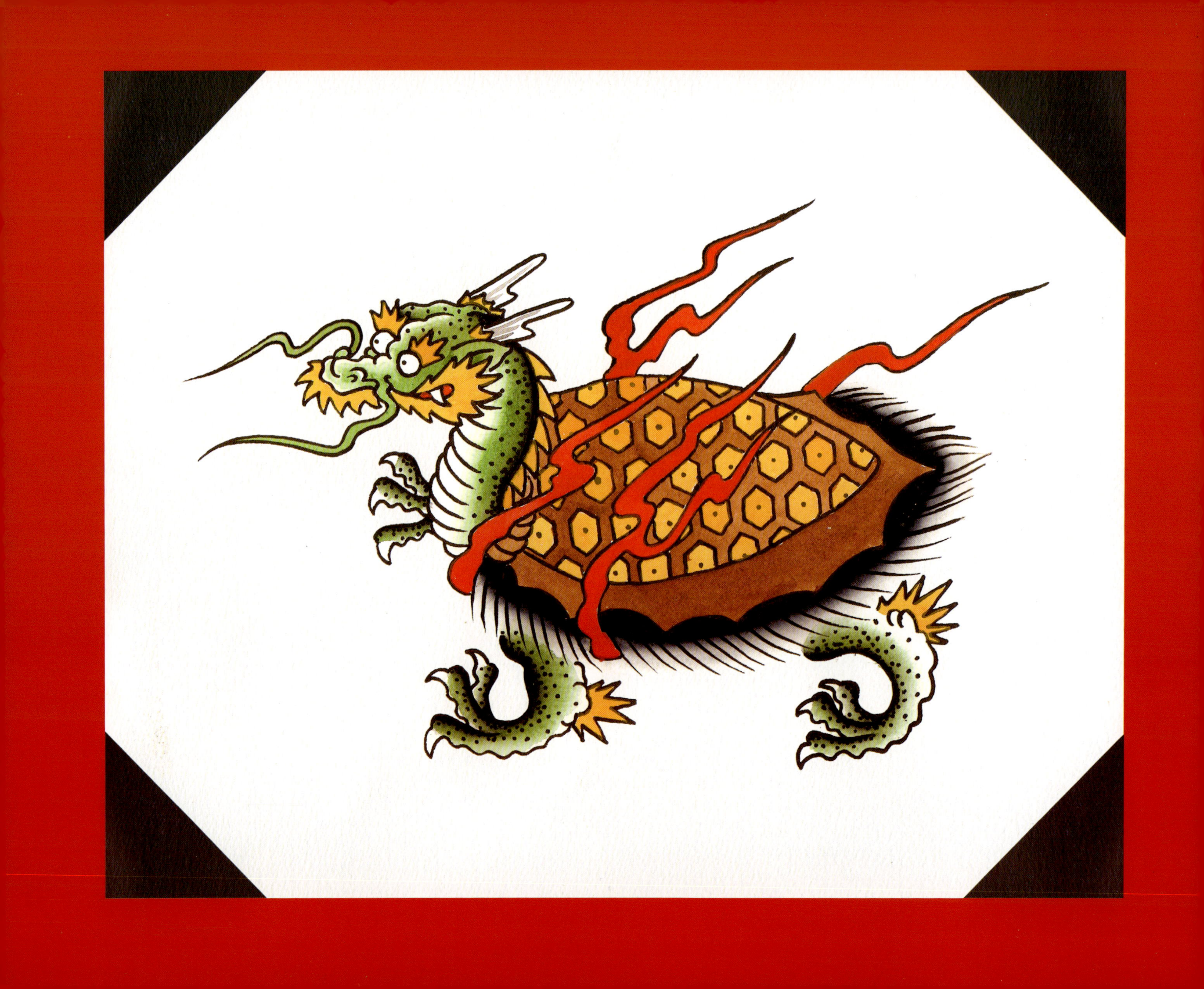

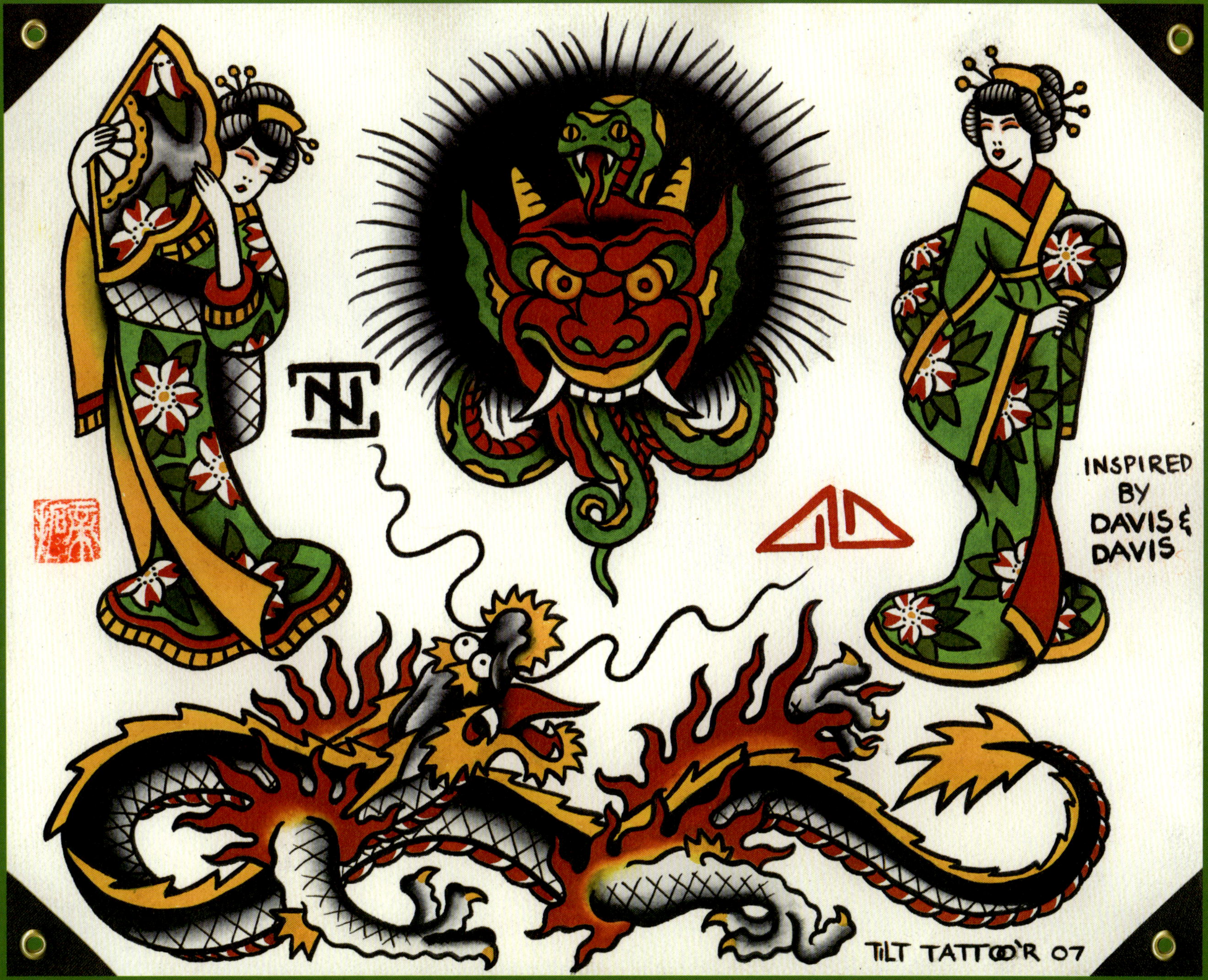
INSPIRED BY DAVIS & DAVIS
TILT TATTOO'R 07

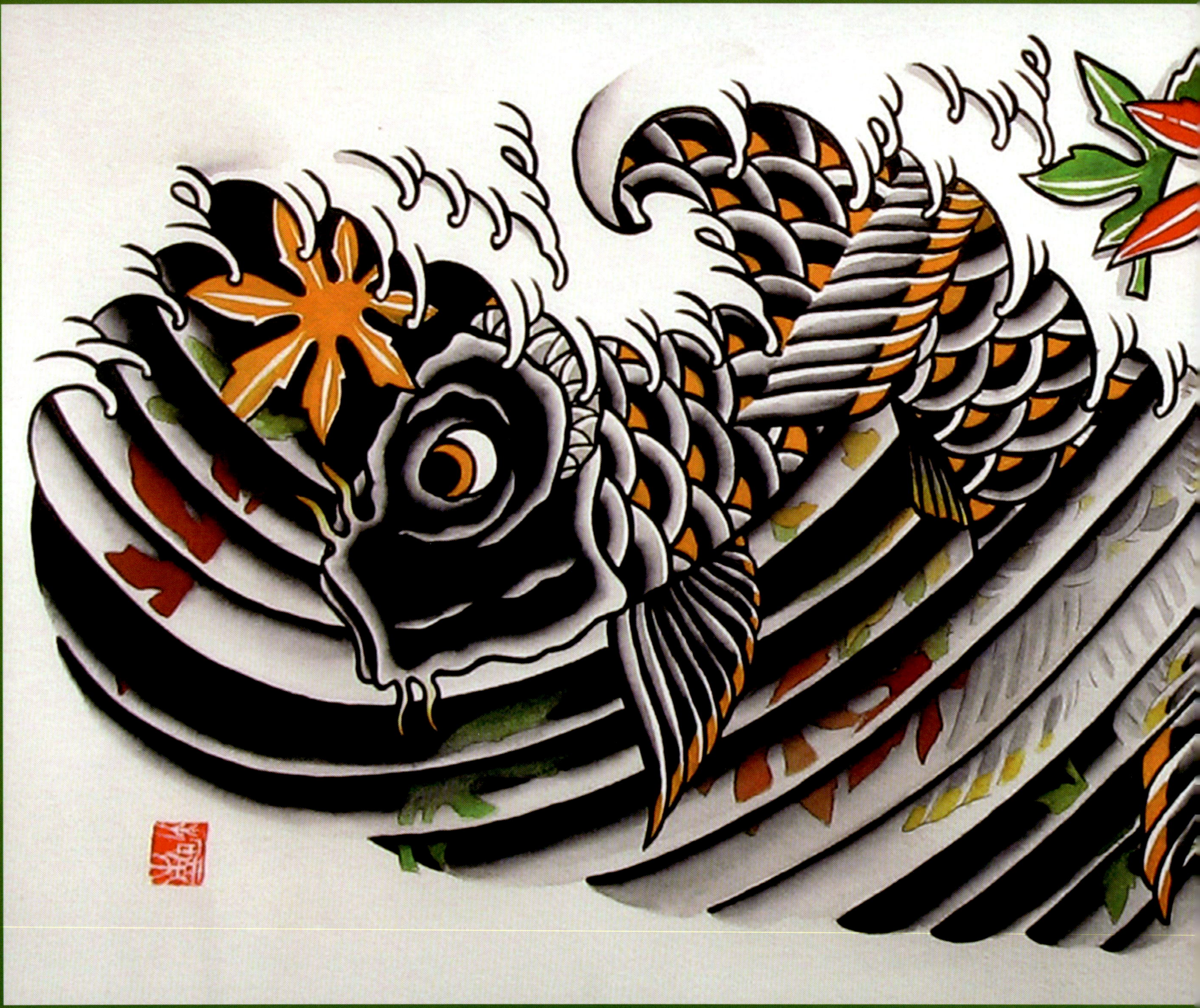

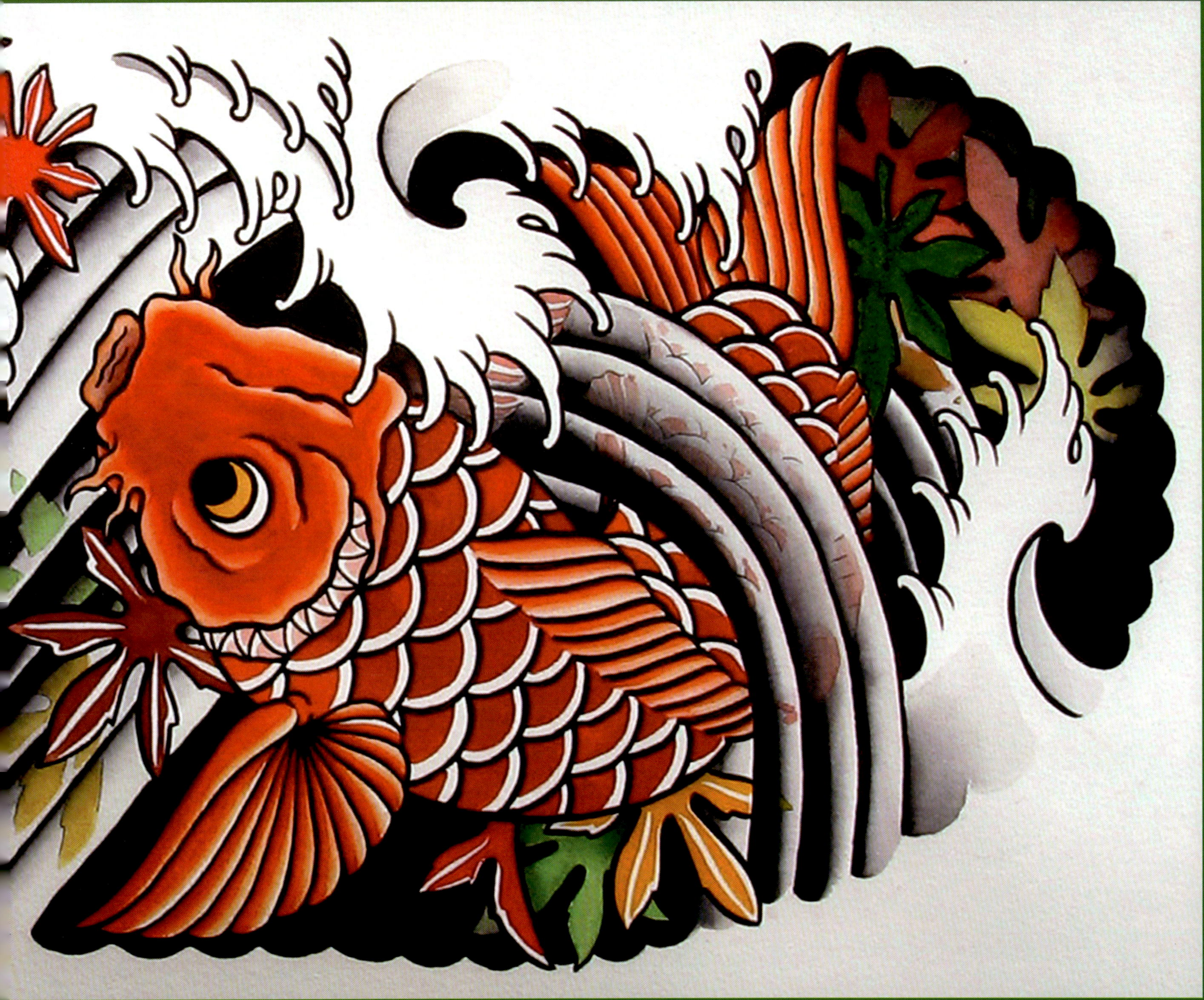

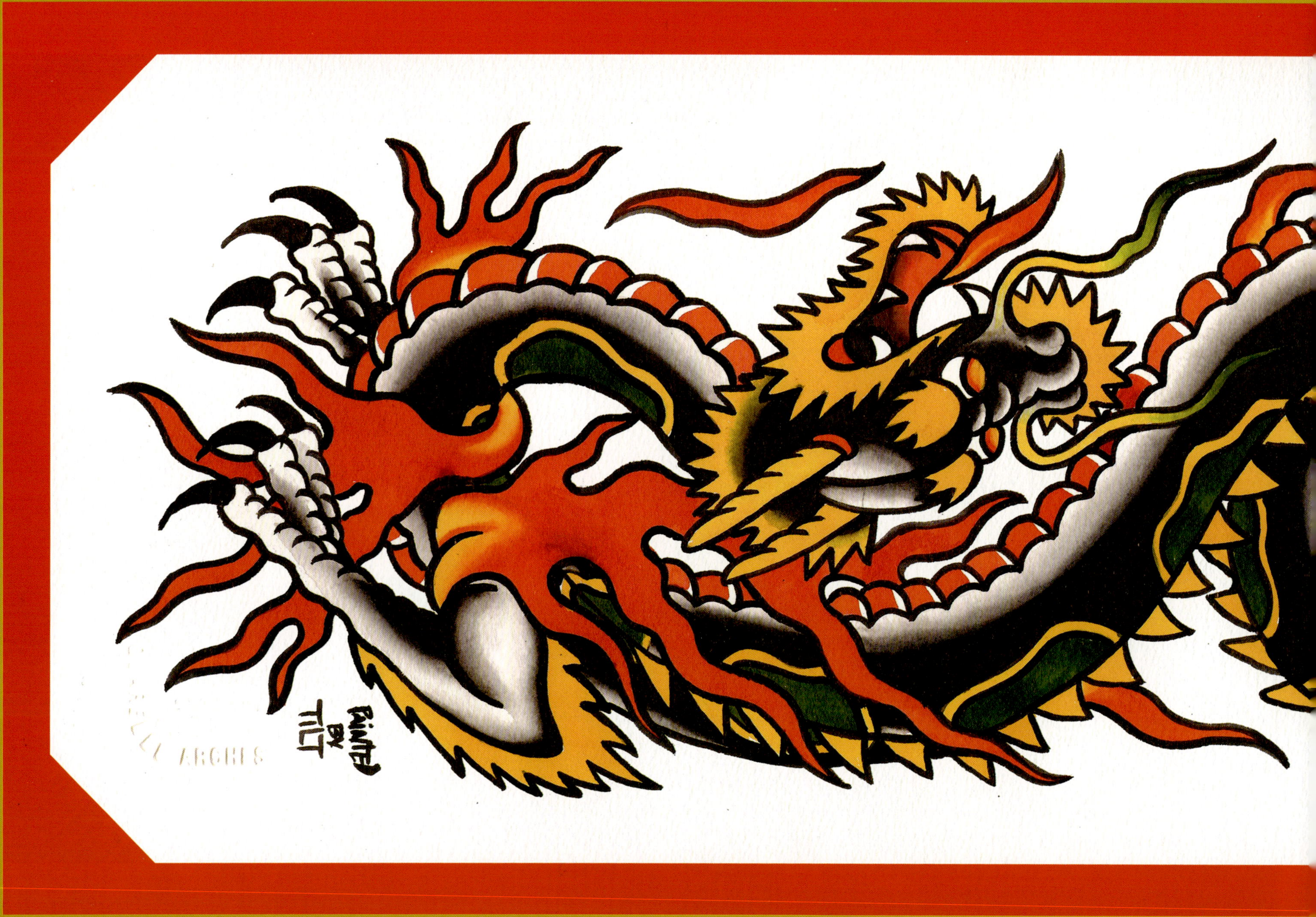
PAINTED BY TILT

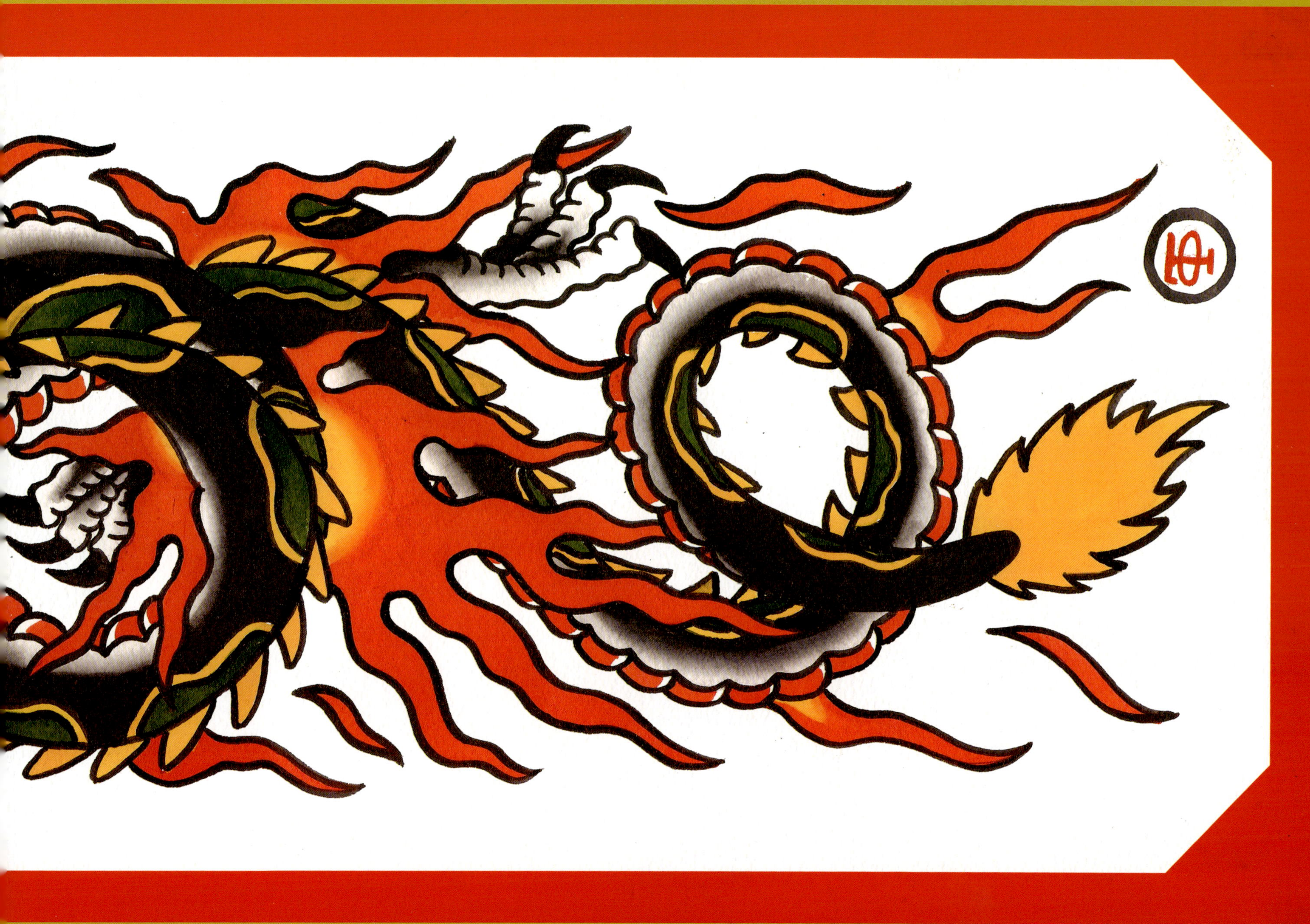

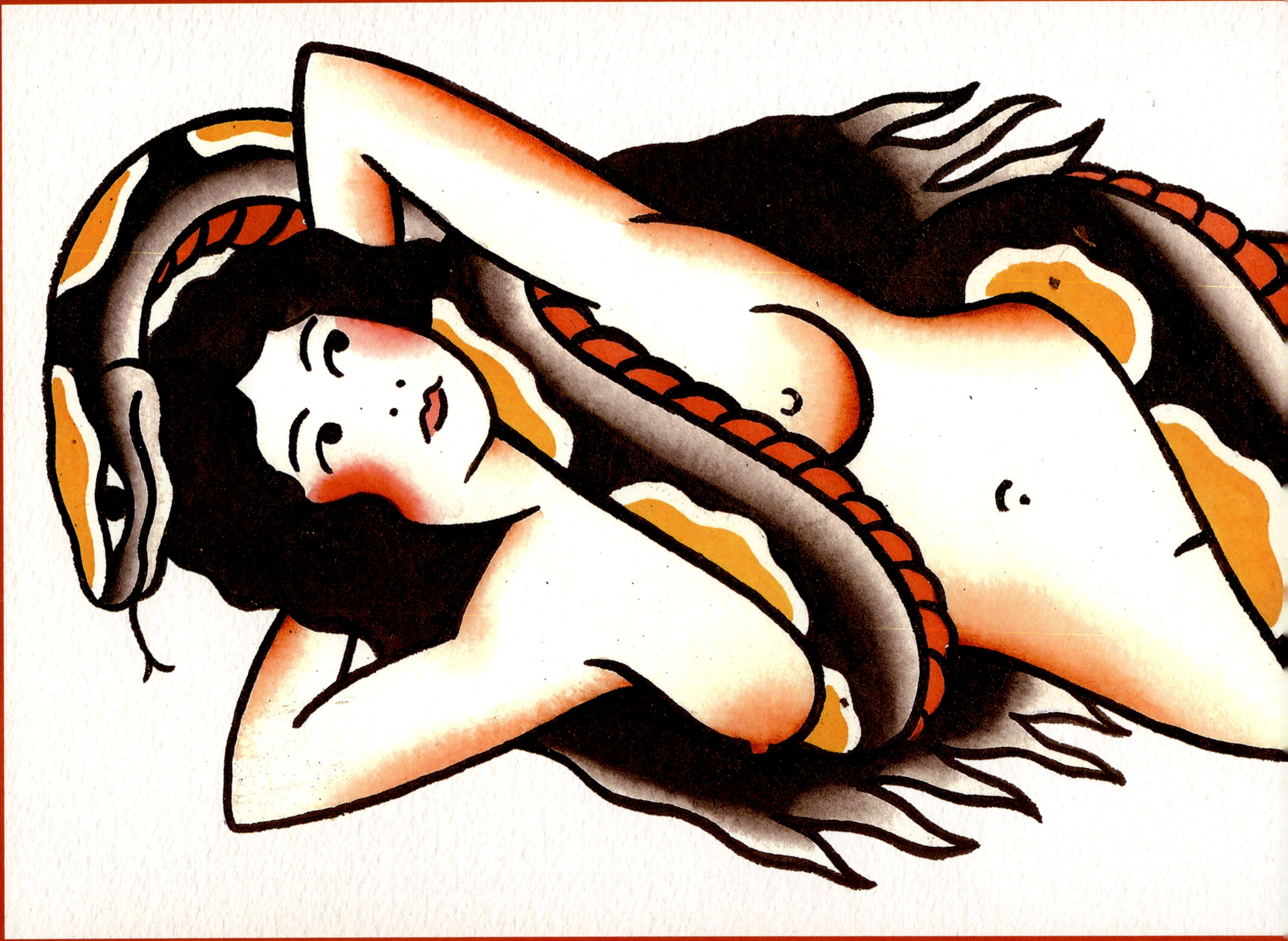

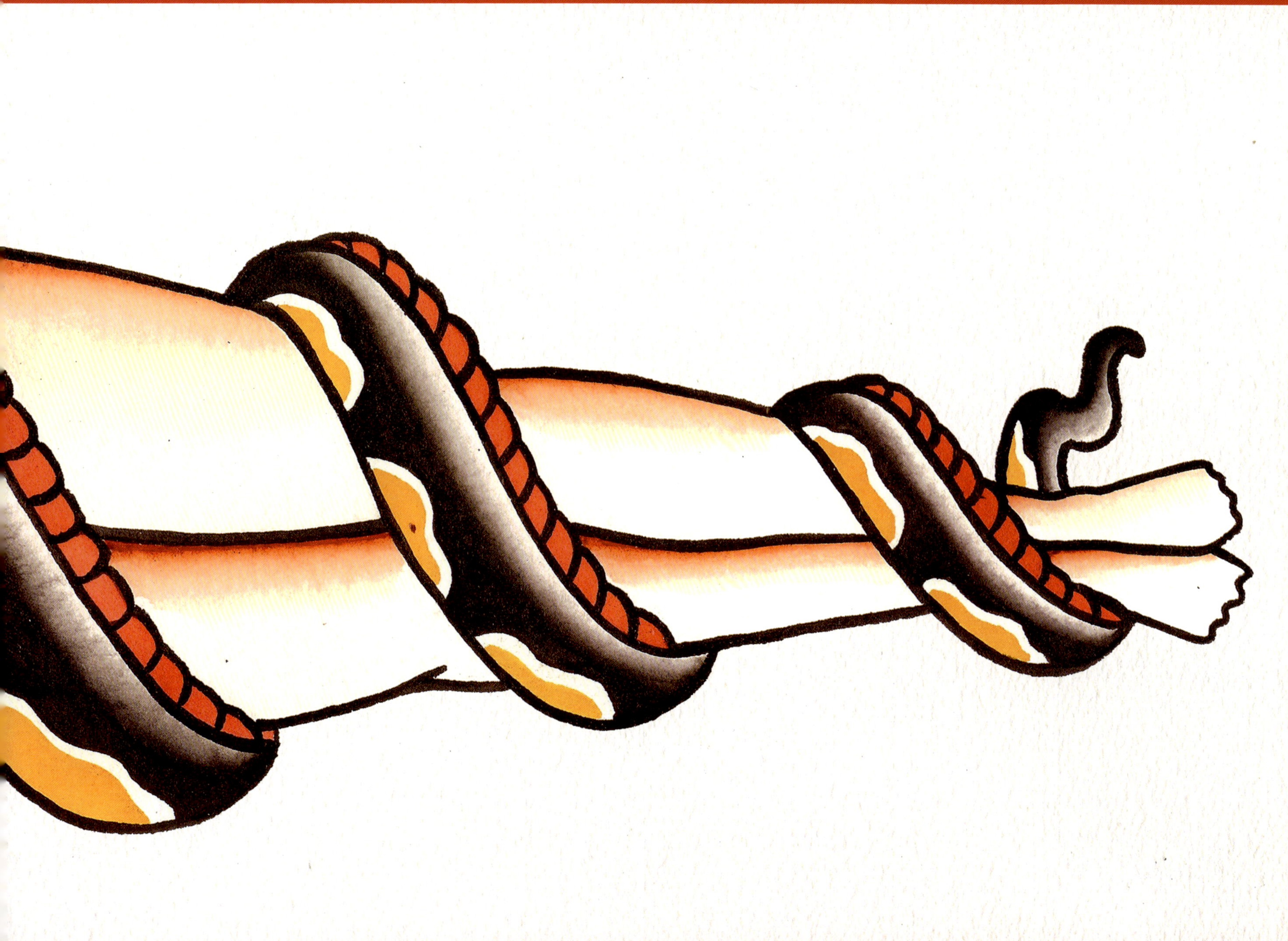

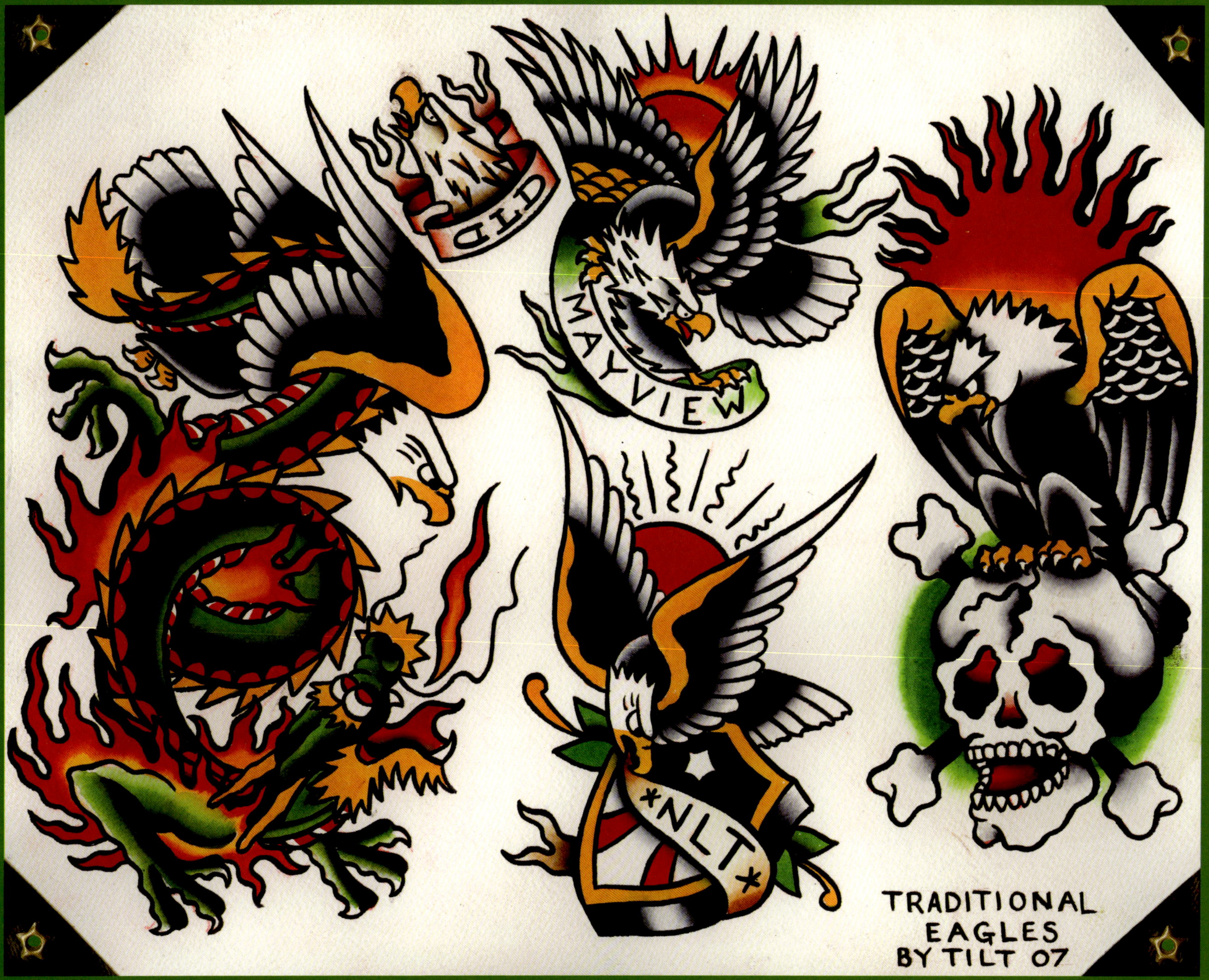
OLD
MAYVIEW
NLT
TRADITIONAL
EAGLES
BY TILT 07

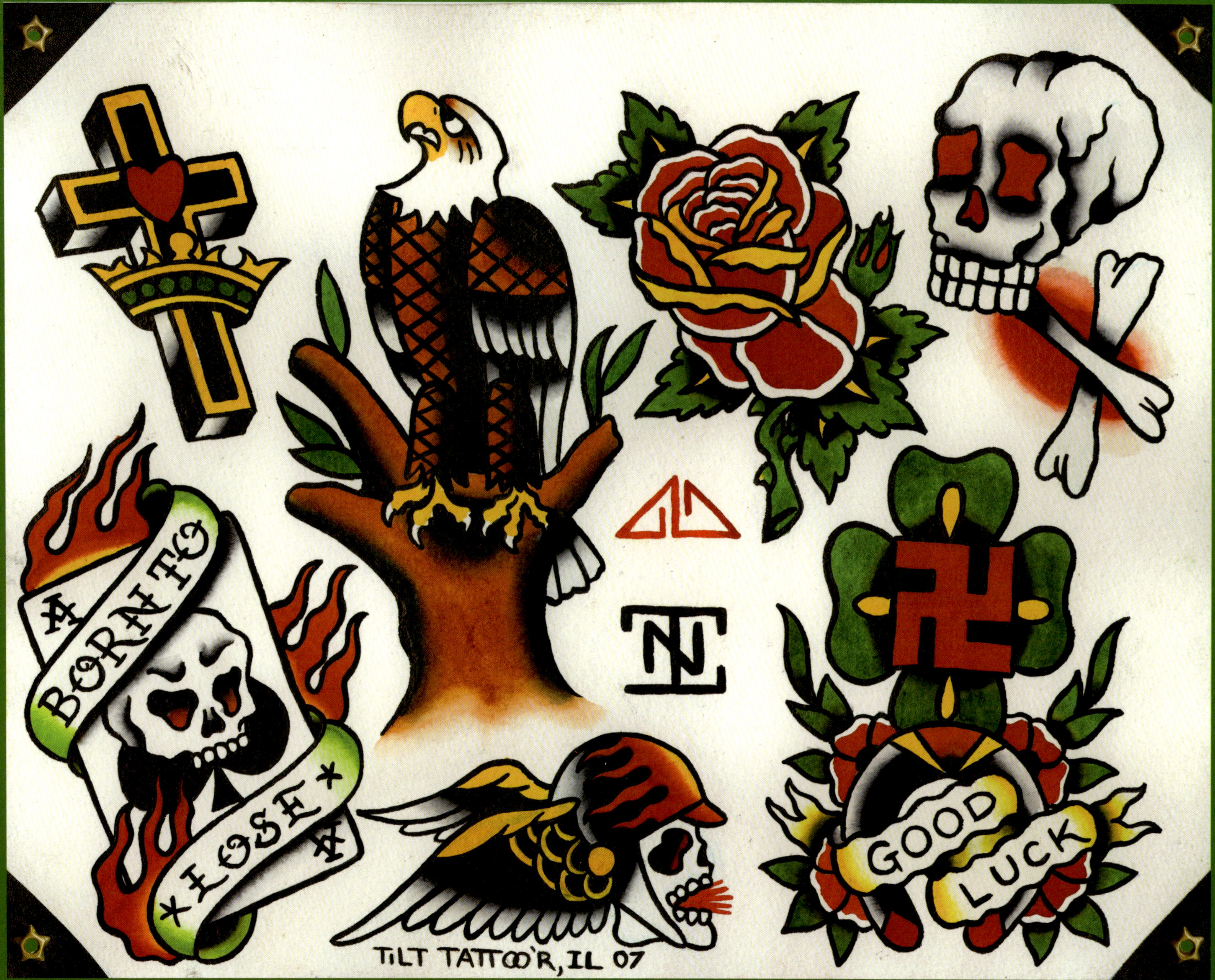
BORN TO
LOSE
GOOD
LUCK
TILT TATTOO'R, IL 07

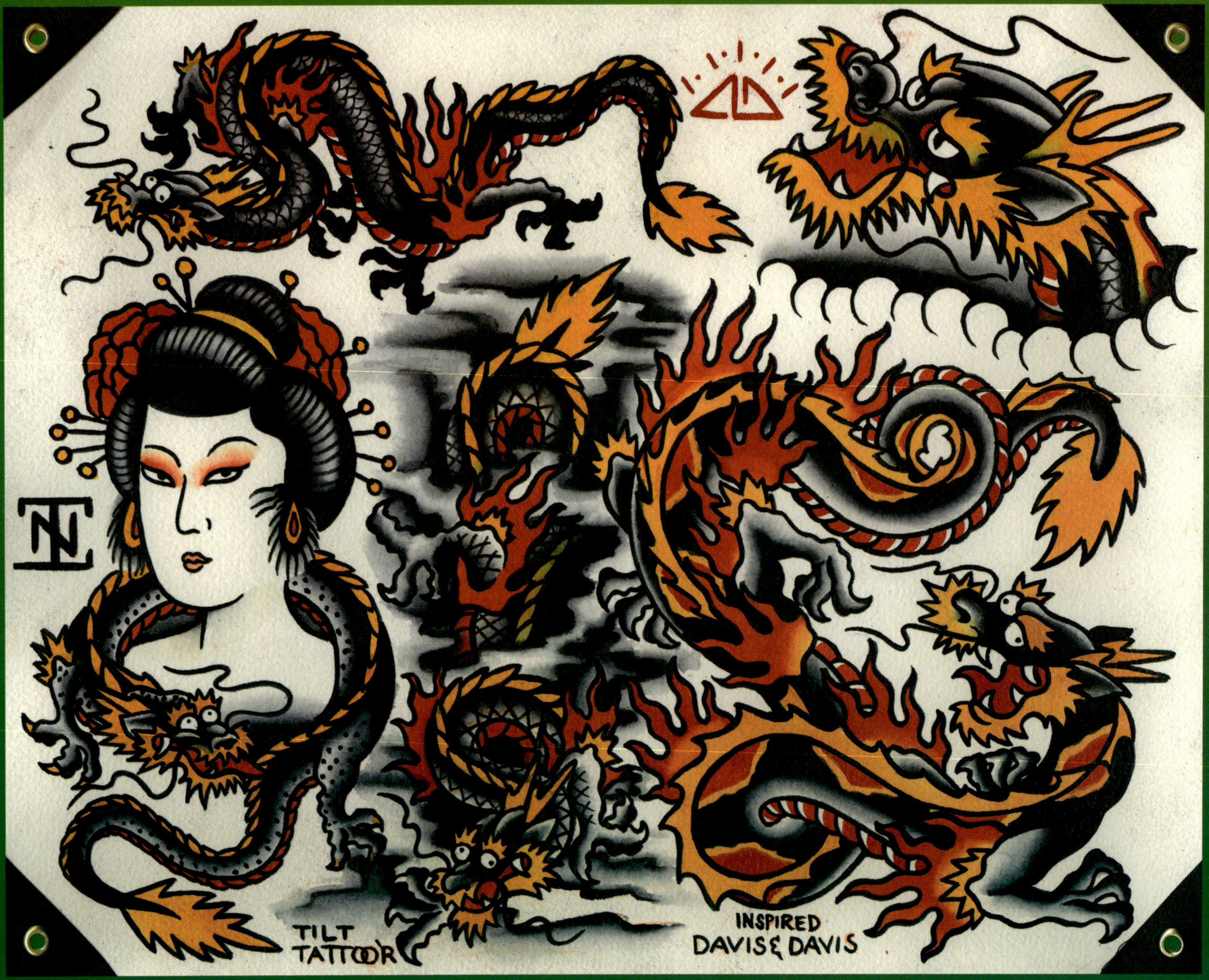
TILT
TATTOO'R
INSPIRED
DAVIS & DAVIS

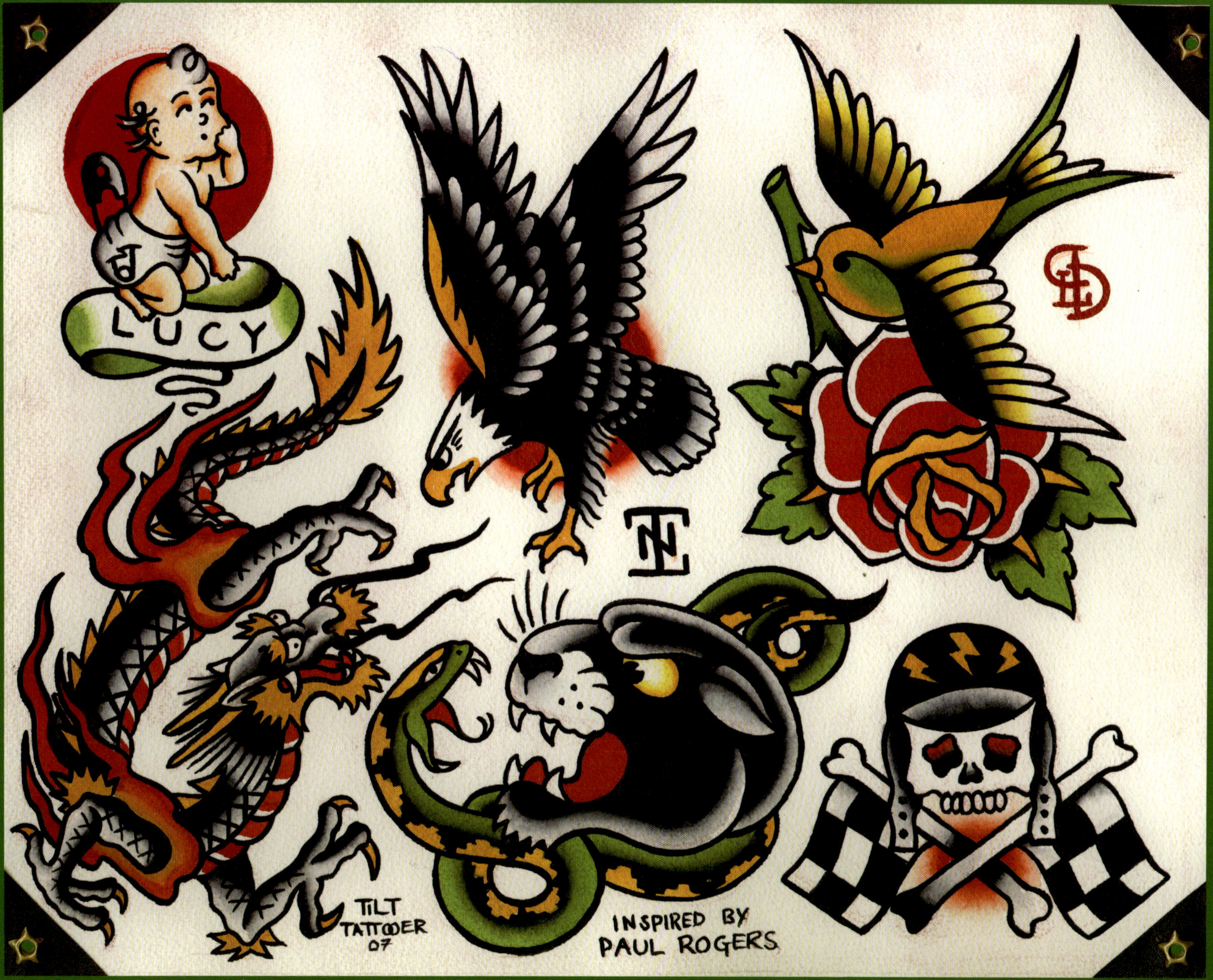
LUCY
TILT
TATTOOER
07
INSPIRED BY
PAUL ROGERS

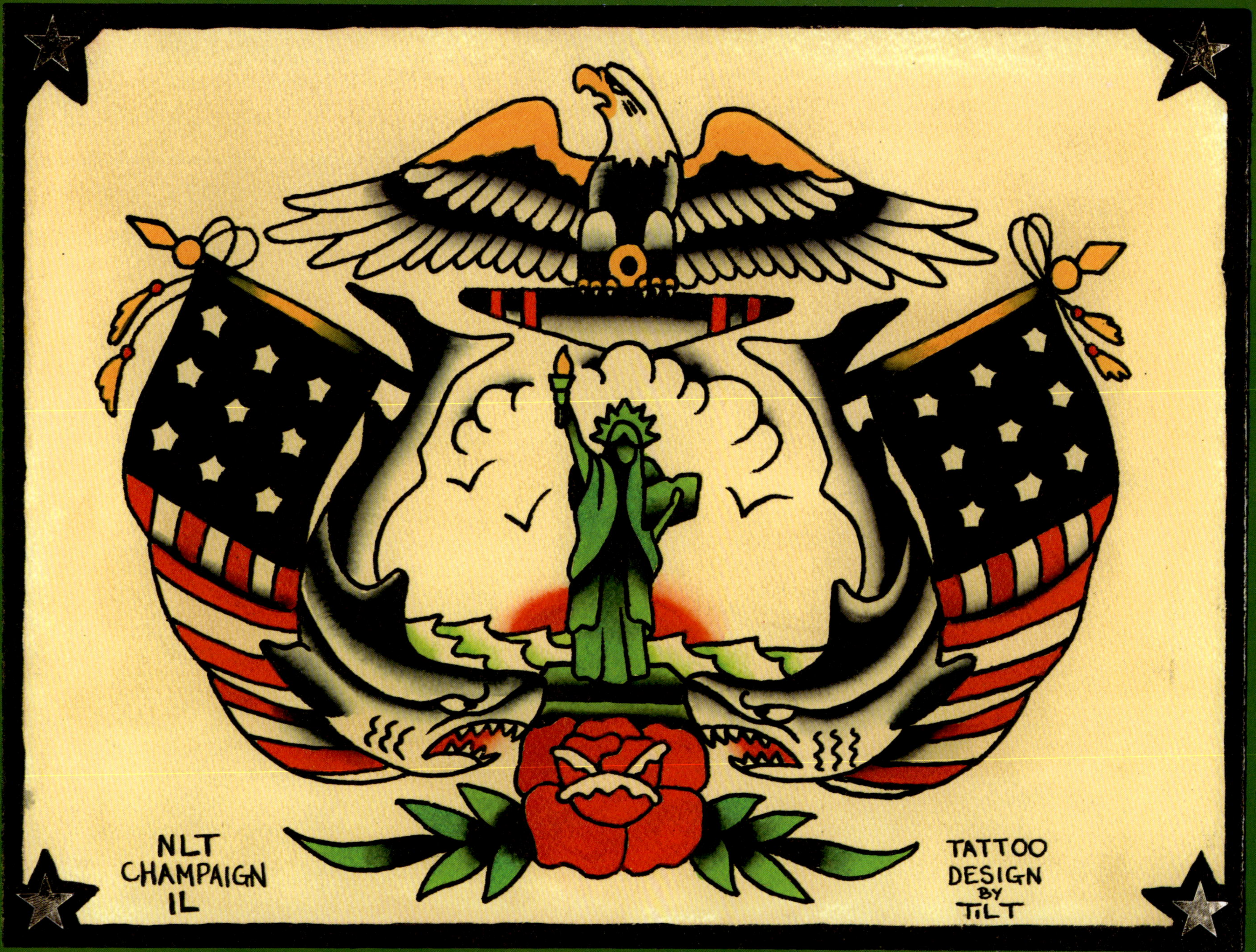
NLT
CHAMPAIGN
IL
TATTOO
DESIGN
BY
TiLT

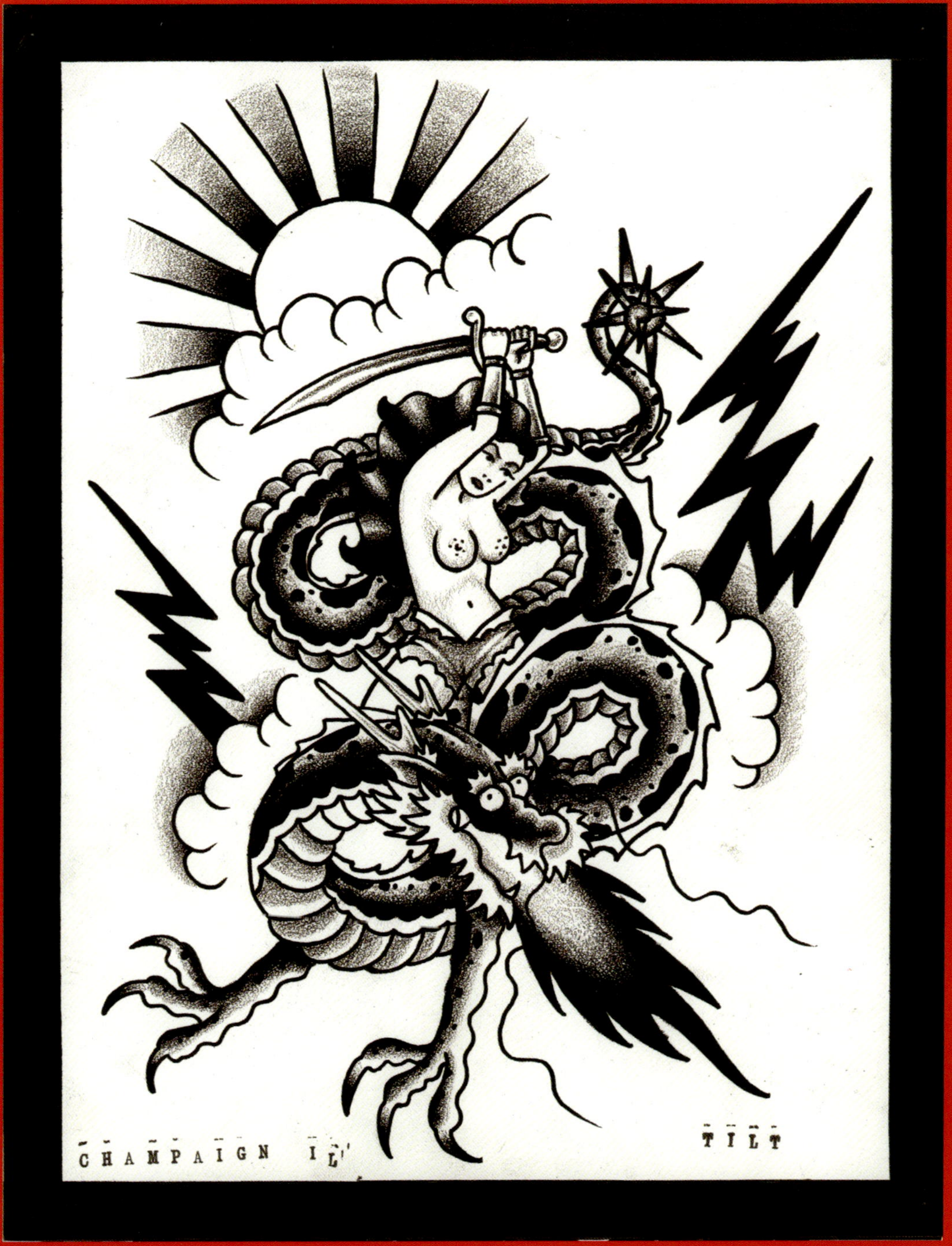
CHAMPAIGN IL
TILT

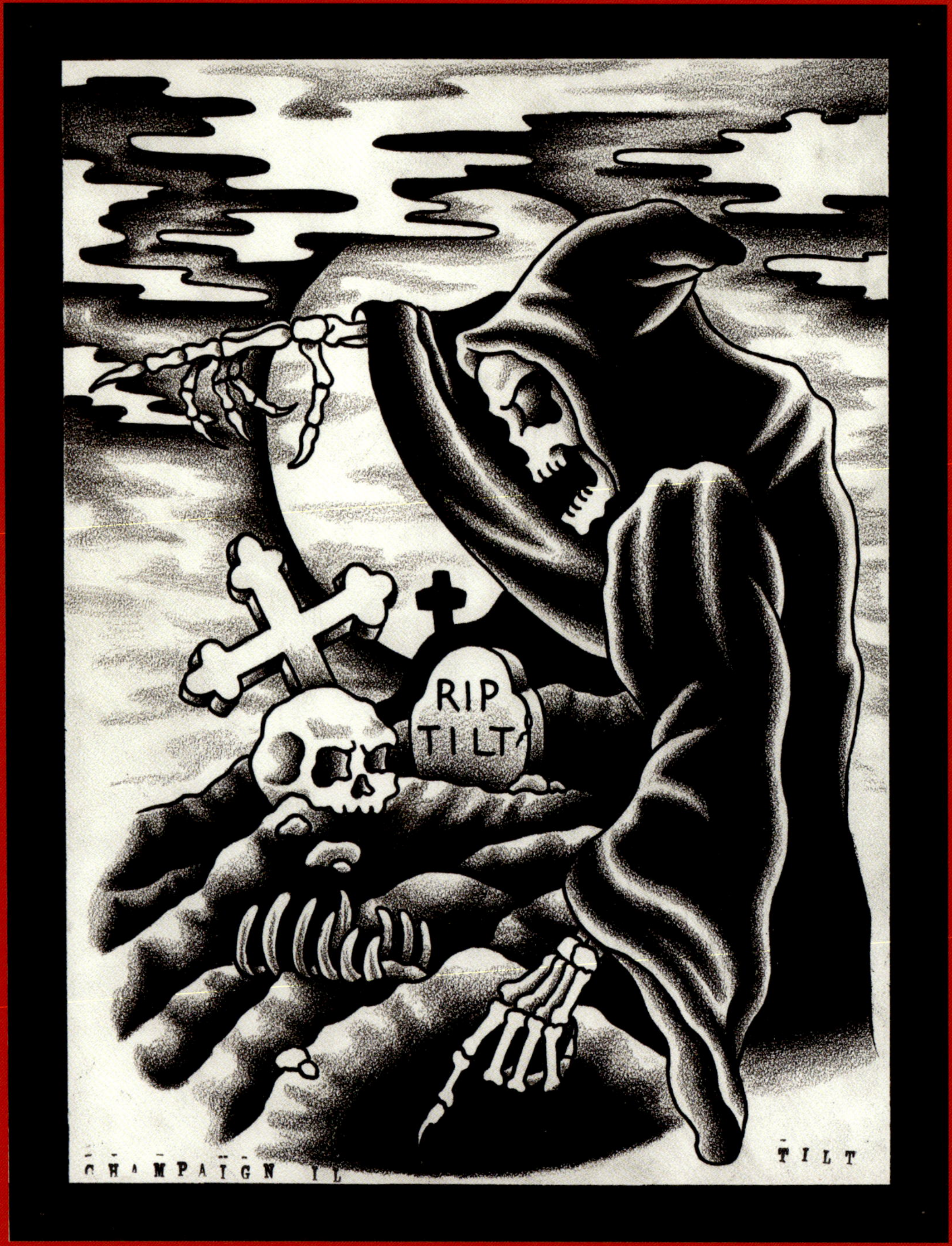
RIP
TILT
CHAMPAIGN IL
TILT

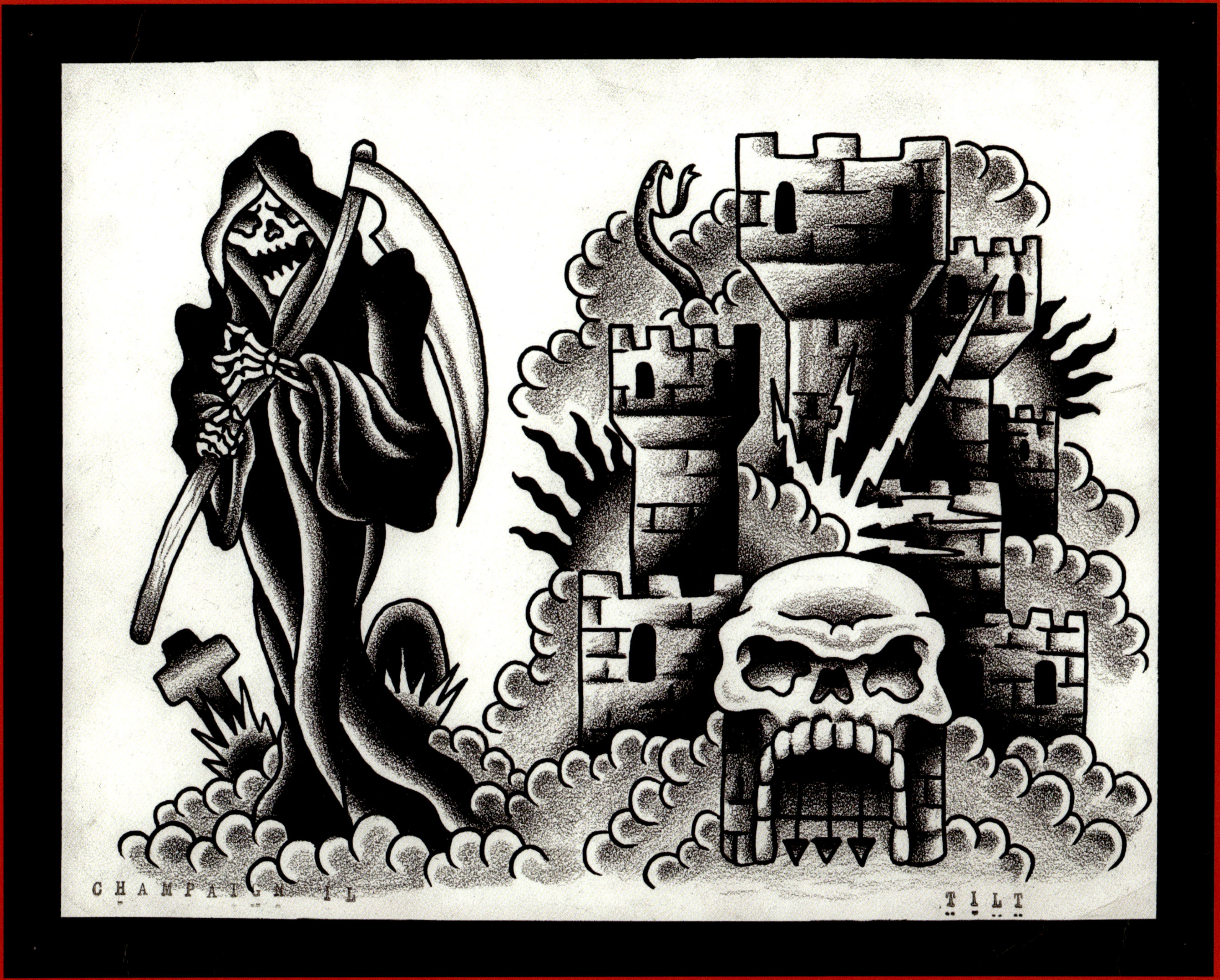
CHAMPAIGN IL
TILT

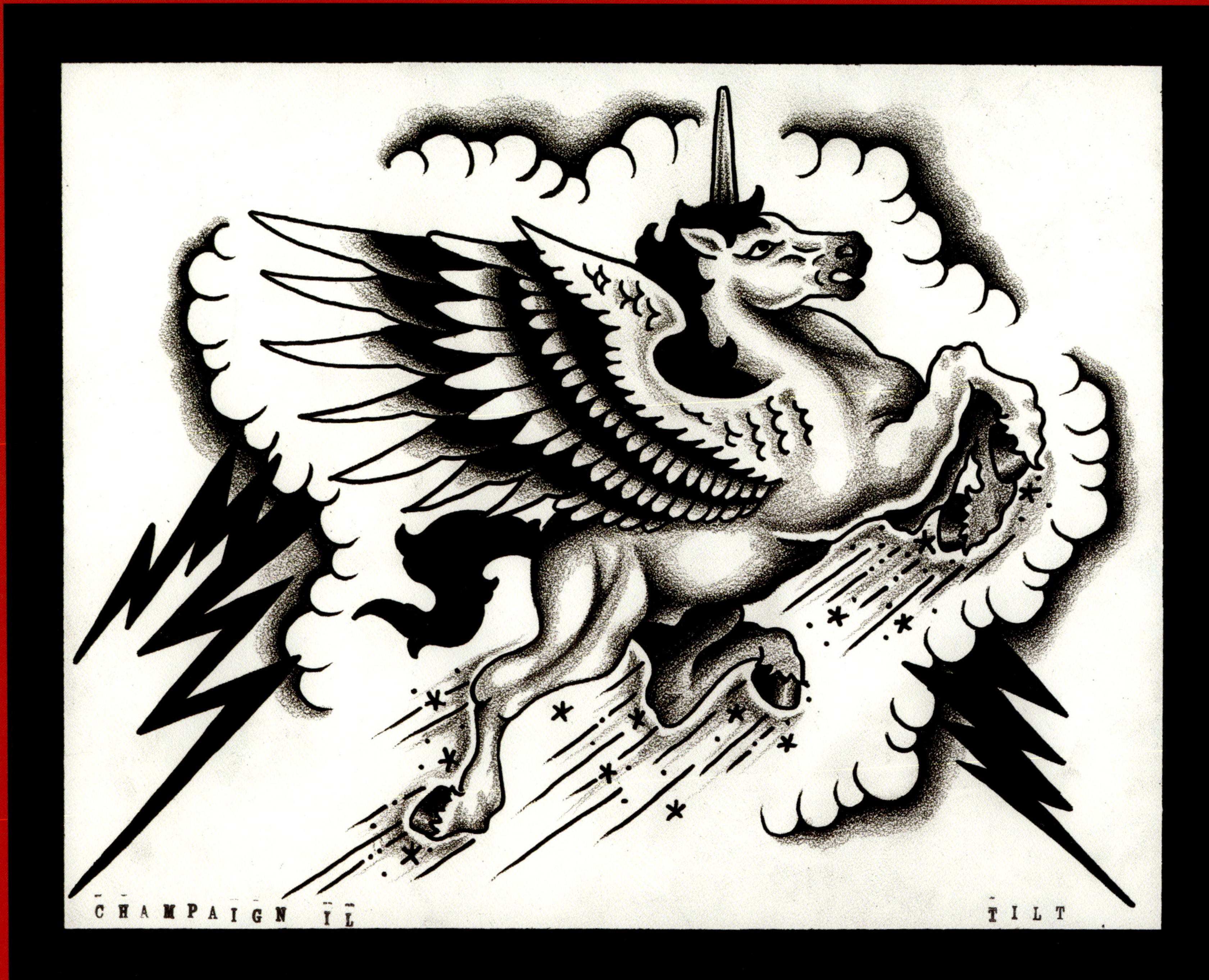
CHAMPAIGN IL
TILT

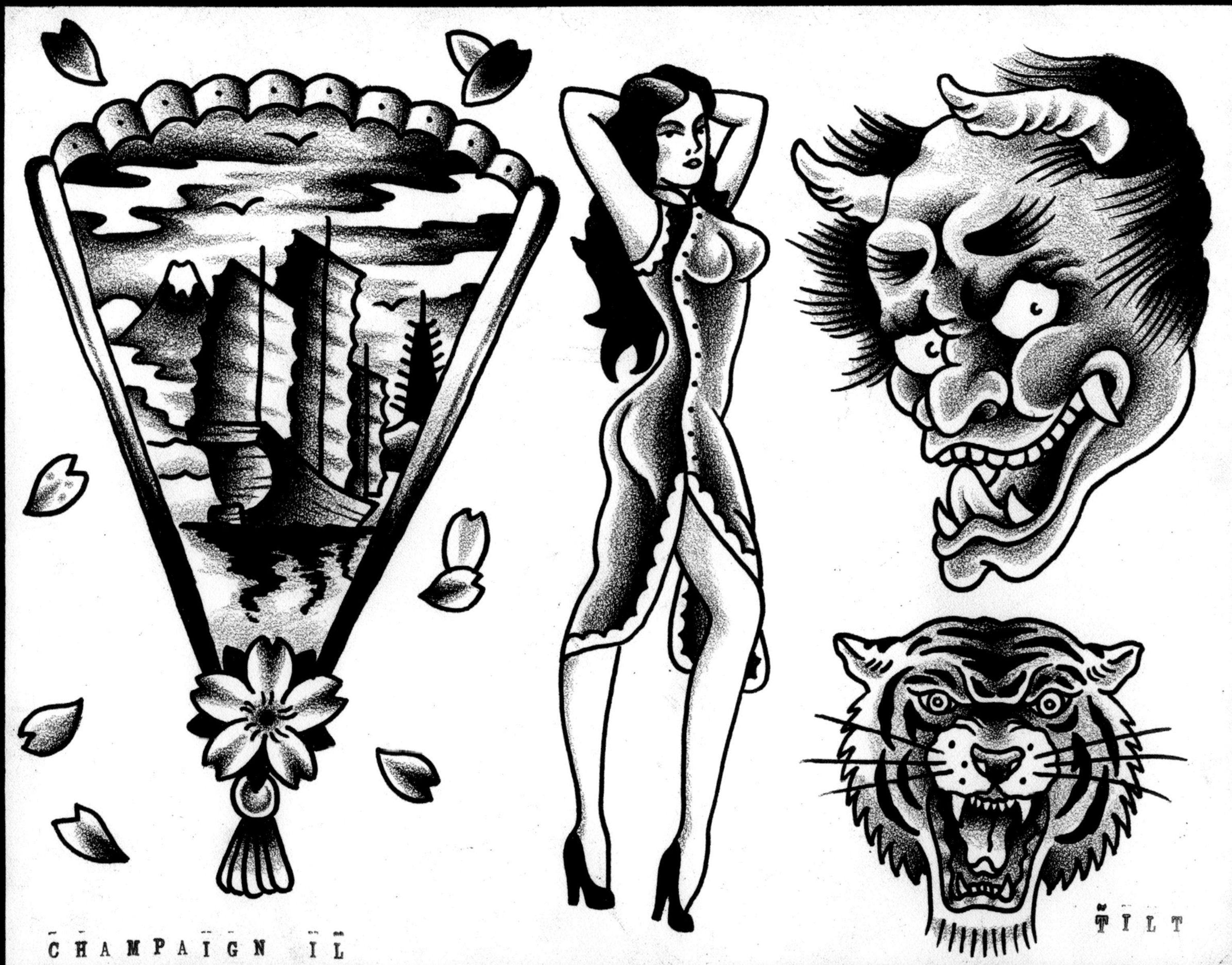
CHAMPAIGN IL
TILT

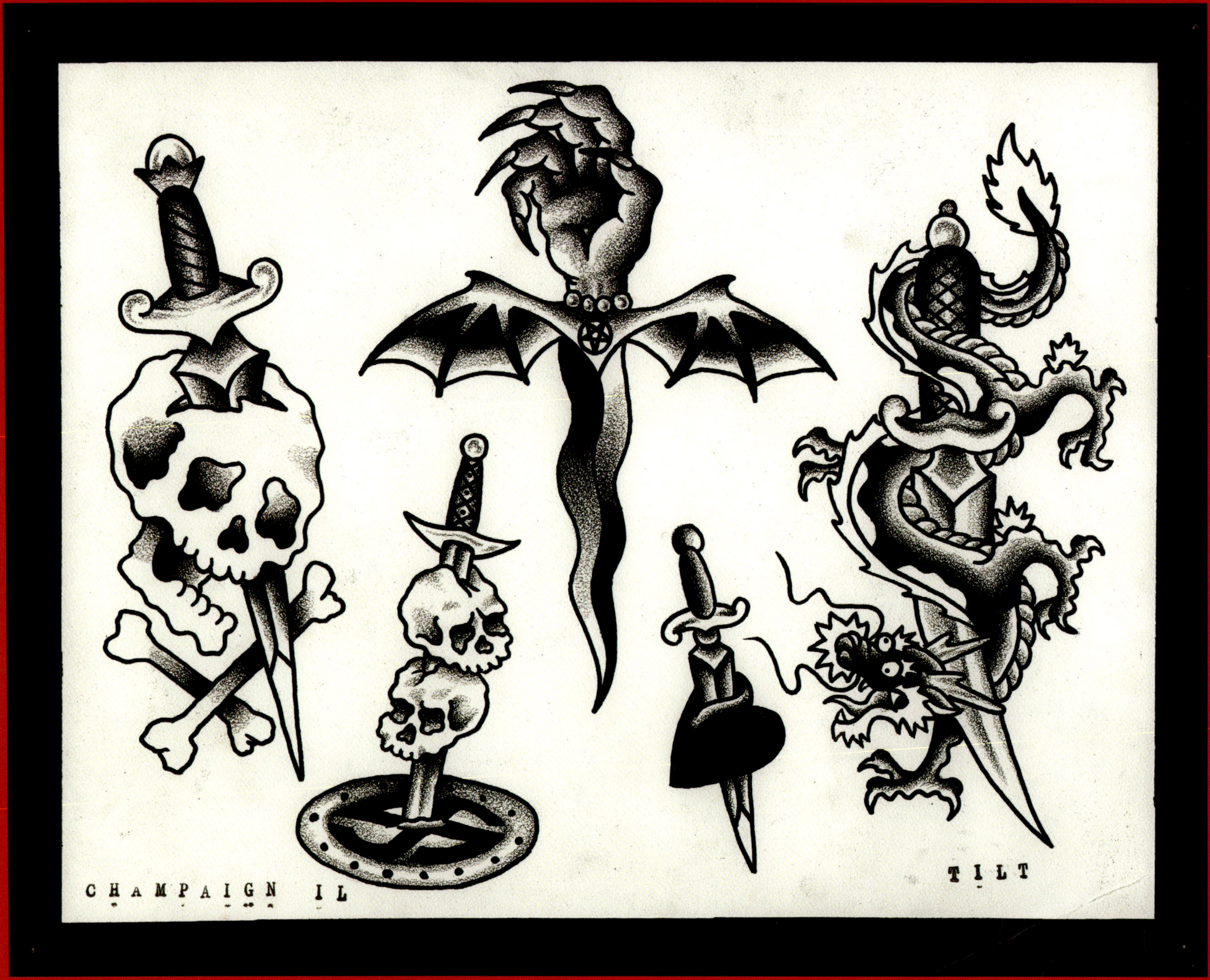
CHAMPAIGN IL
TILT

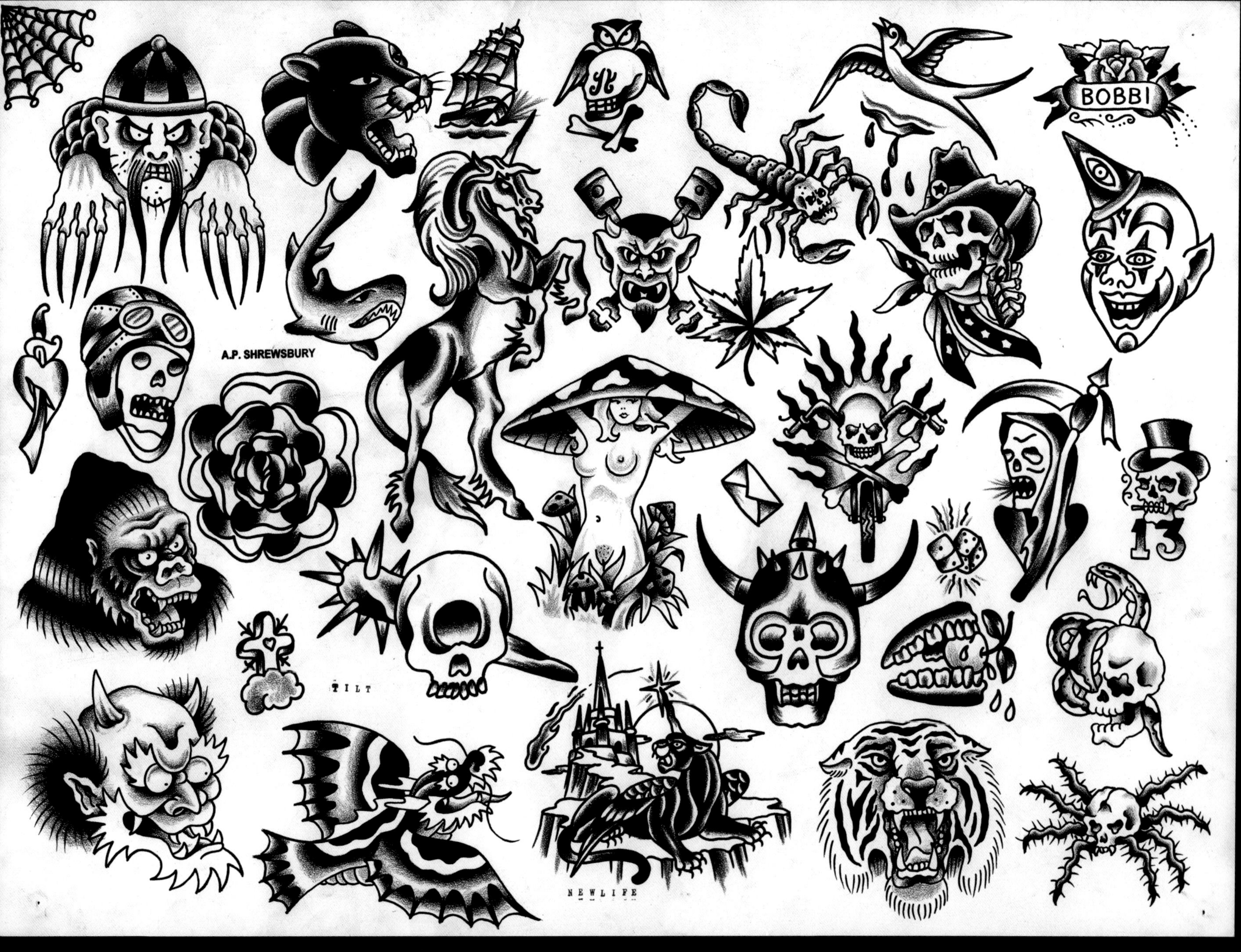

A.P. Shrewsbury & Tilt

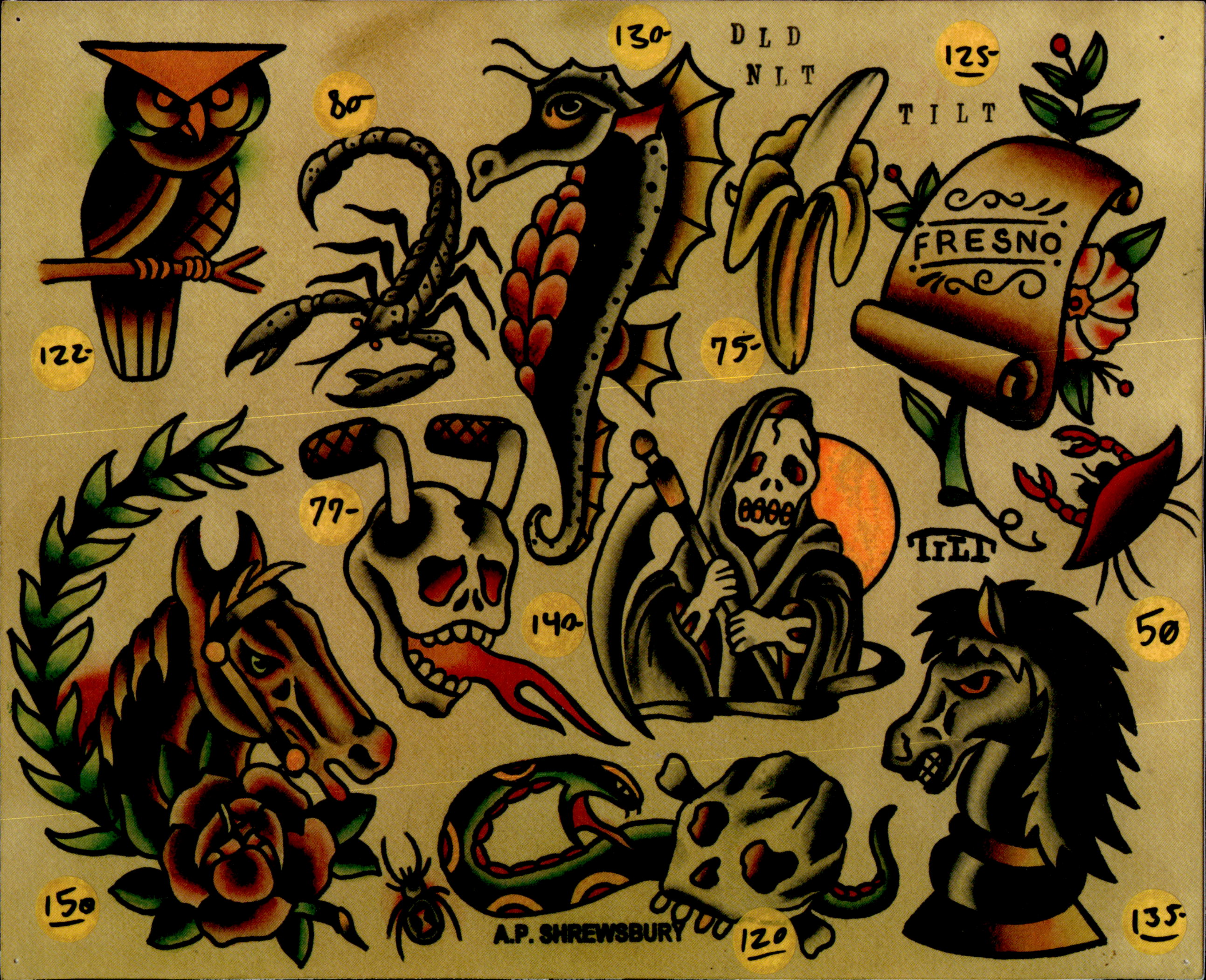

A.P. Shrewsbury & Tilt

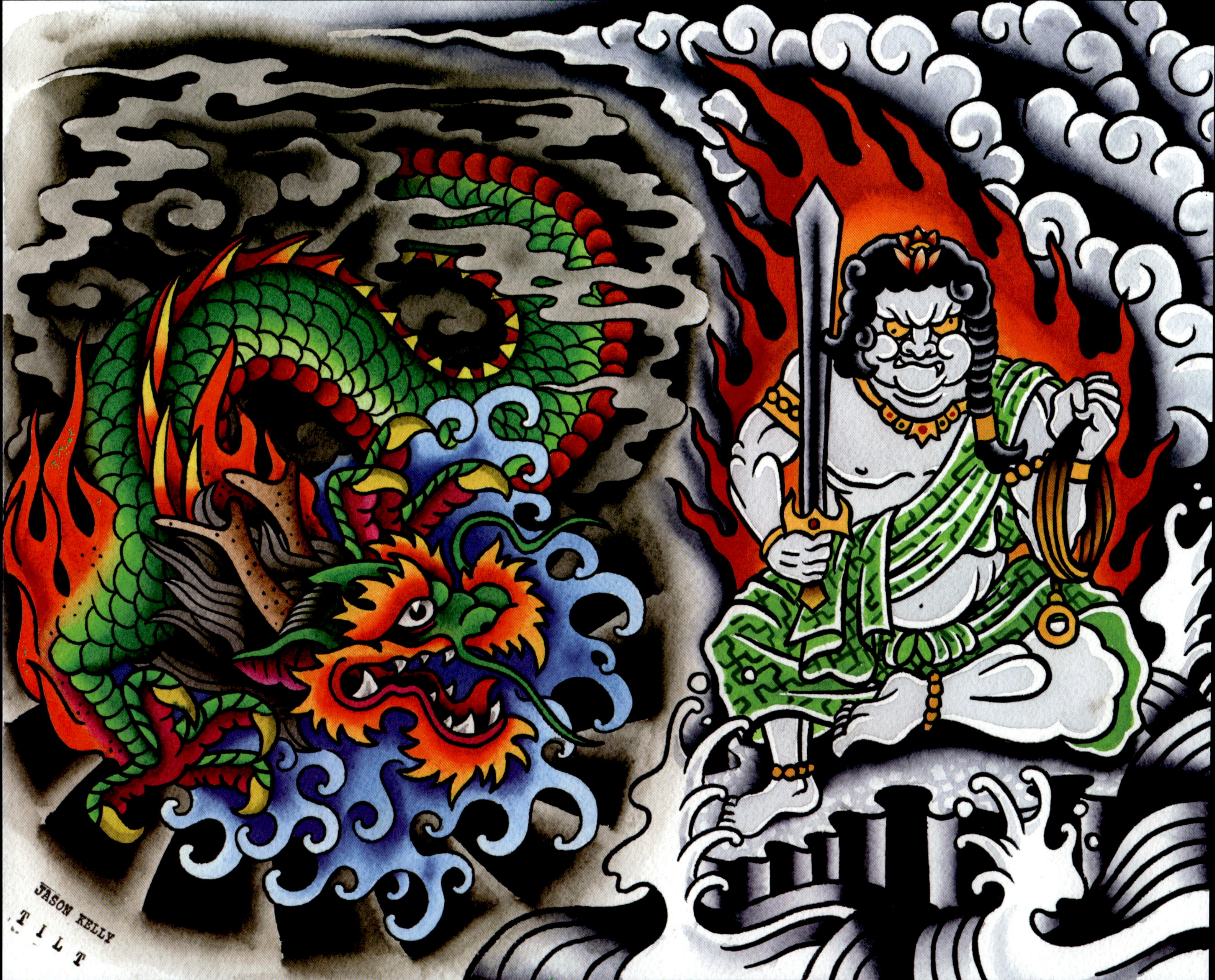
JASON KELLY
TILT

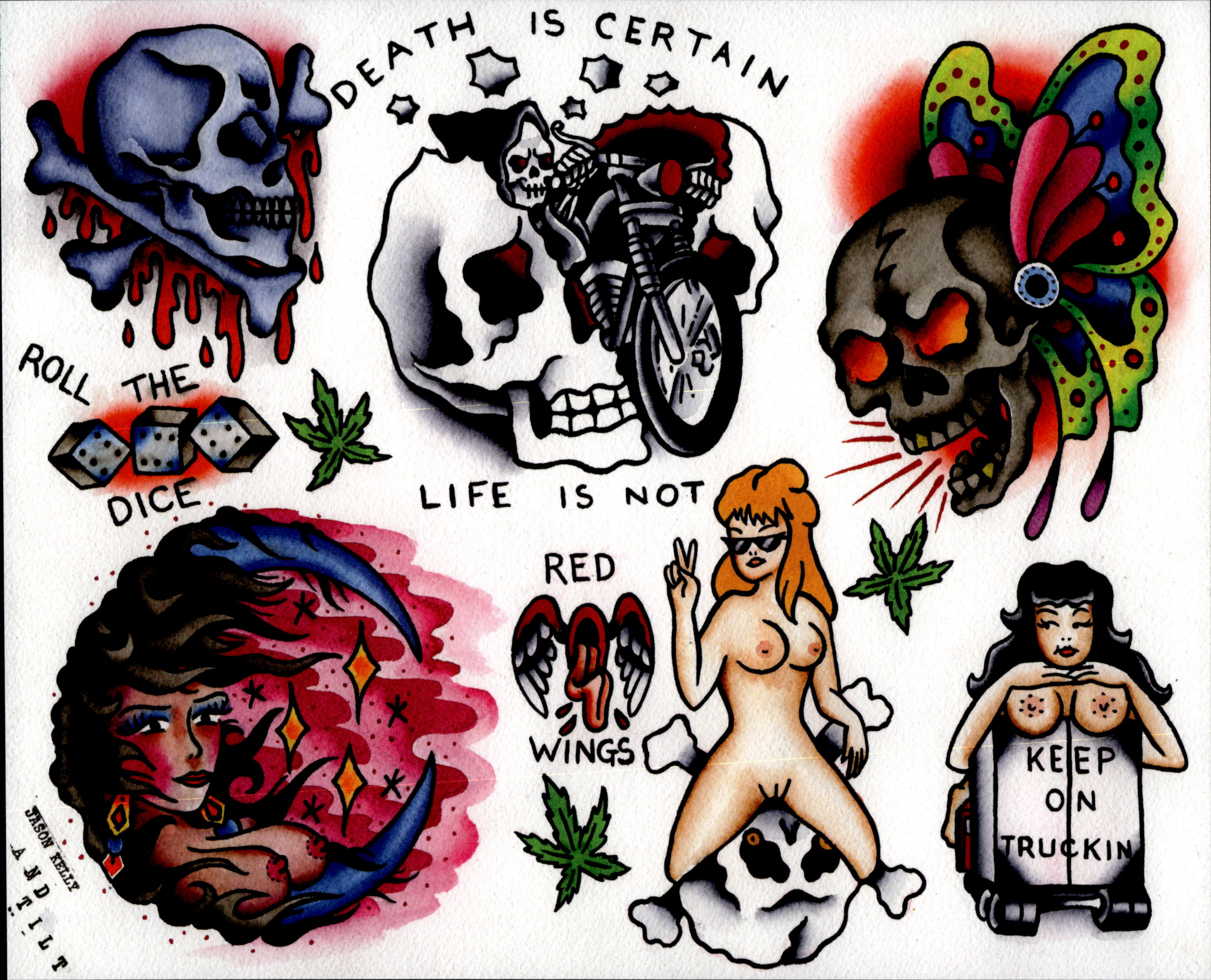

Jason Kelly & Tilt

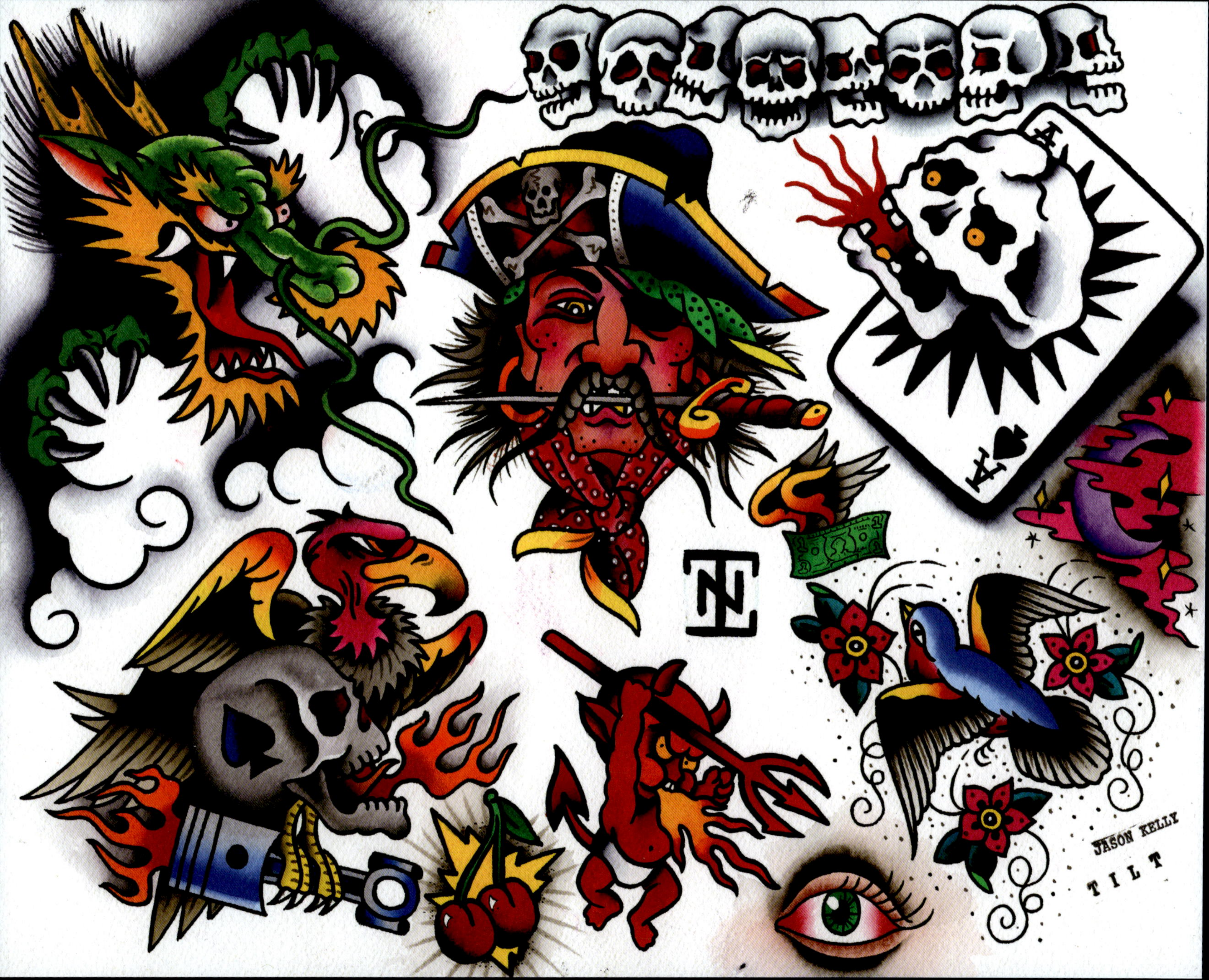

Jason Kelly & Tilt

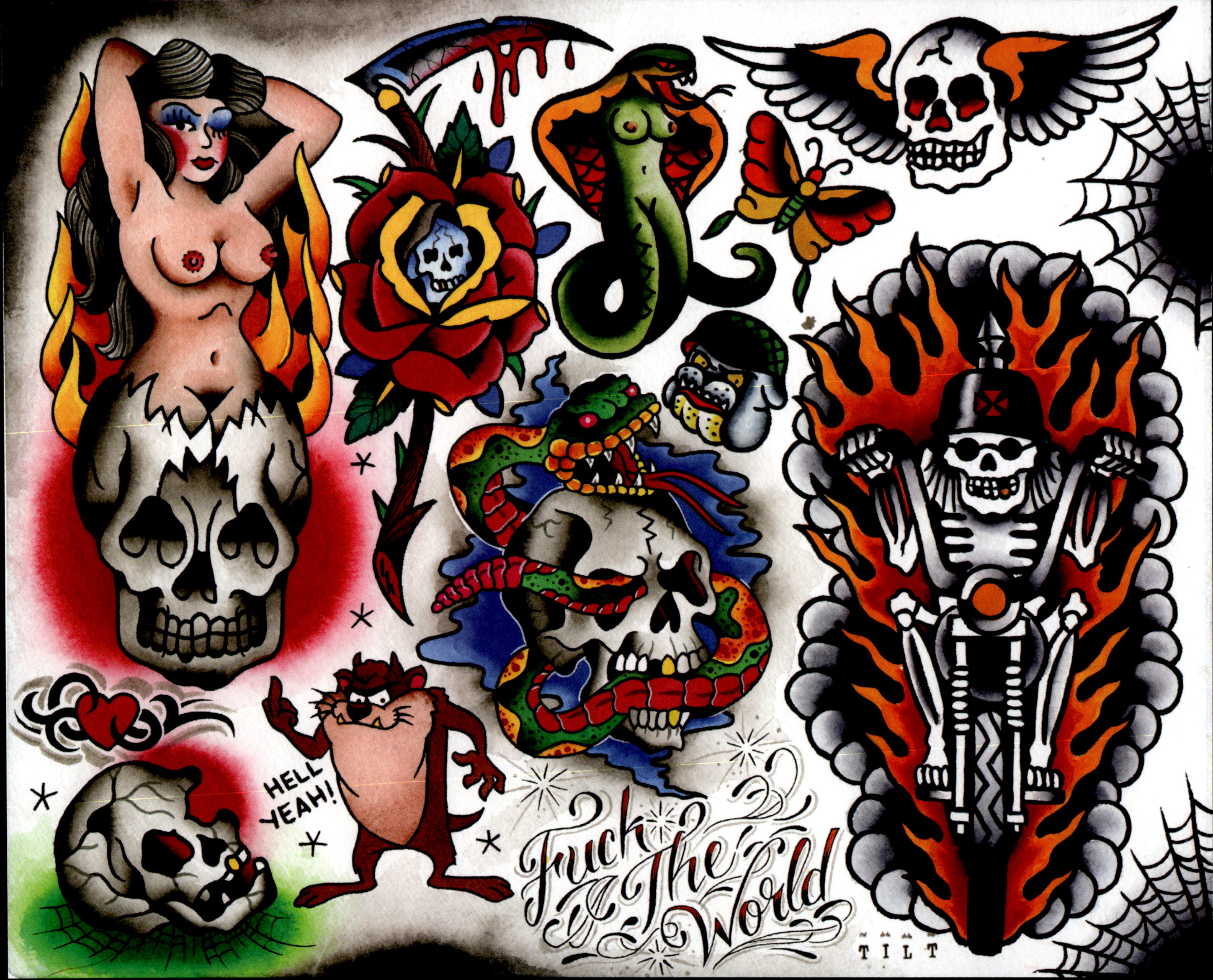

Jason Kelly & Tilt

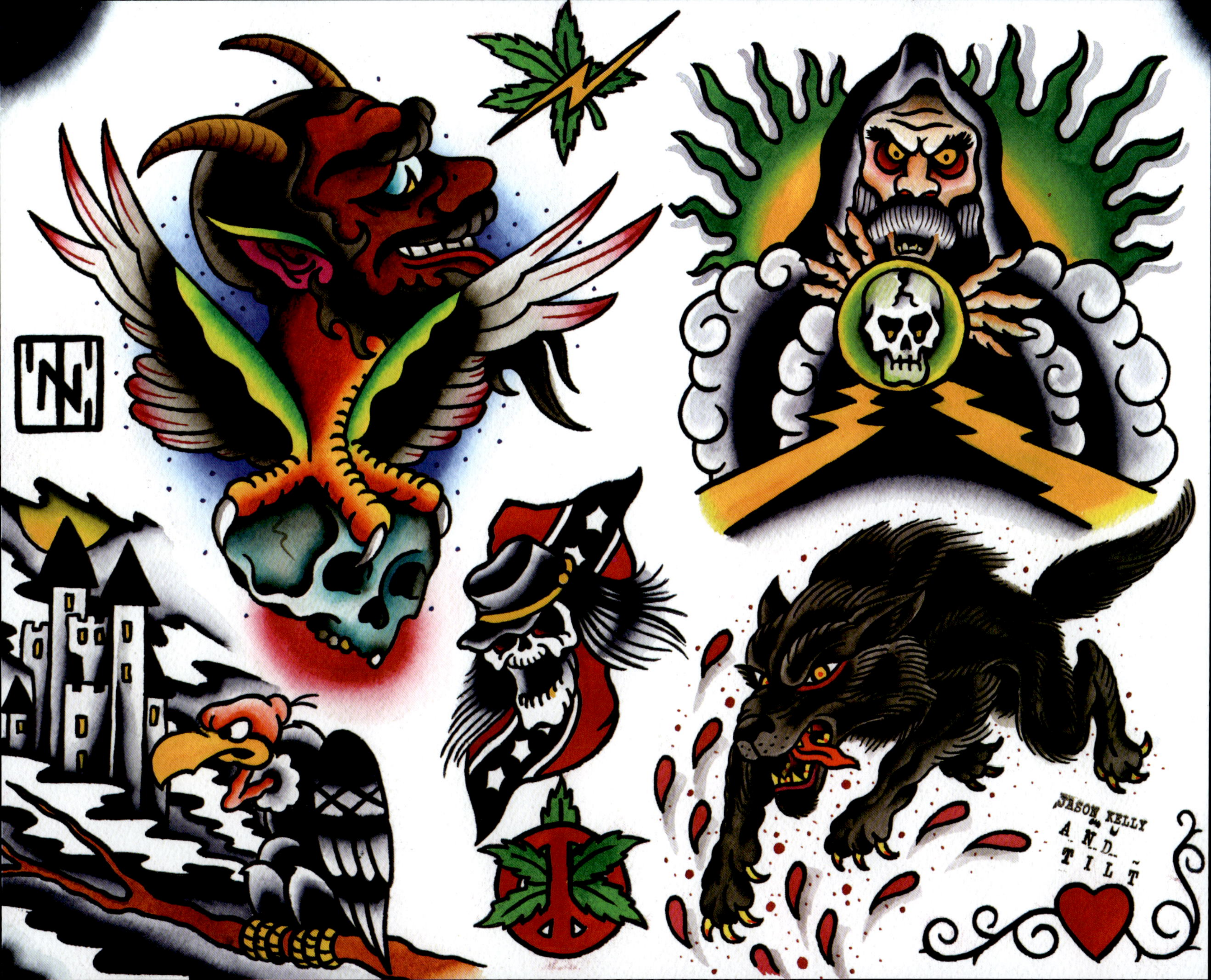

Jason Kelly & Tilt

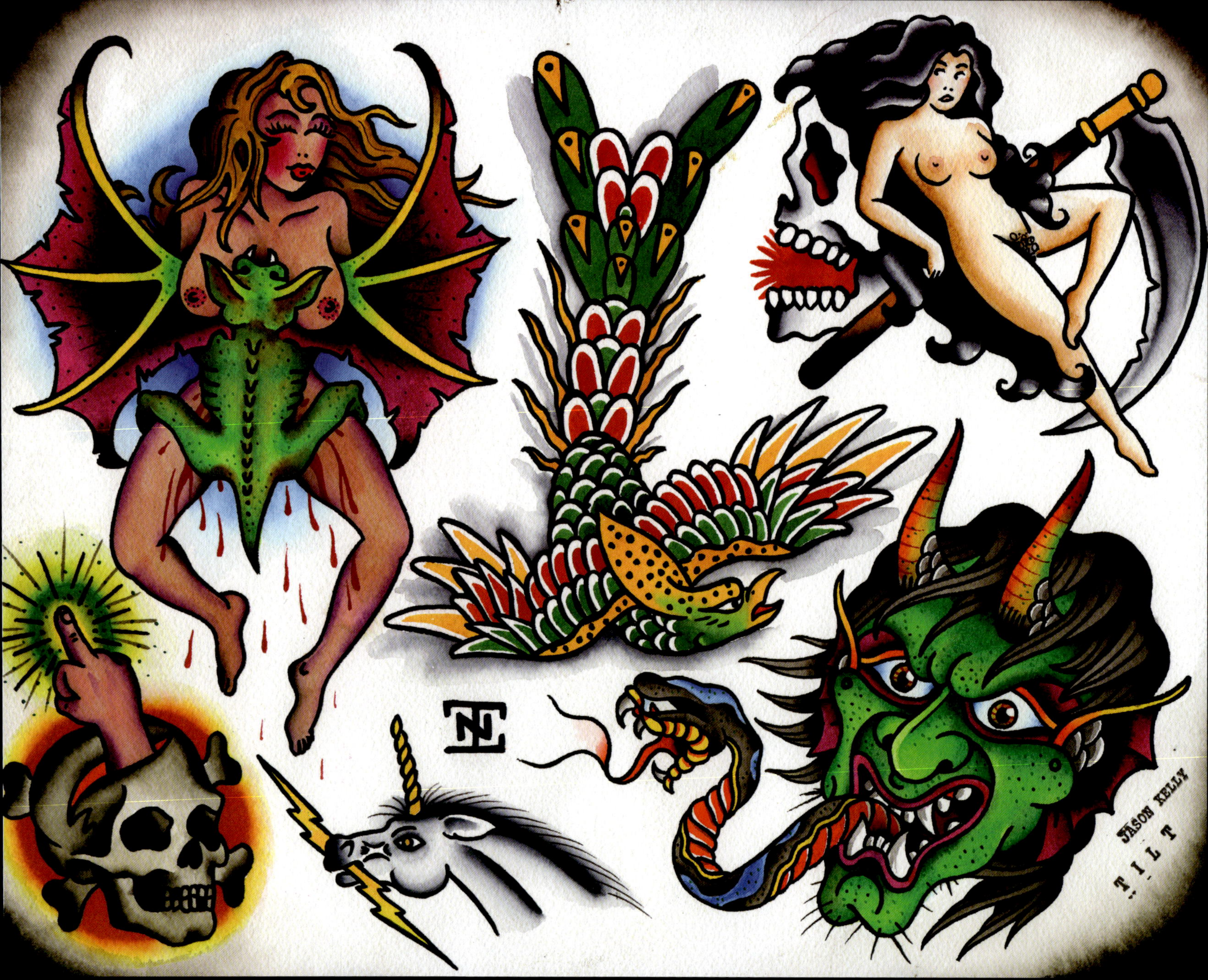

Jason Kelly & Tilt

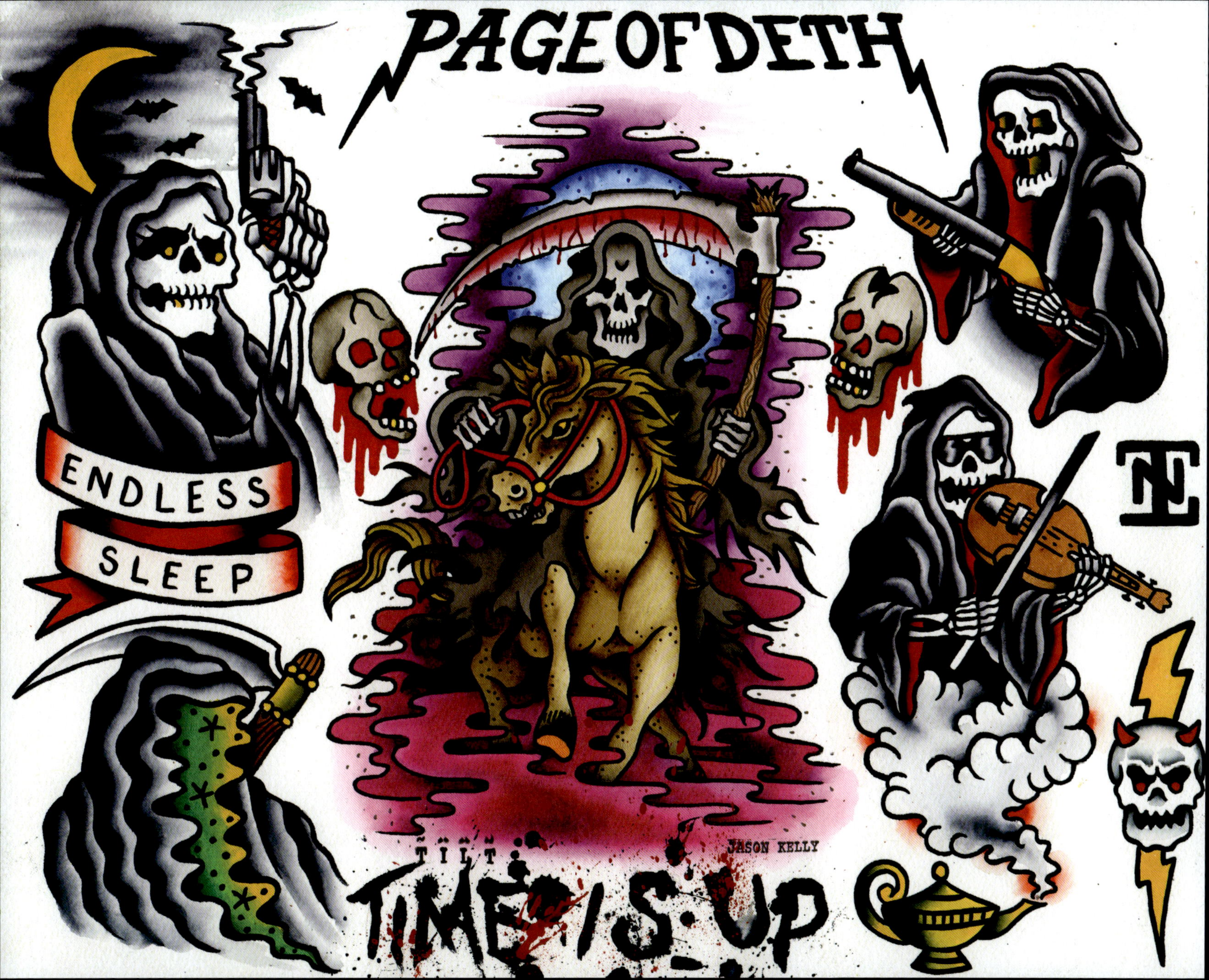

Jason Kelly & Tilt

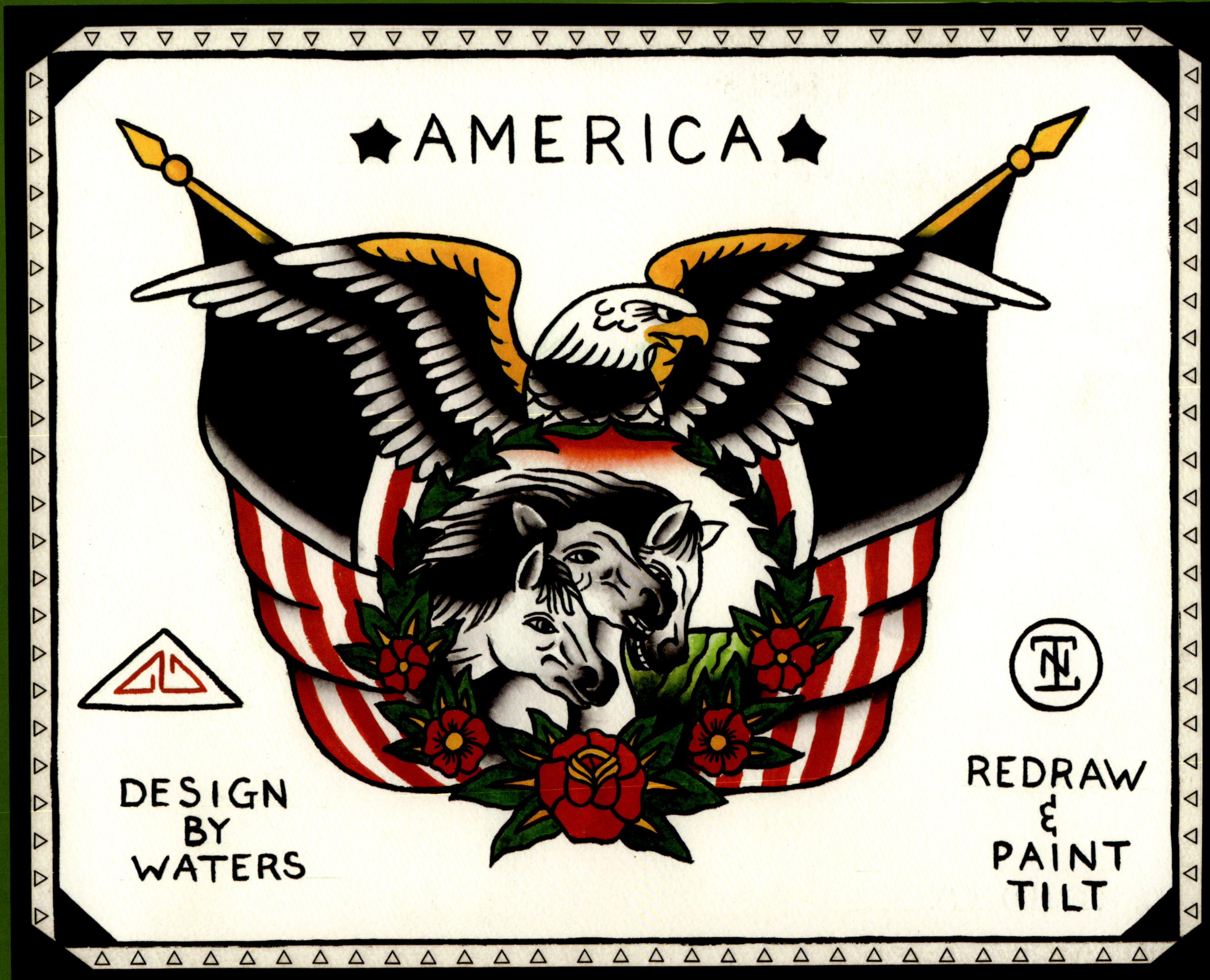

Andrew Stickler & Tilt

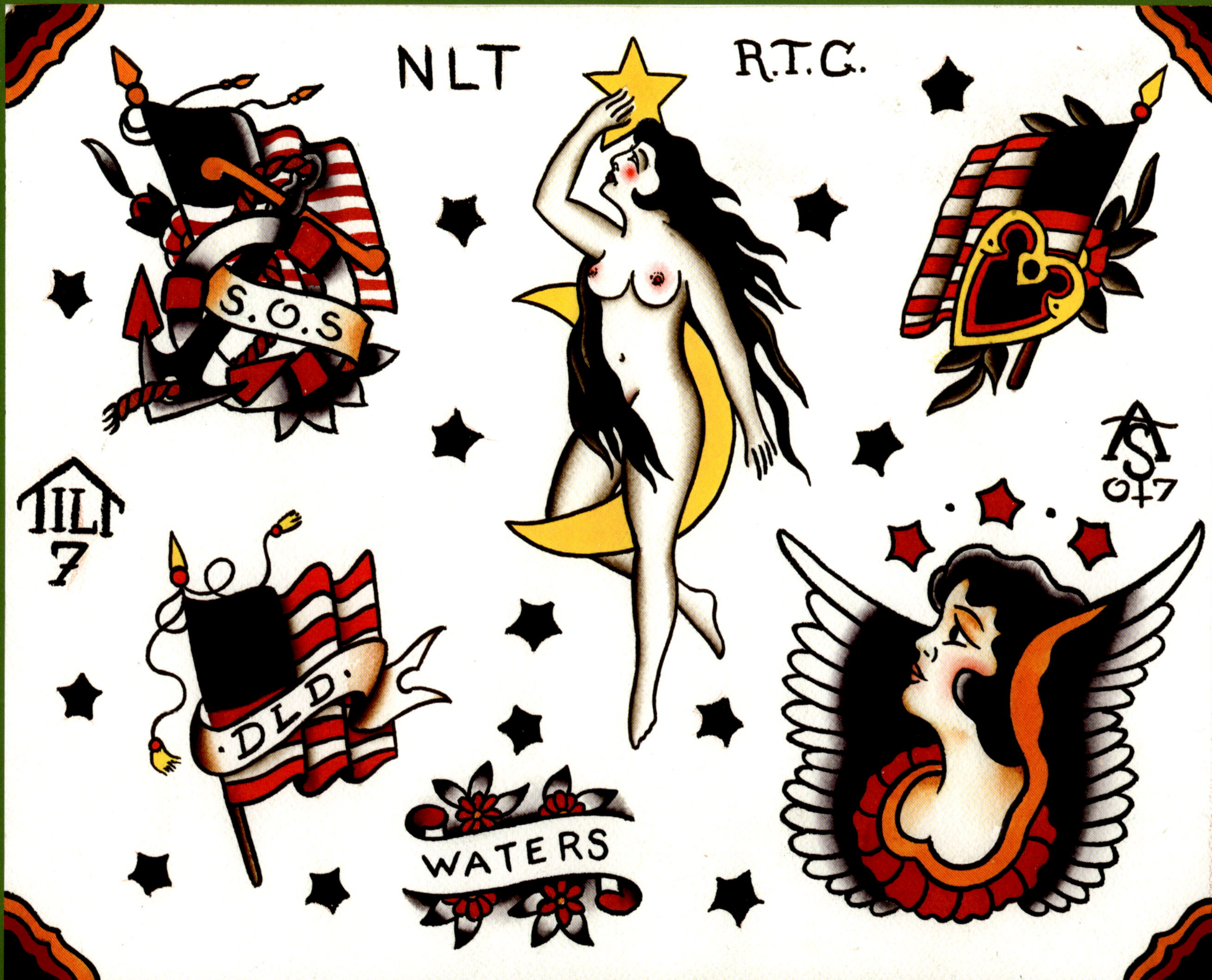

Andrew Stickler & Tilt

Andrew Stickler & Tilt

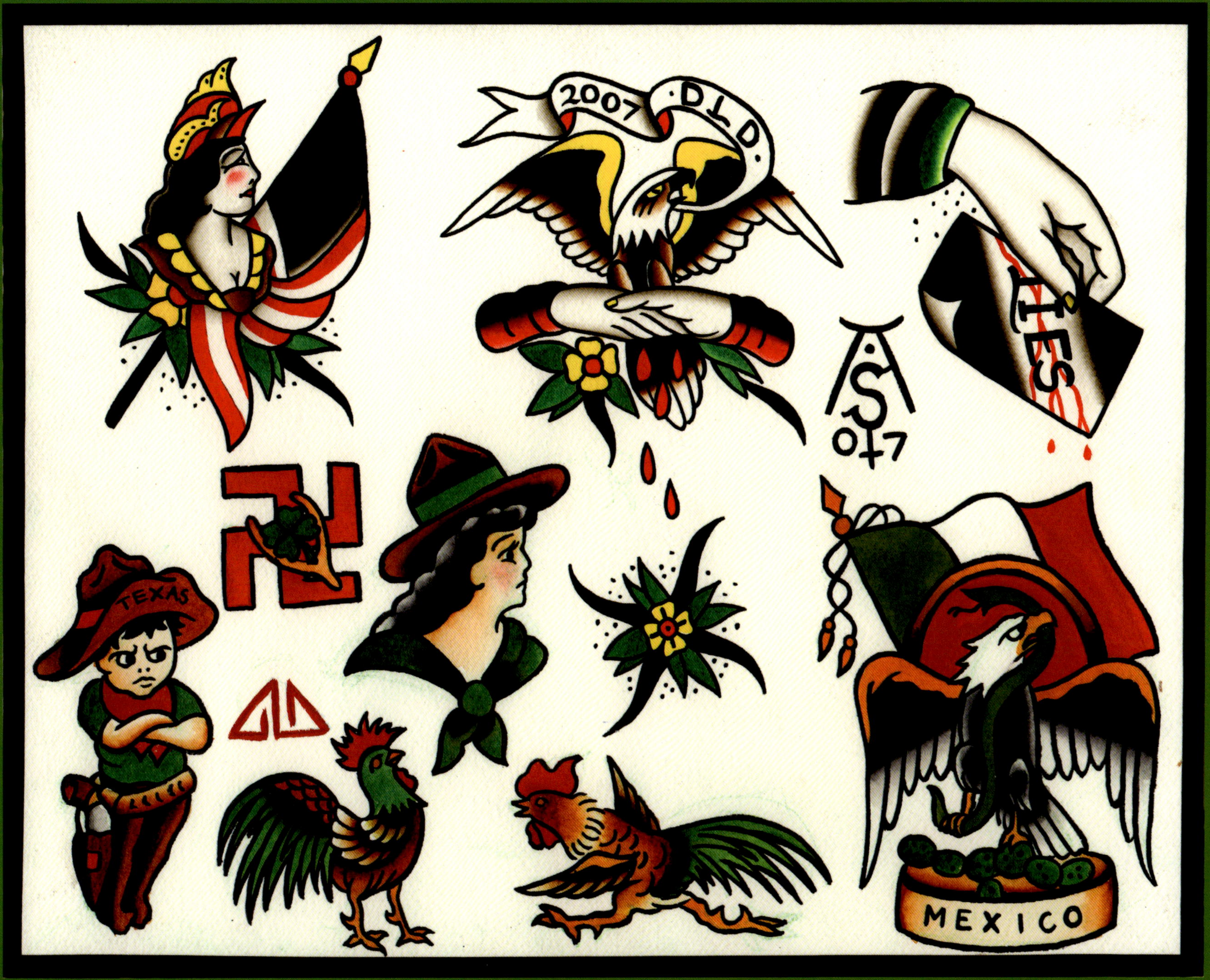

Andrew Stickler & Tilt

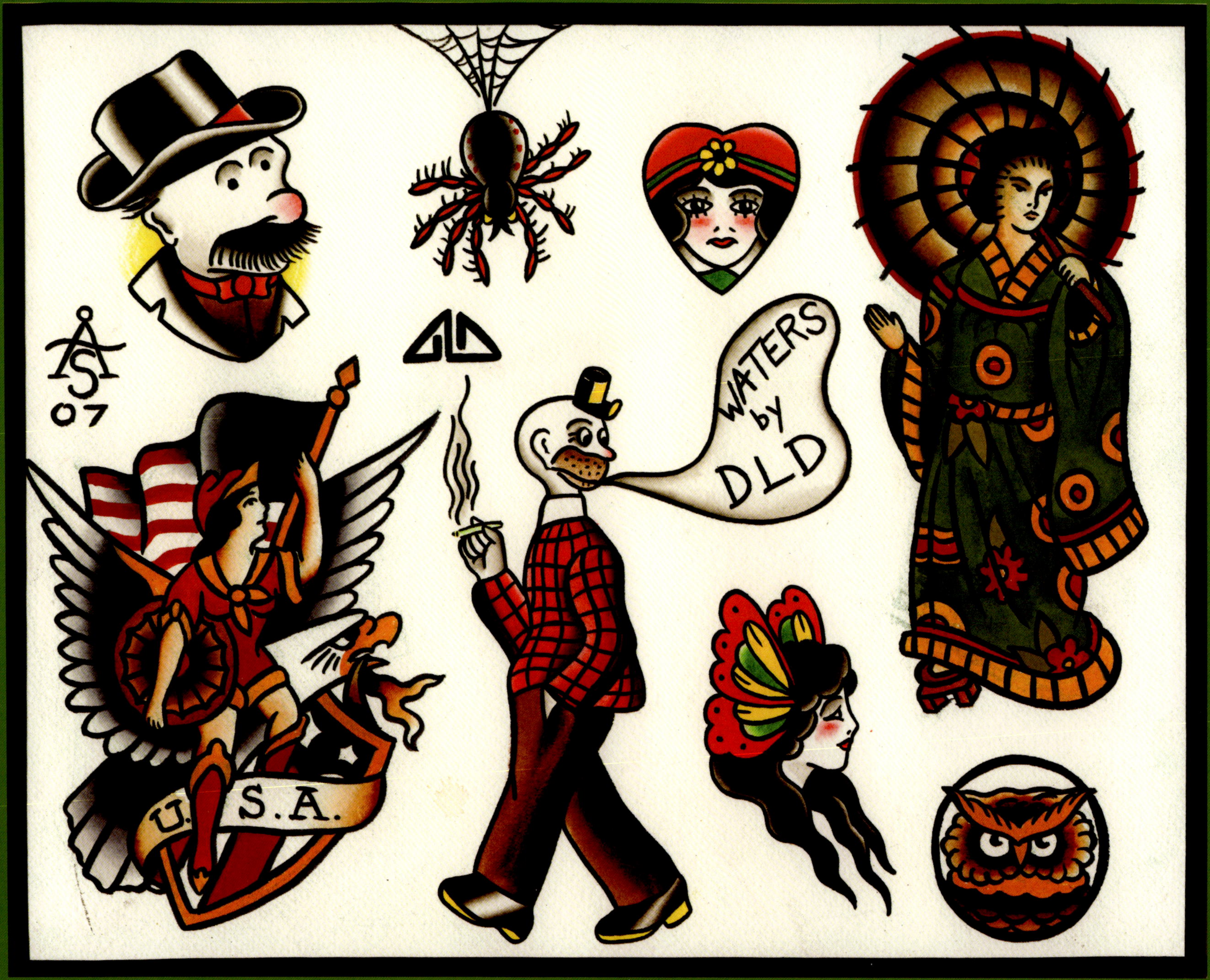

Andrew Stickler & Tilt

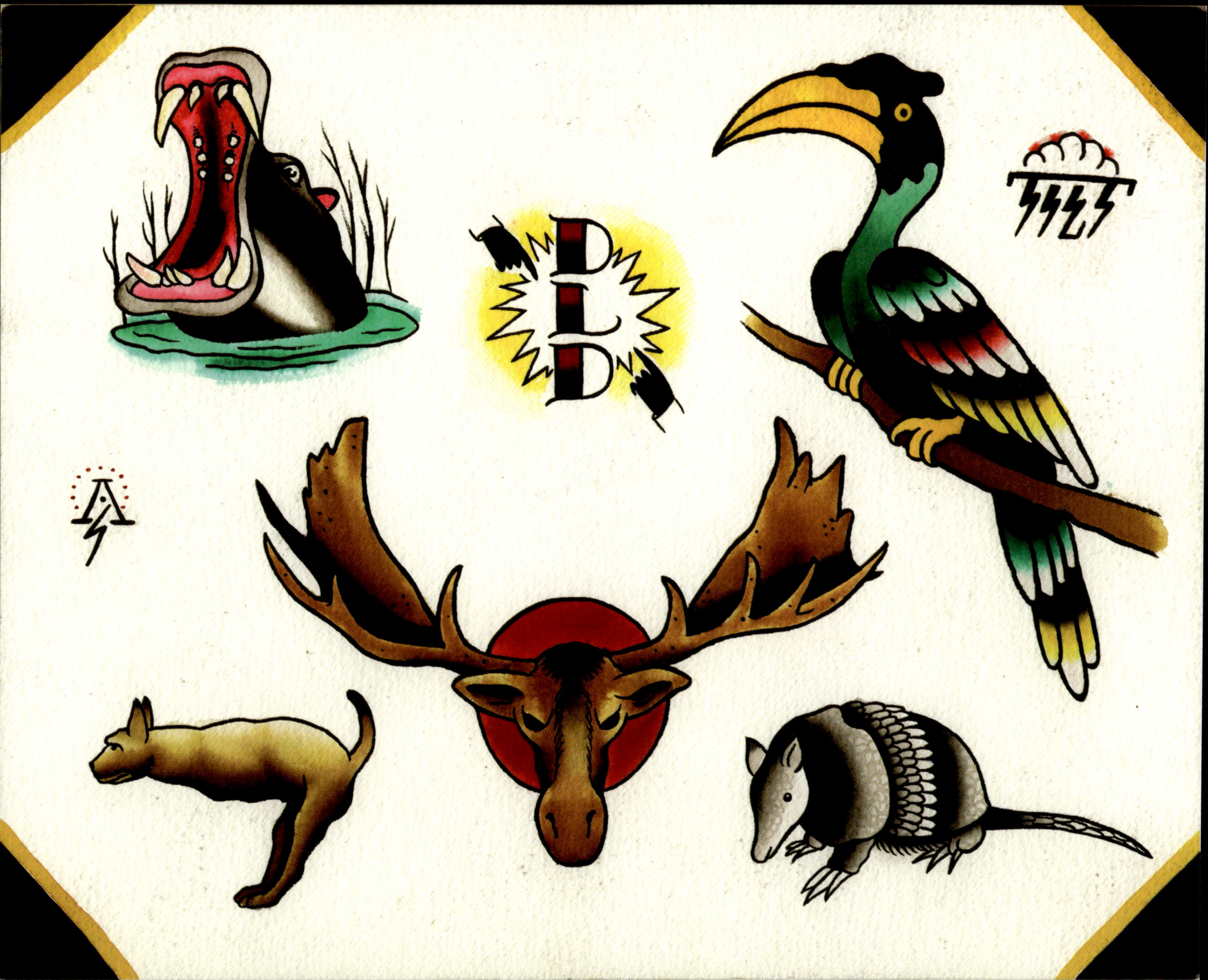

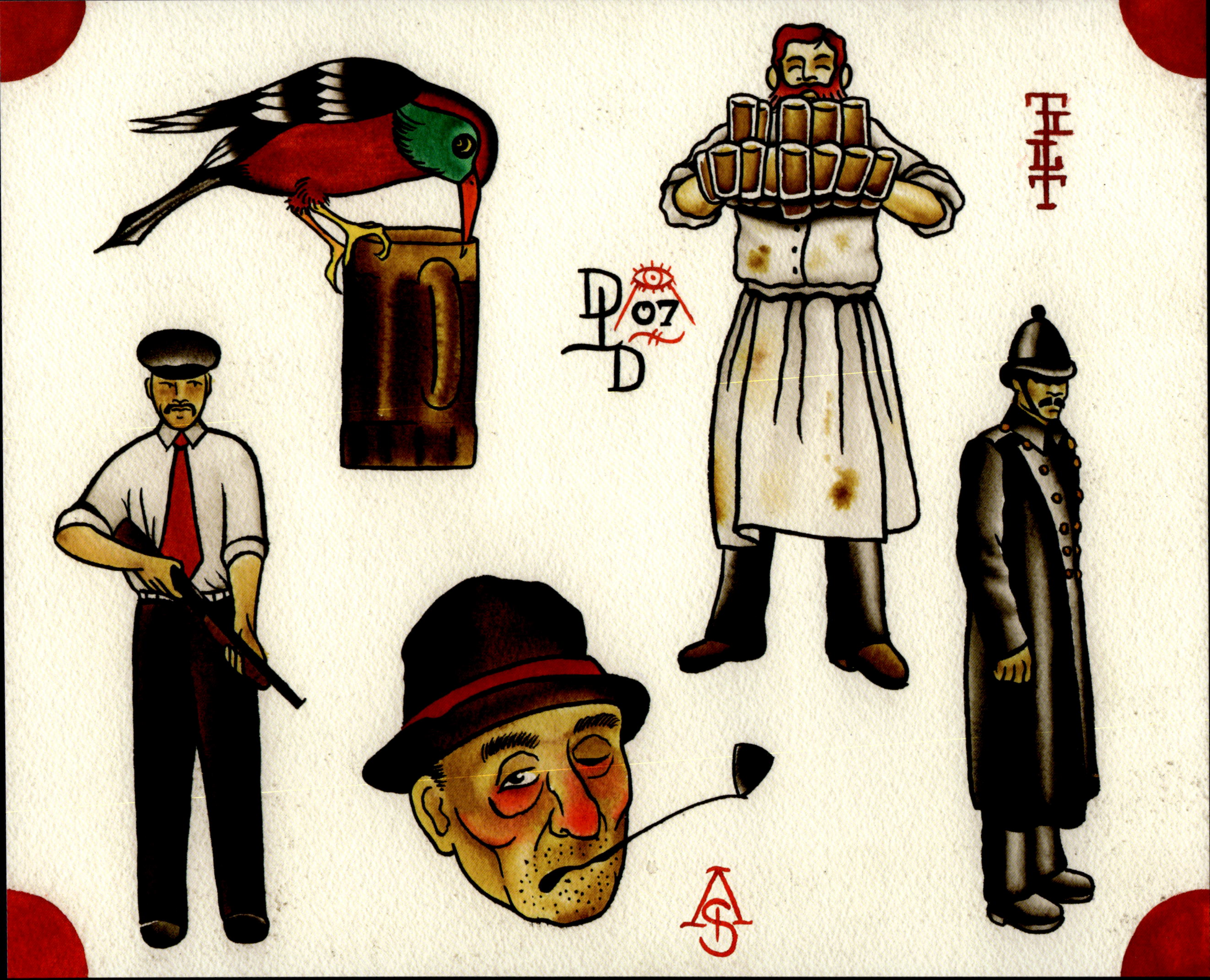

Andrew Stickler & Tilt

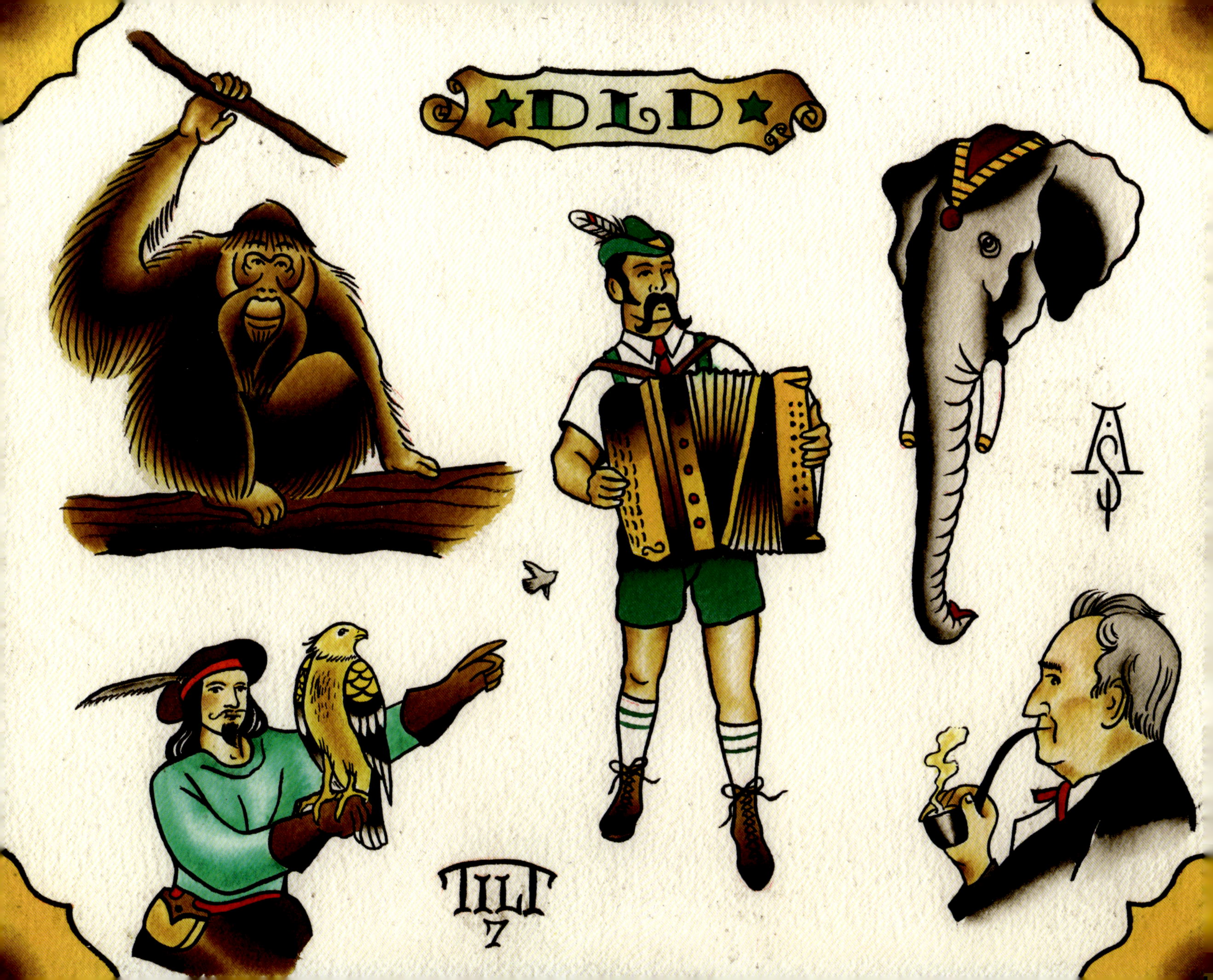
DLD
TILT
7

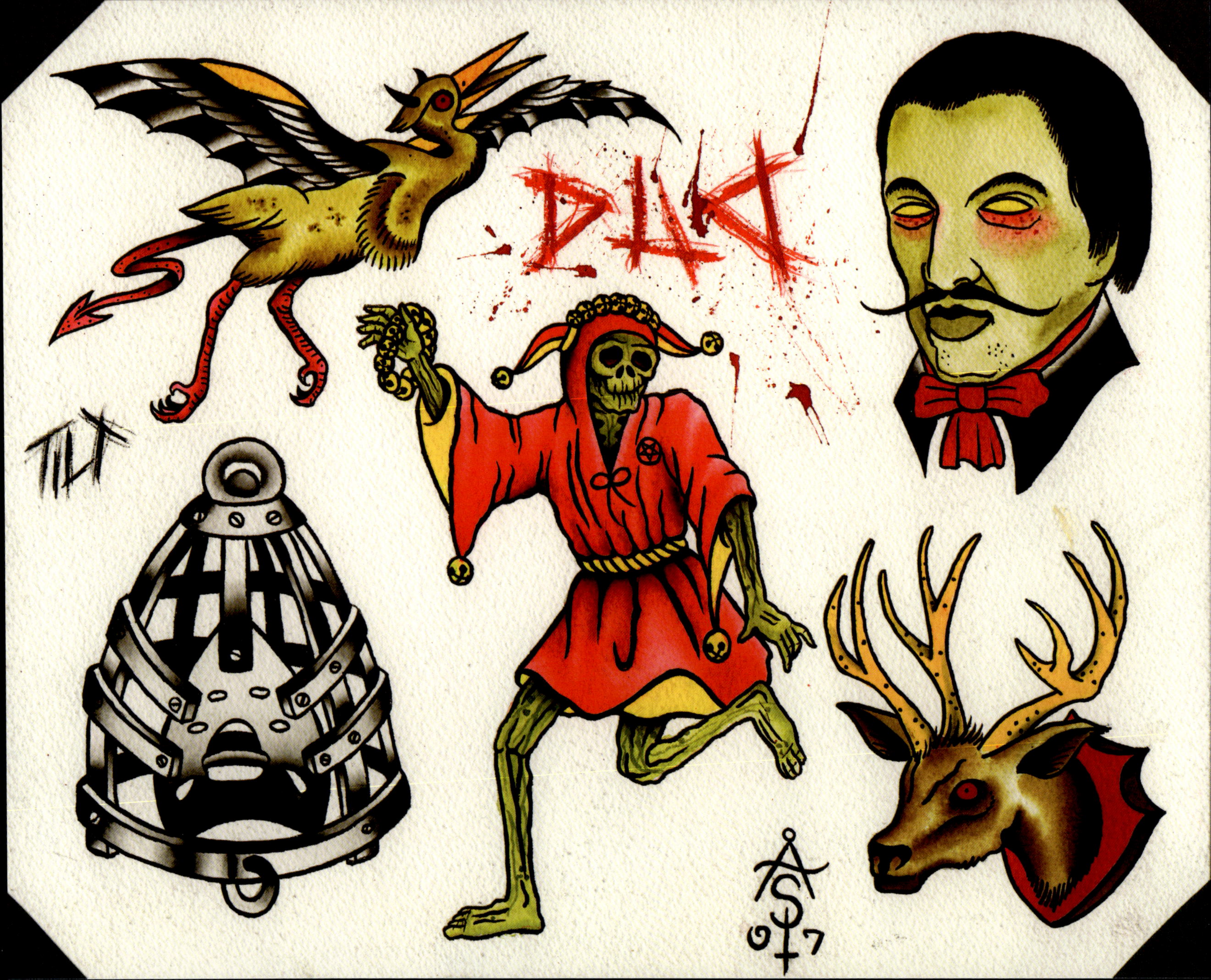

Andrew Stickler & Tilt

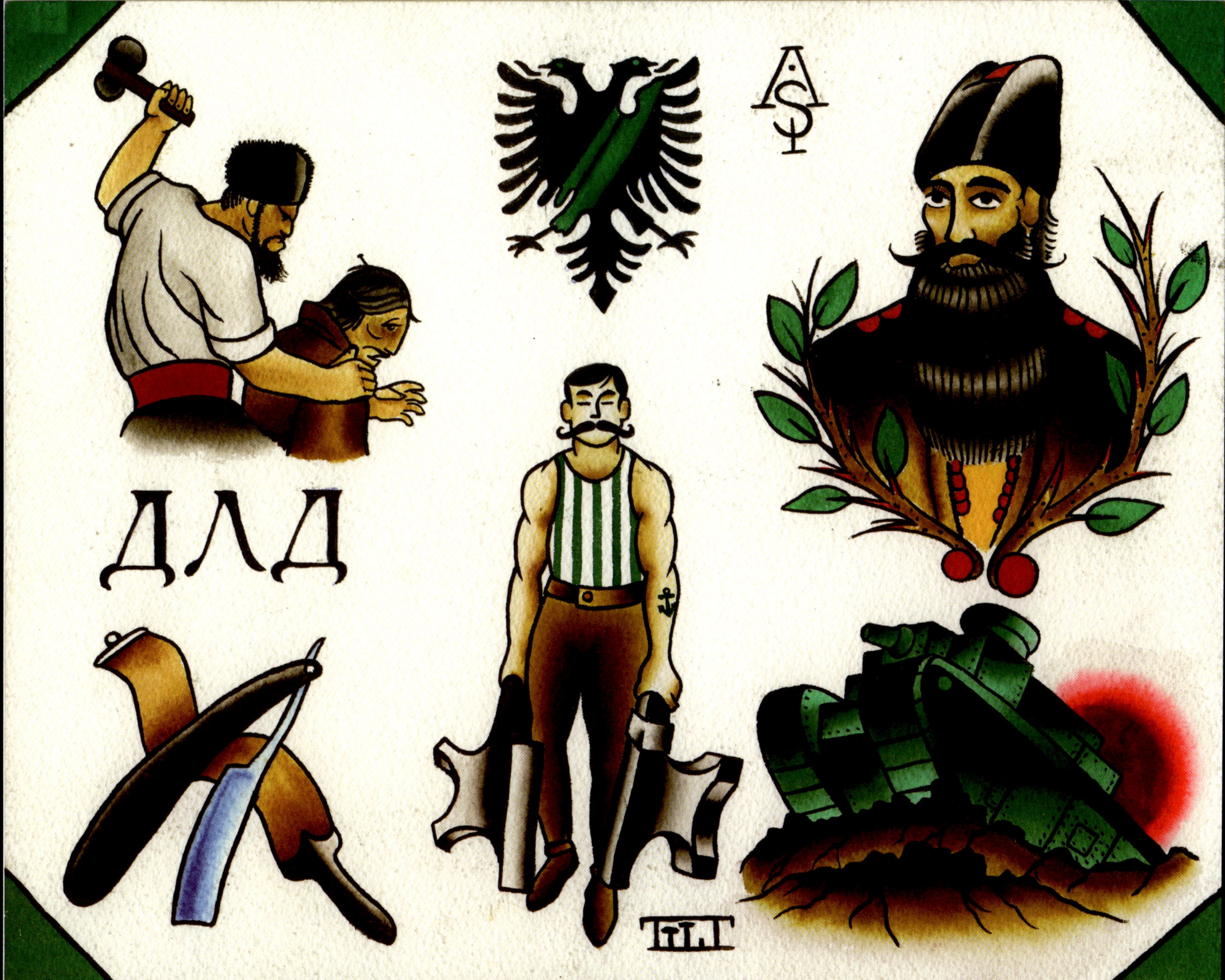

Andrew Stickler & Tilt

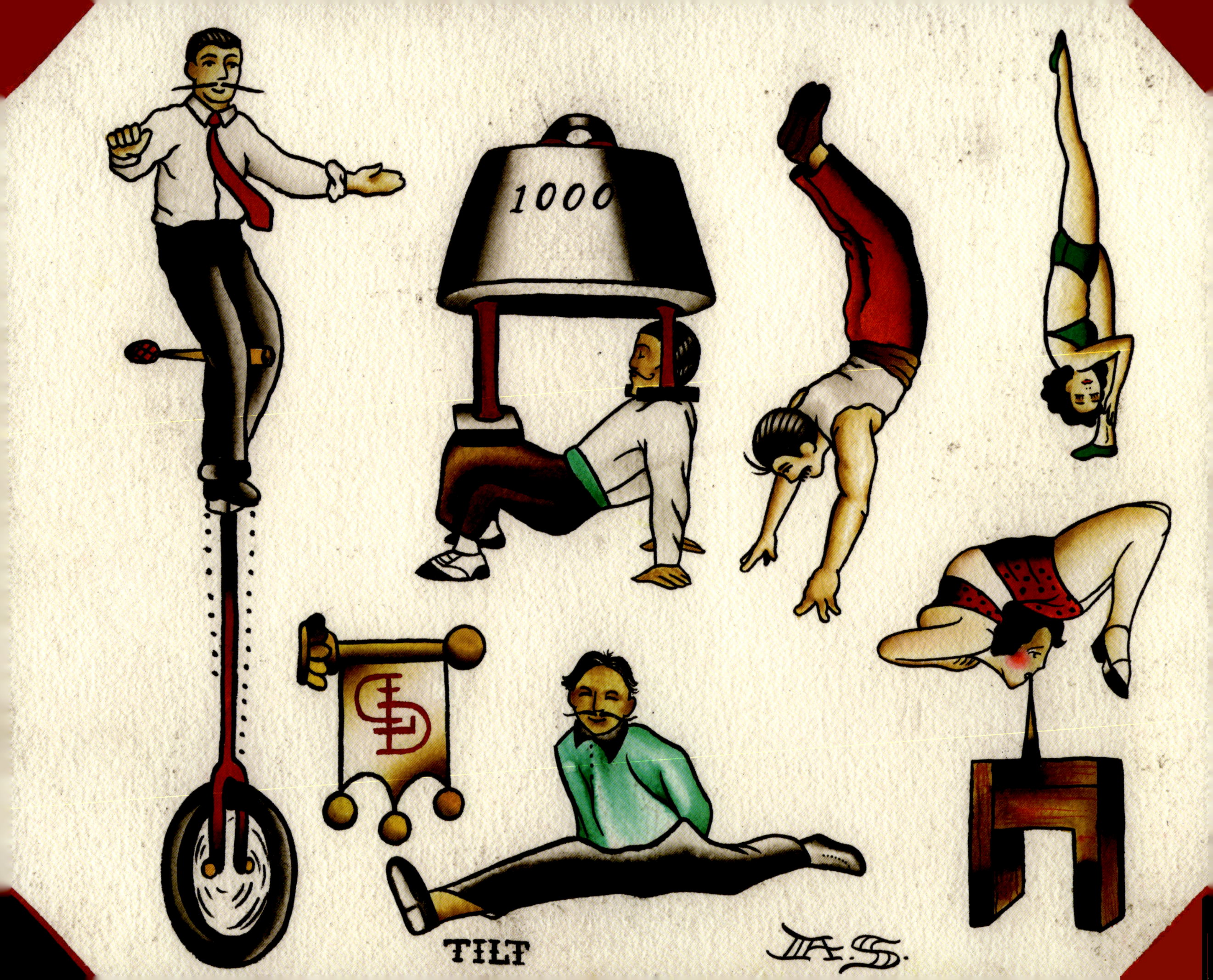
1000
TILT

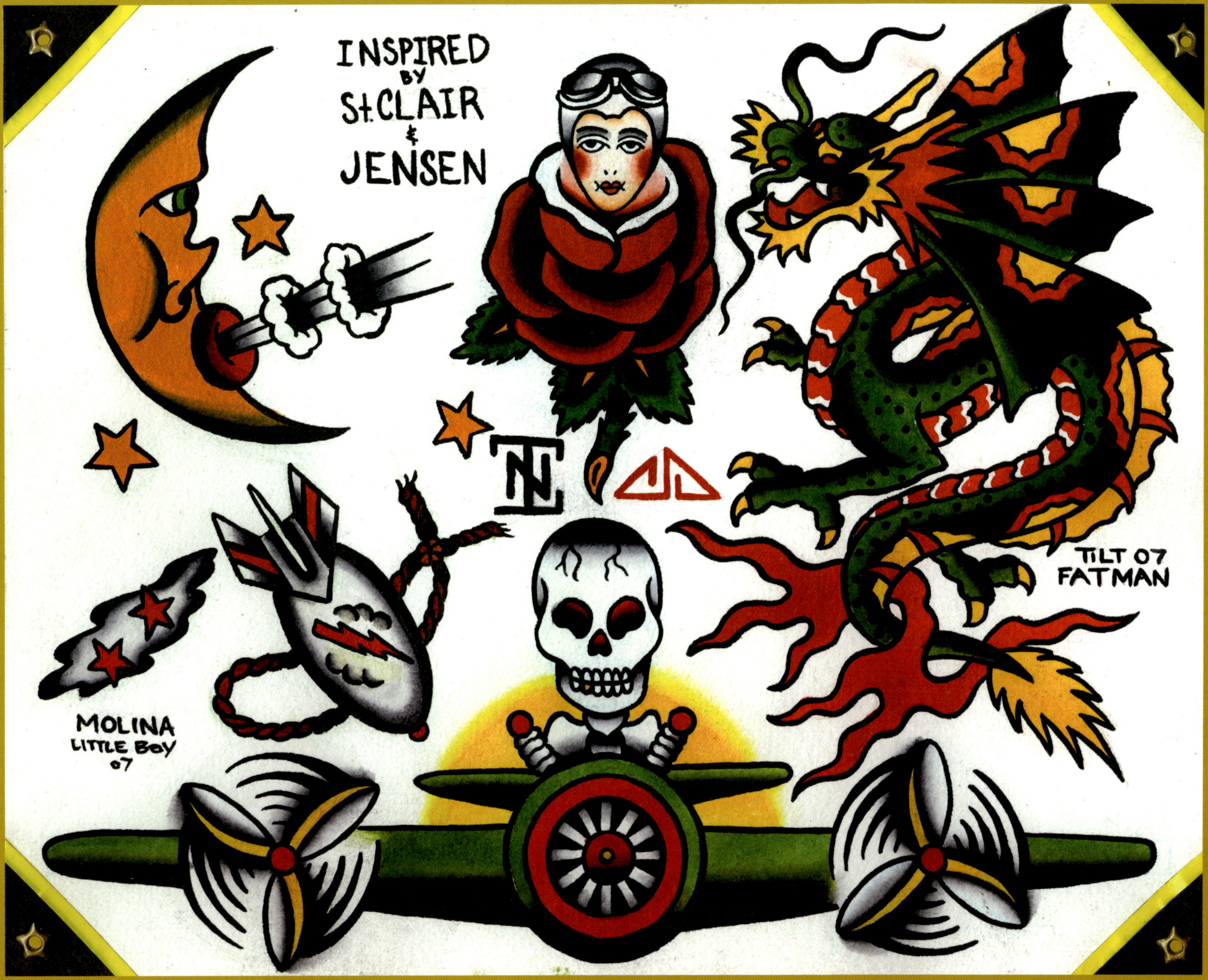

Joel Molina & Tilt

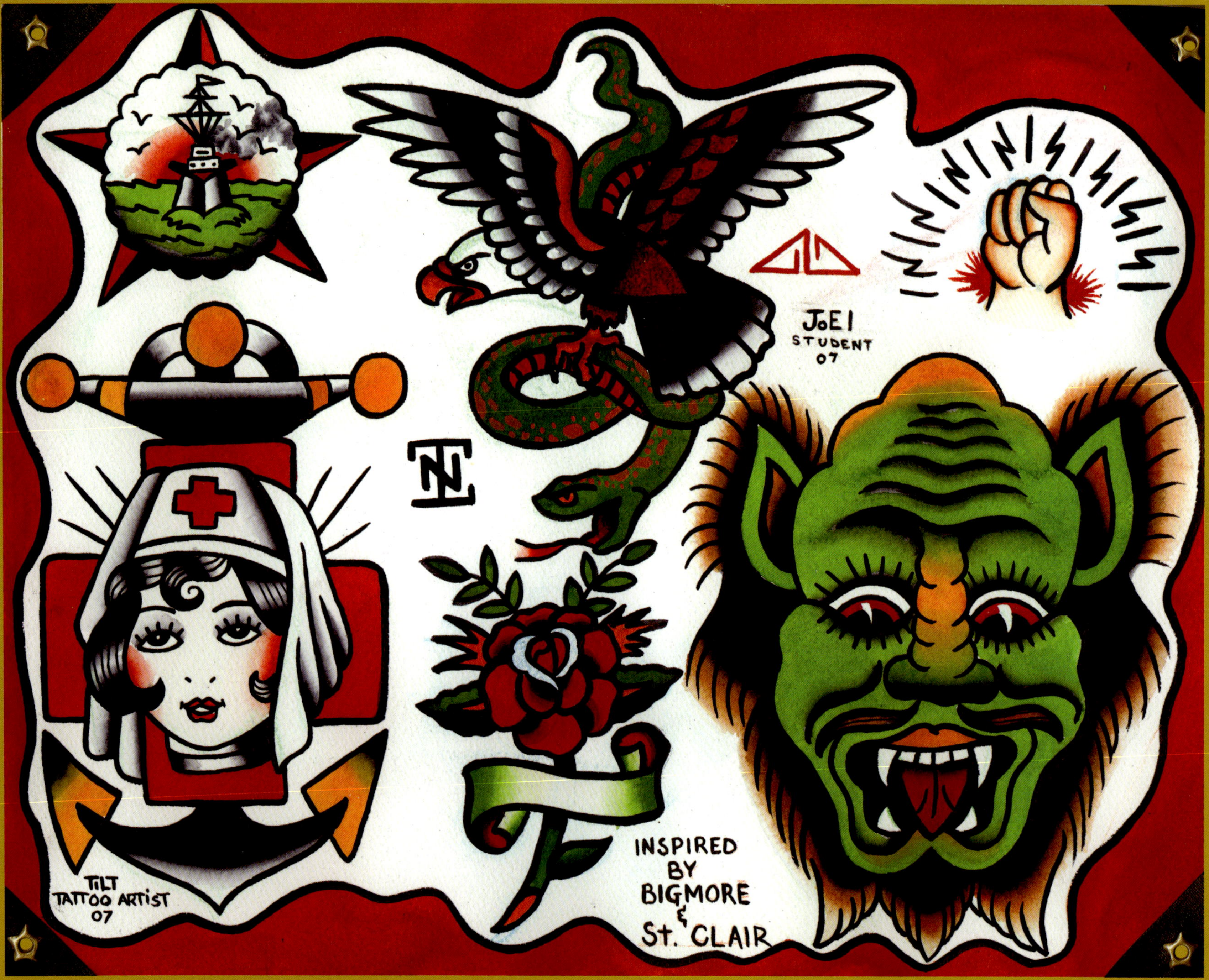

Joel Molina & Tilt

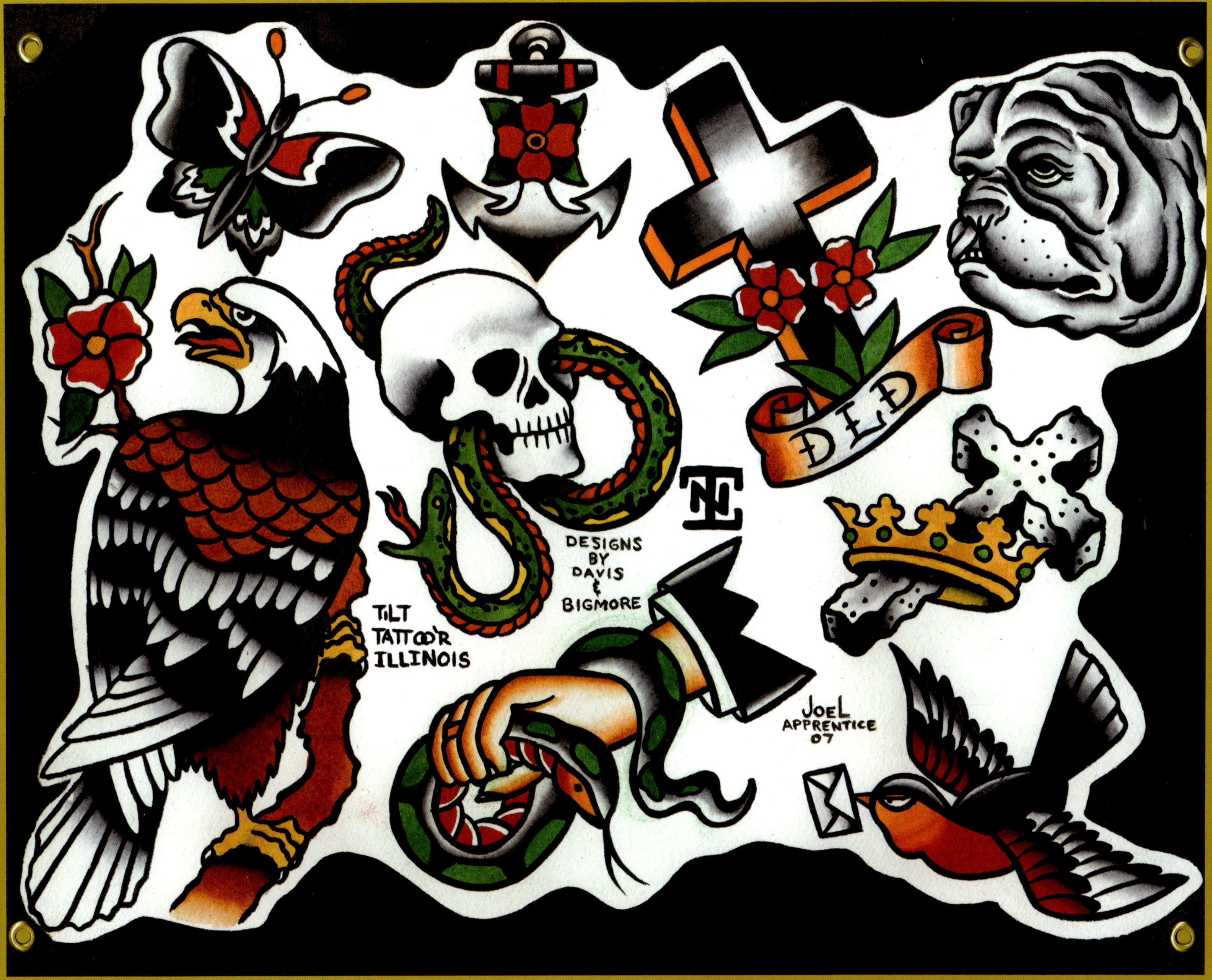

Joel Molina & Tilt

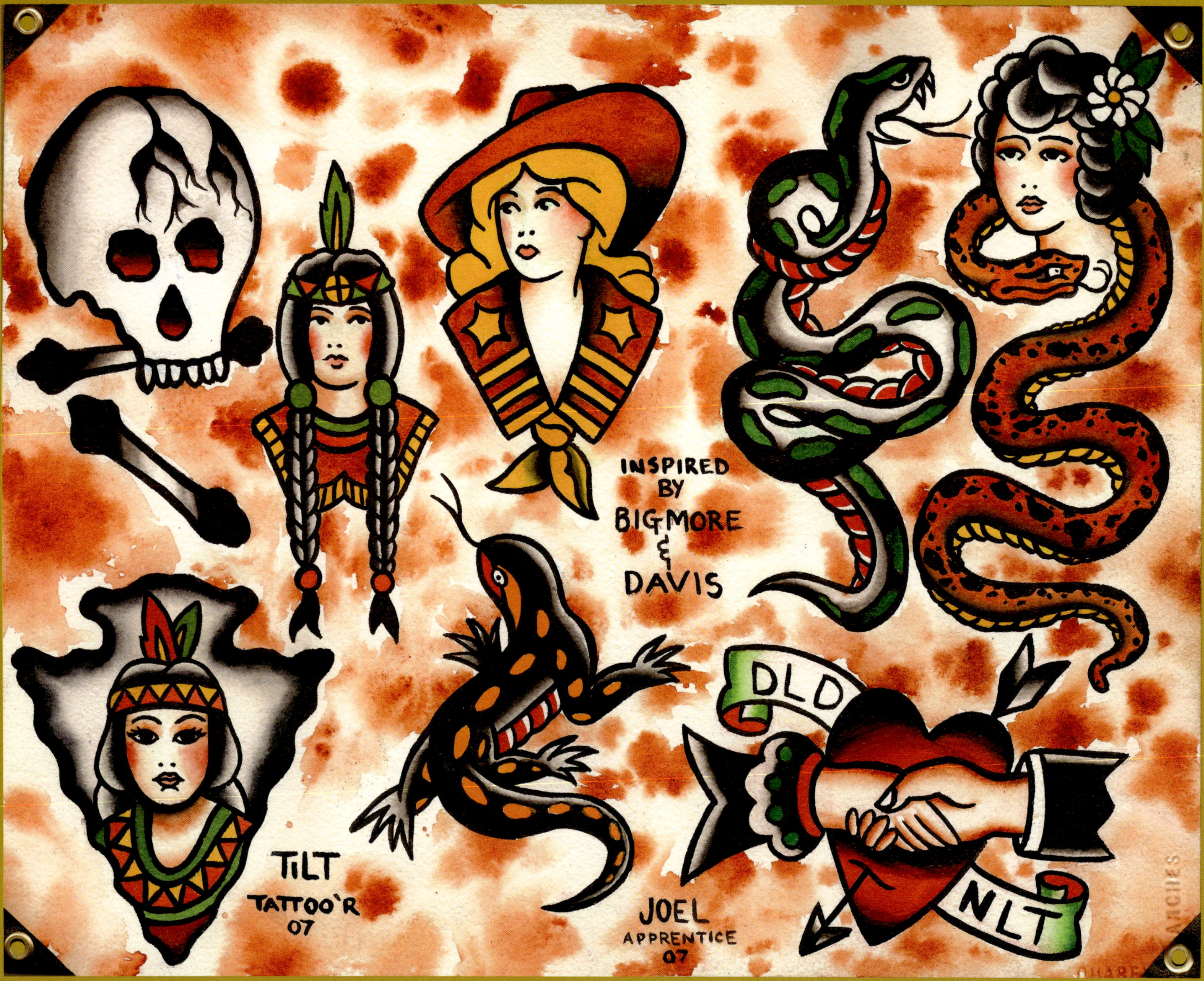

Joel Molina & Tilt

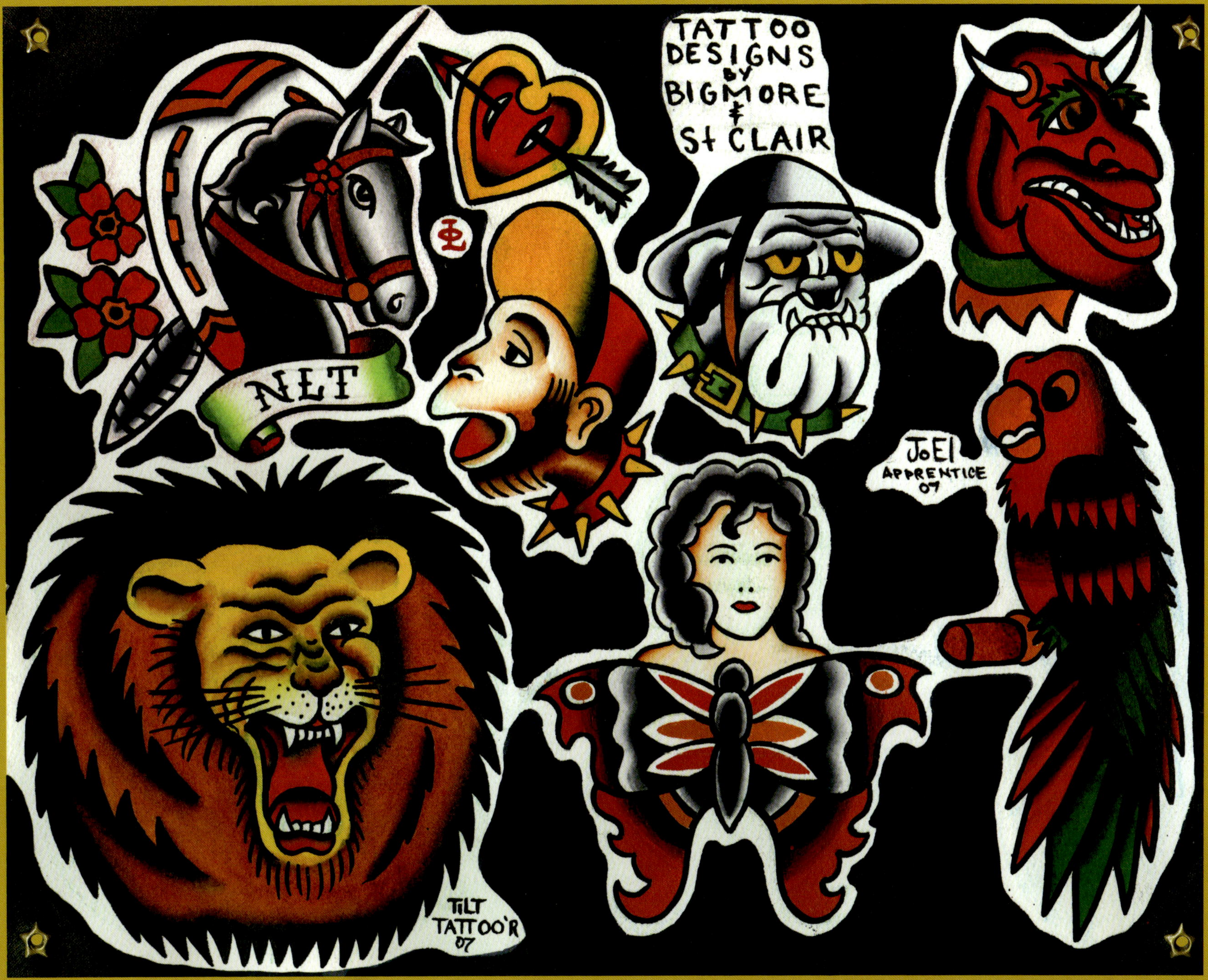

Joel Molina & Tilt

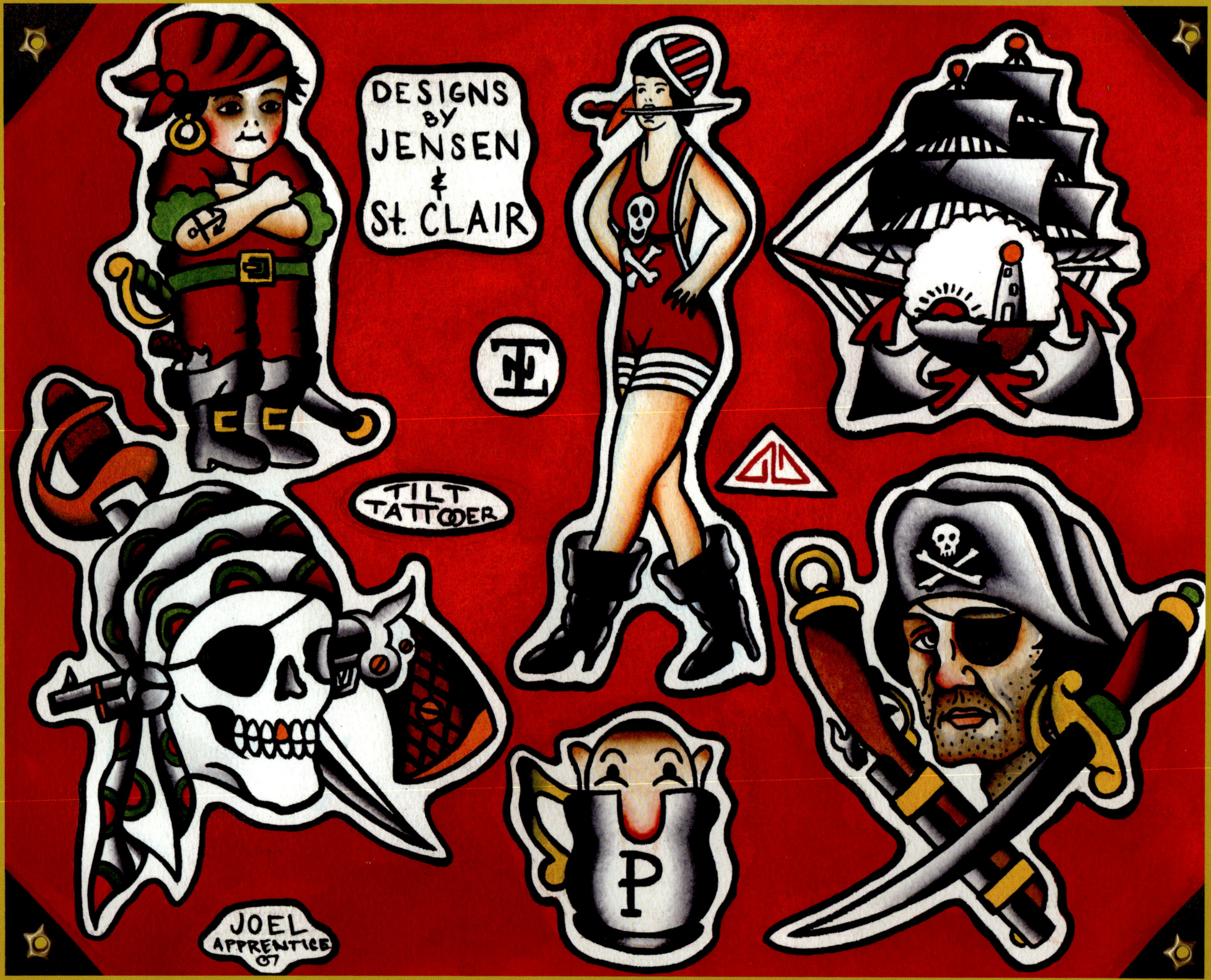

Joel Molina & Tilt

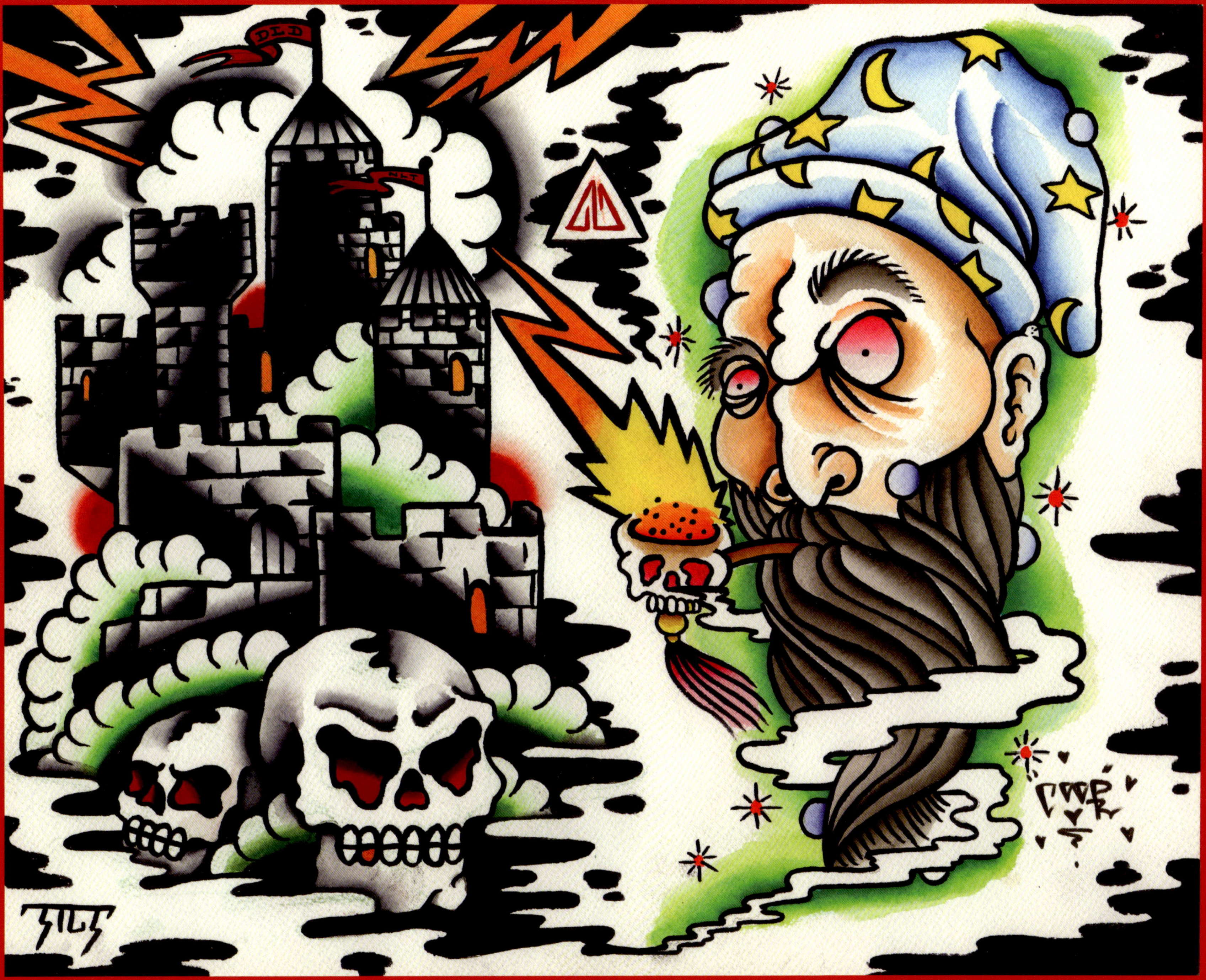

Coopr & Tilt

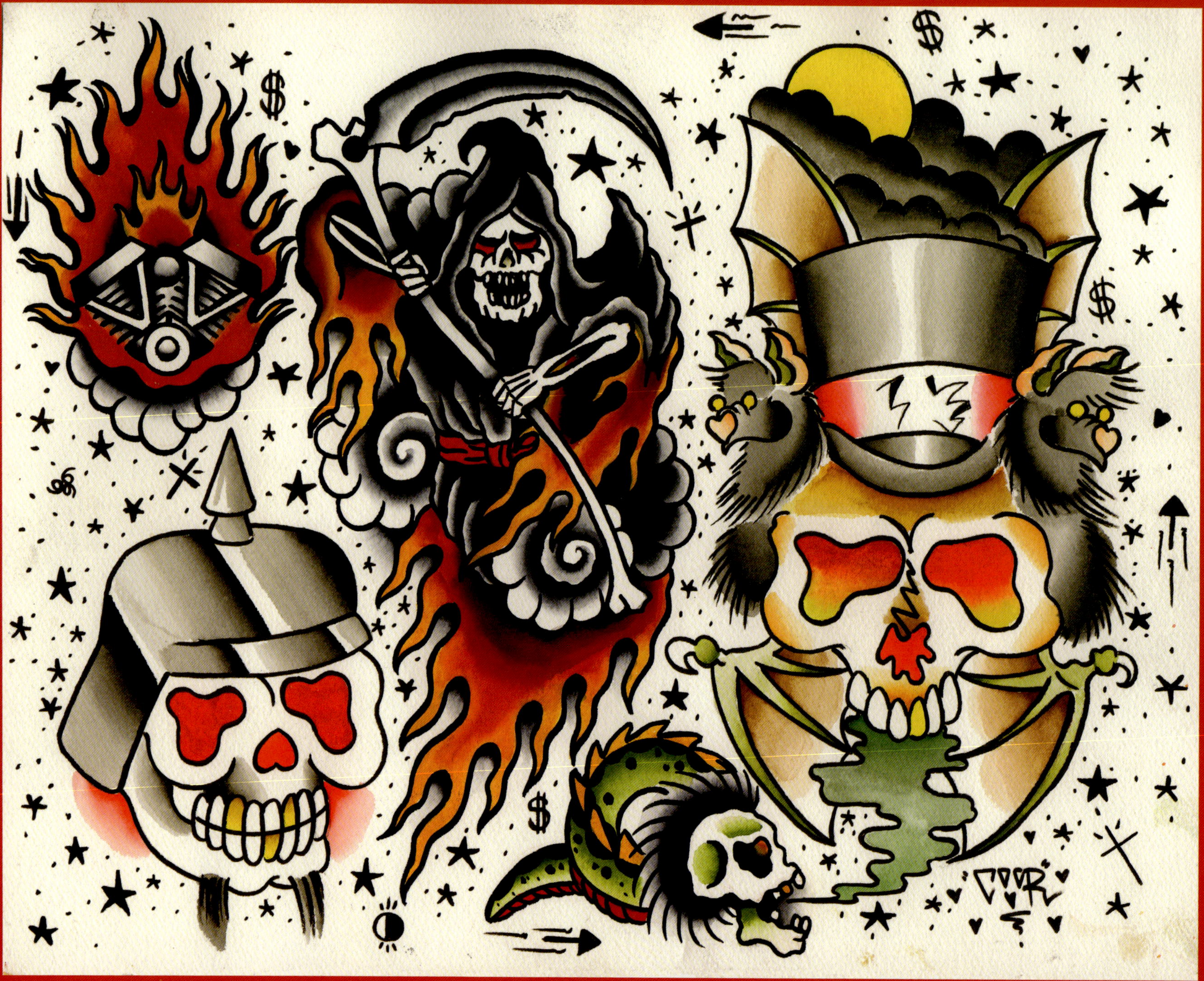

Coopr & Tilt

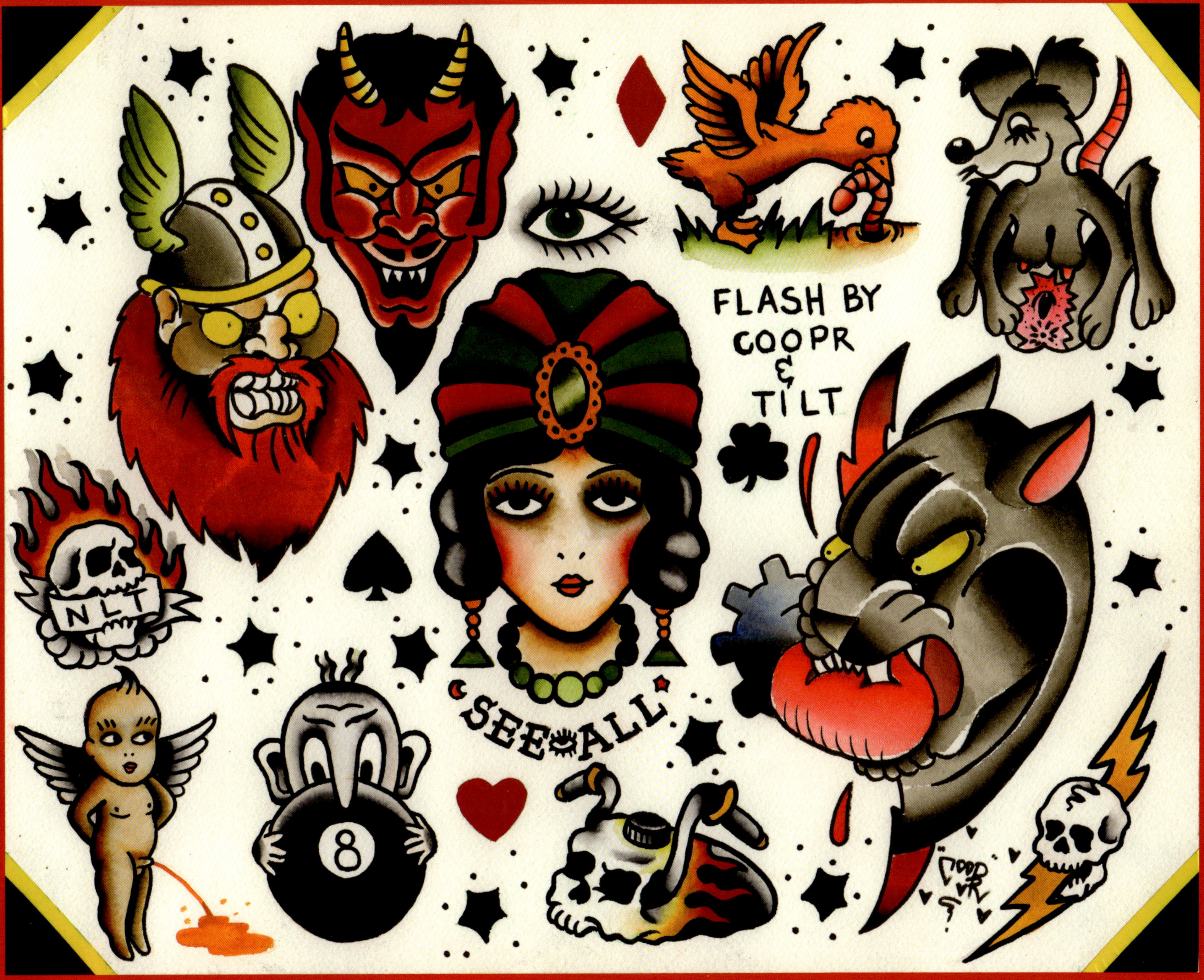

Coopr & Tilt

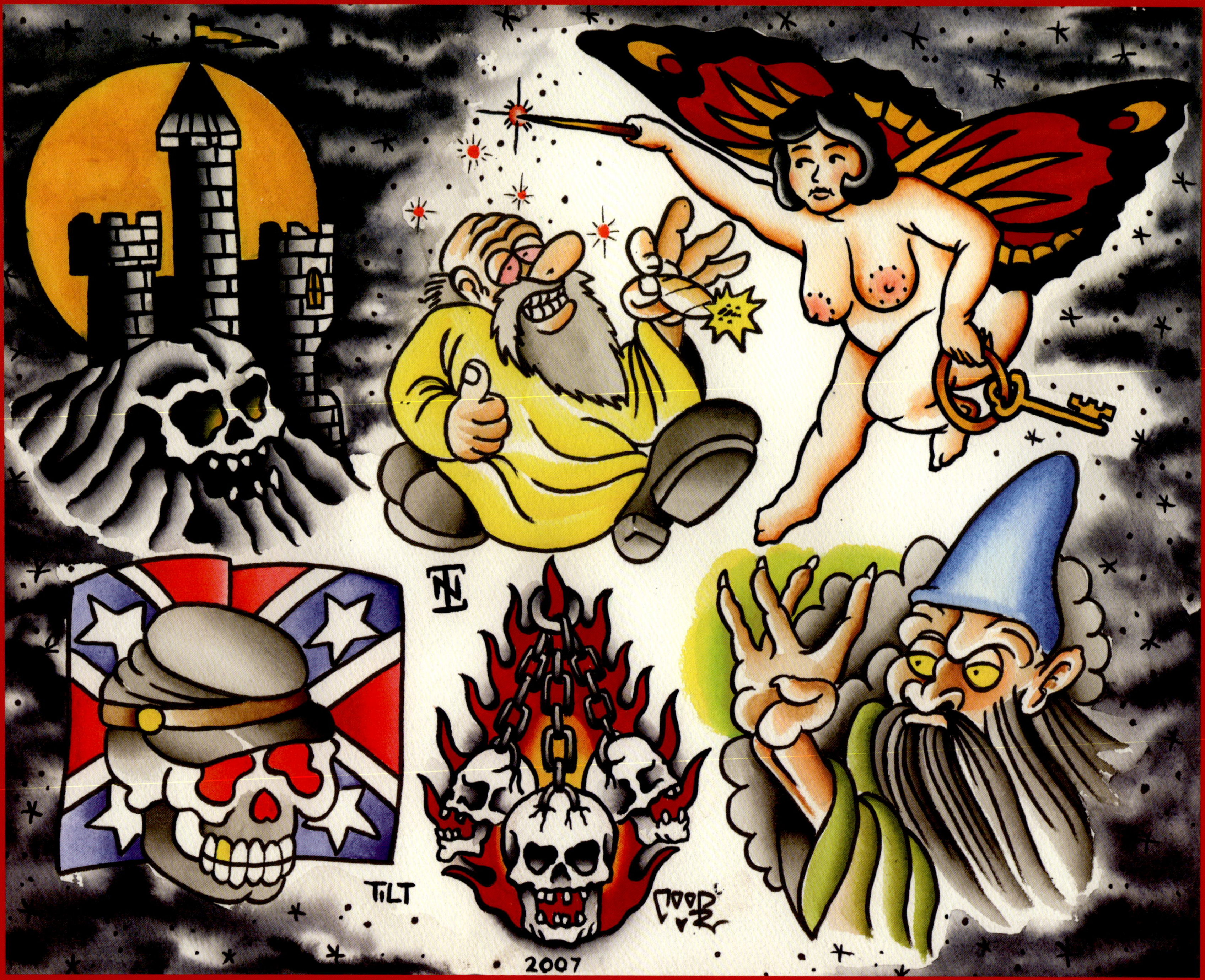

Coopr & Tilt

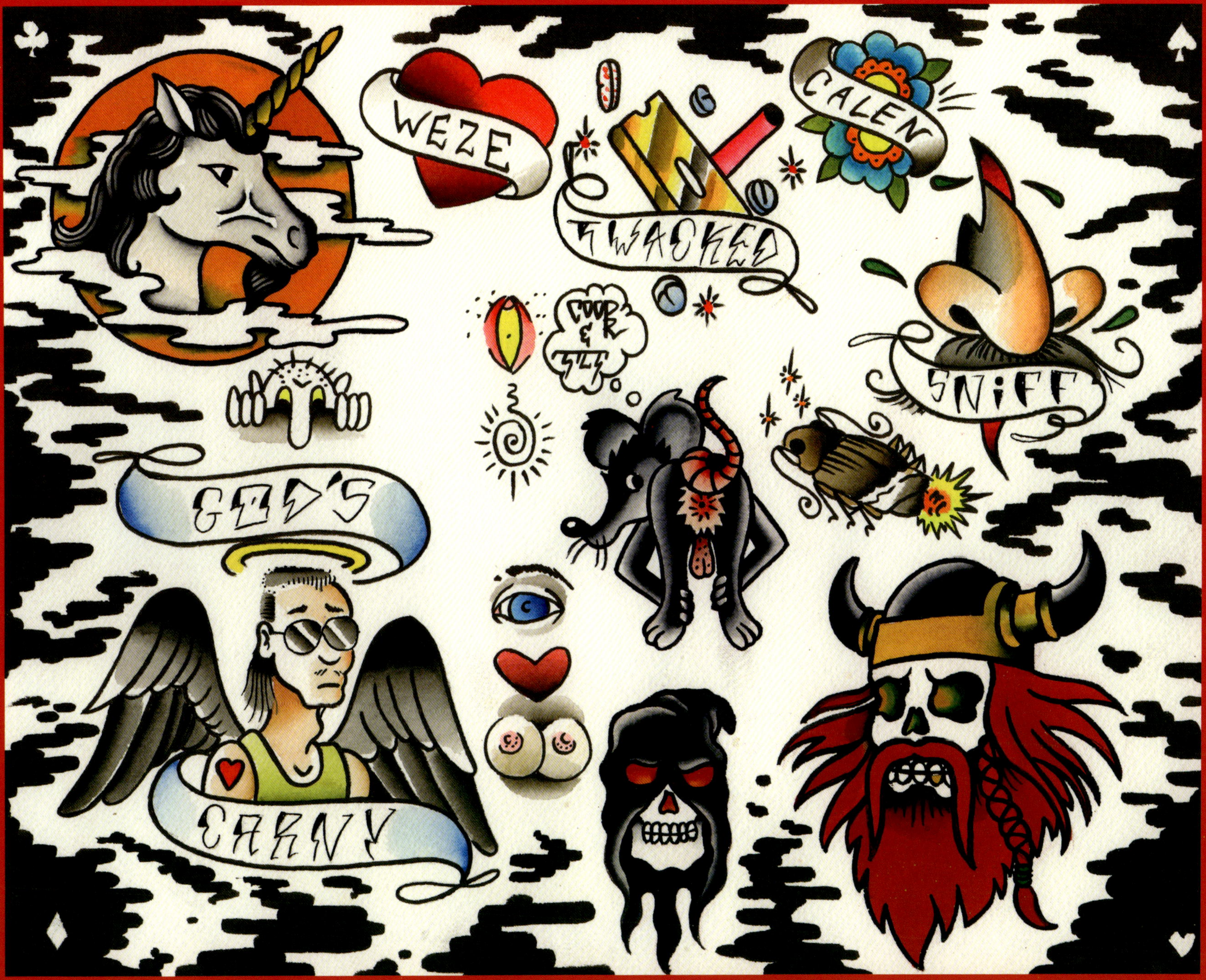

Coopr & Tilt

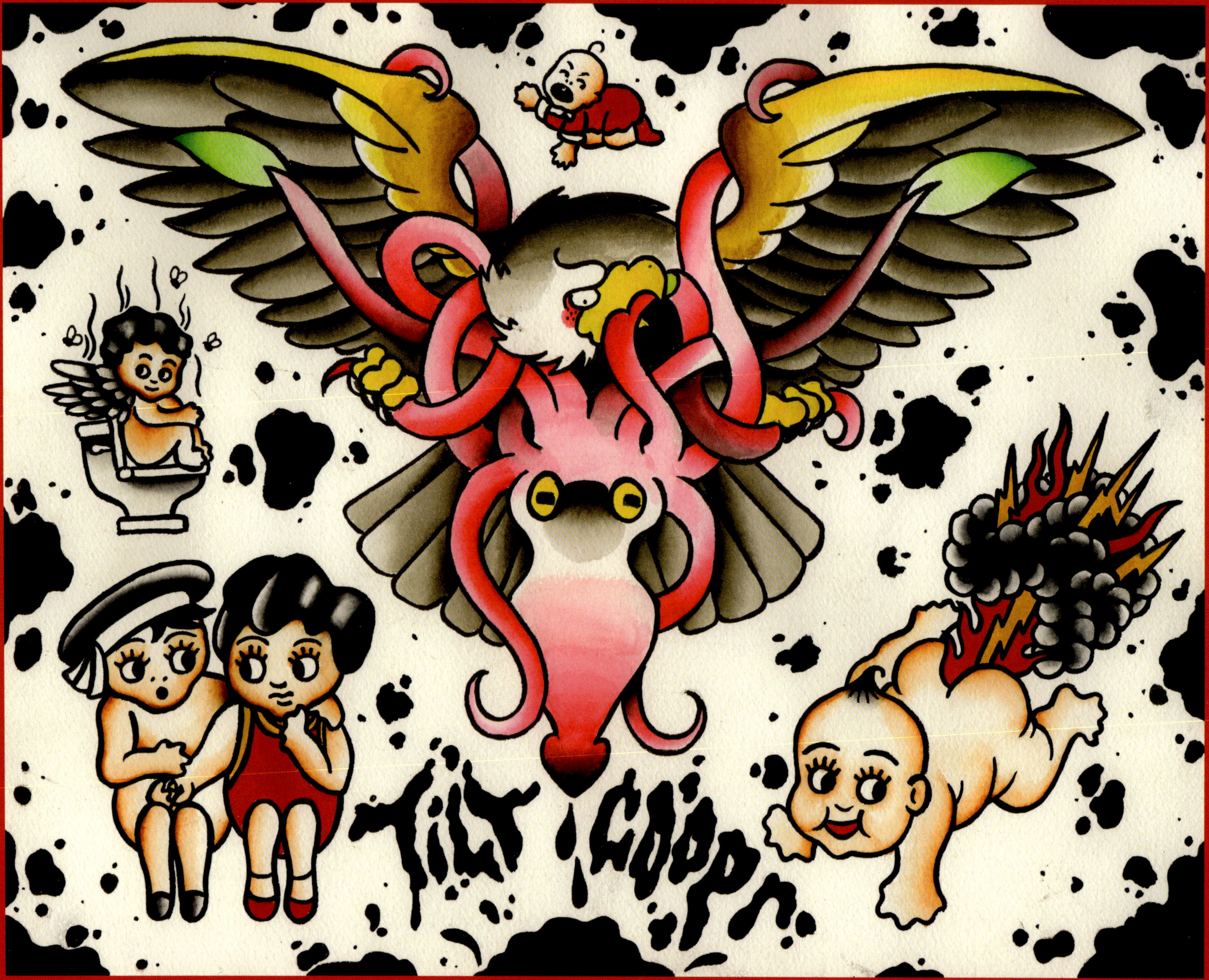

Coopr & Tilt

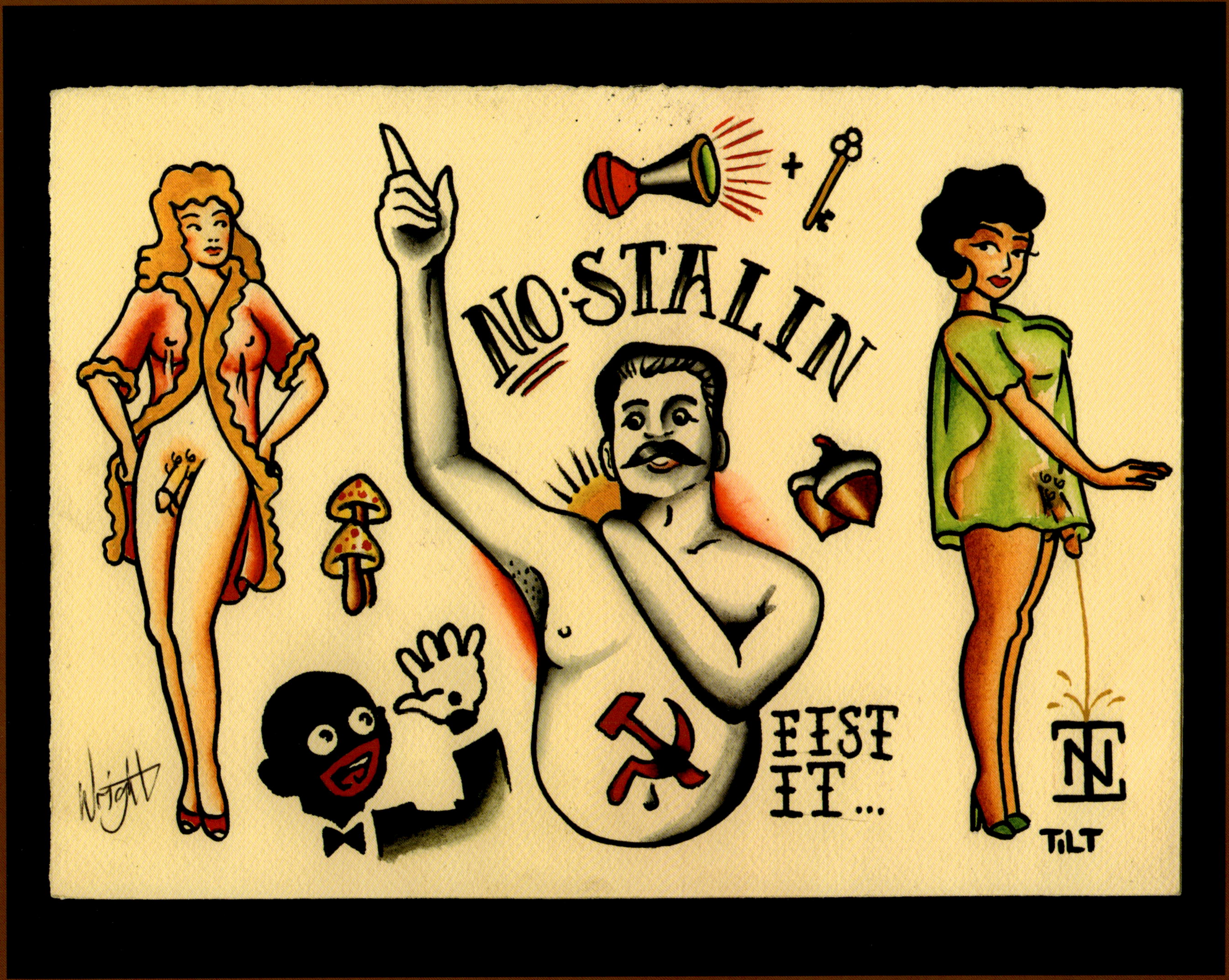

Jef Wright & Tilt

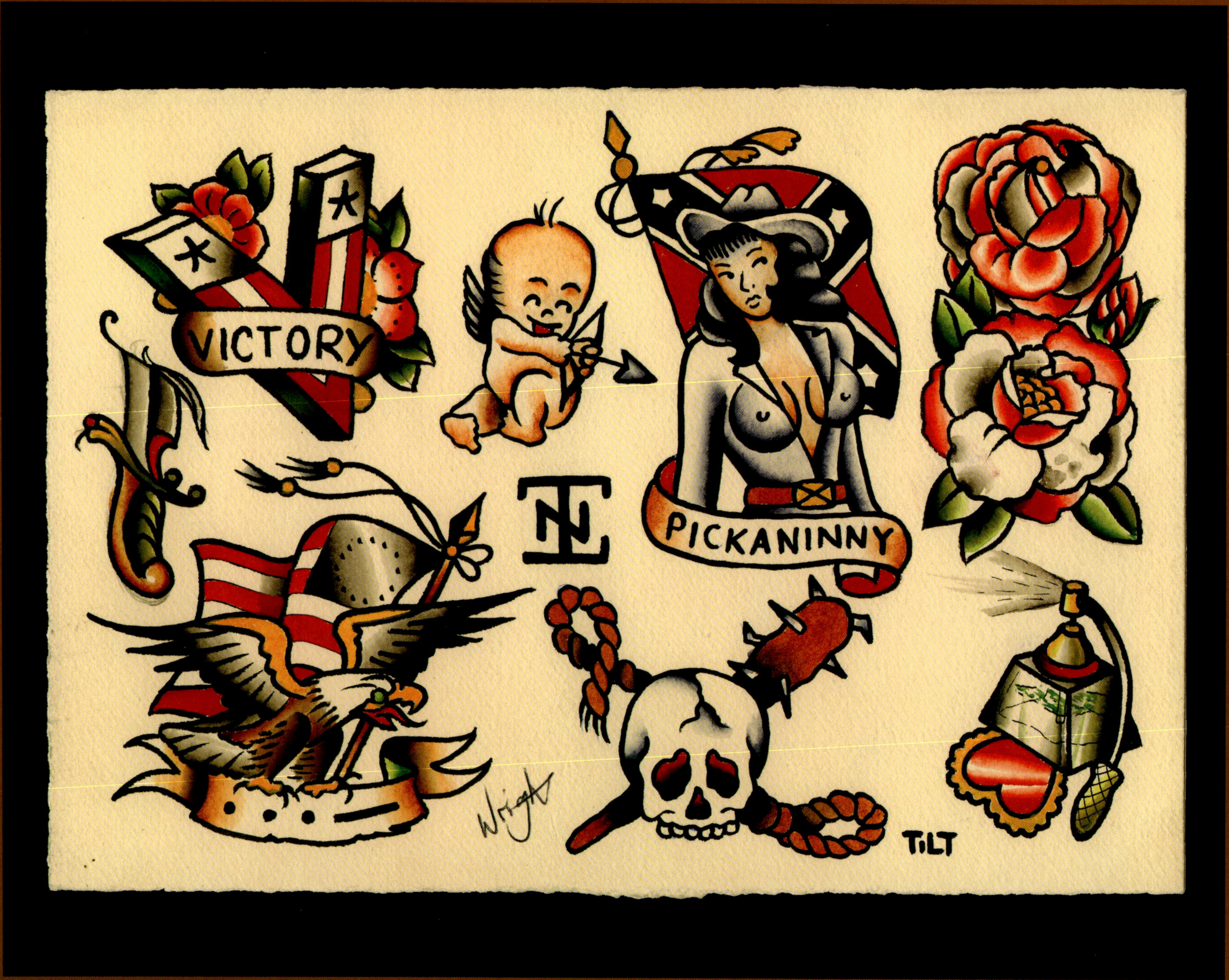

Jef Wright & Tilt

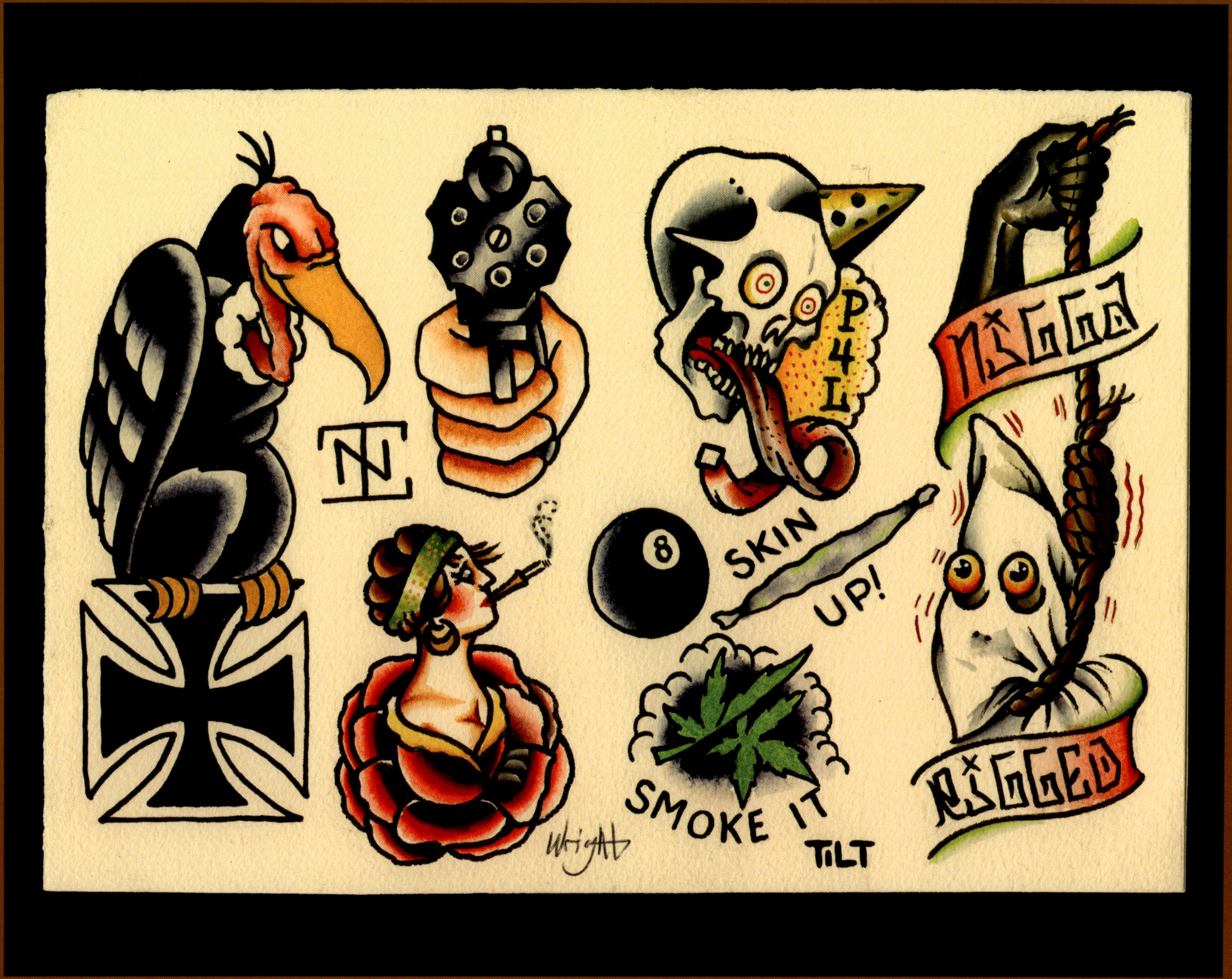

Jef Wright & Tilt

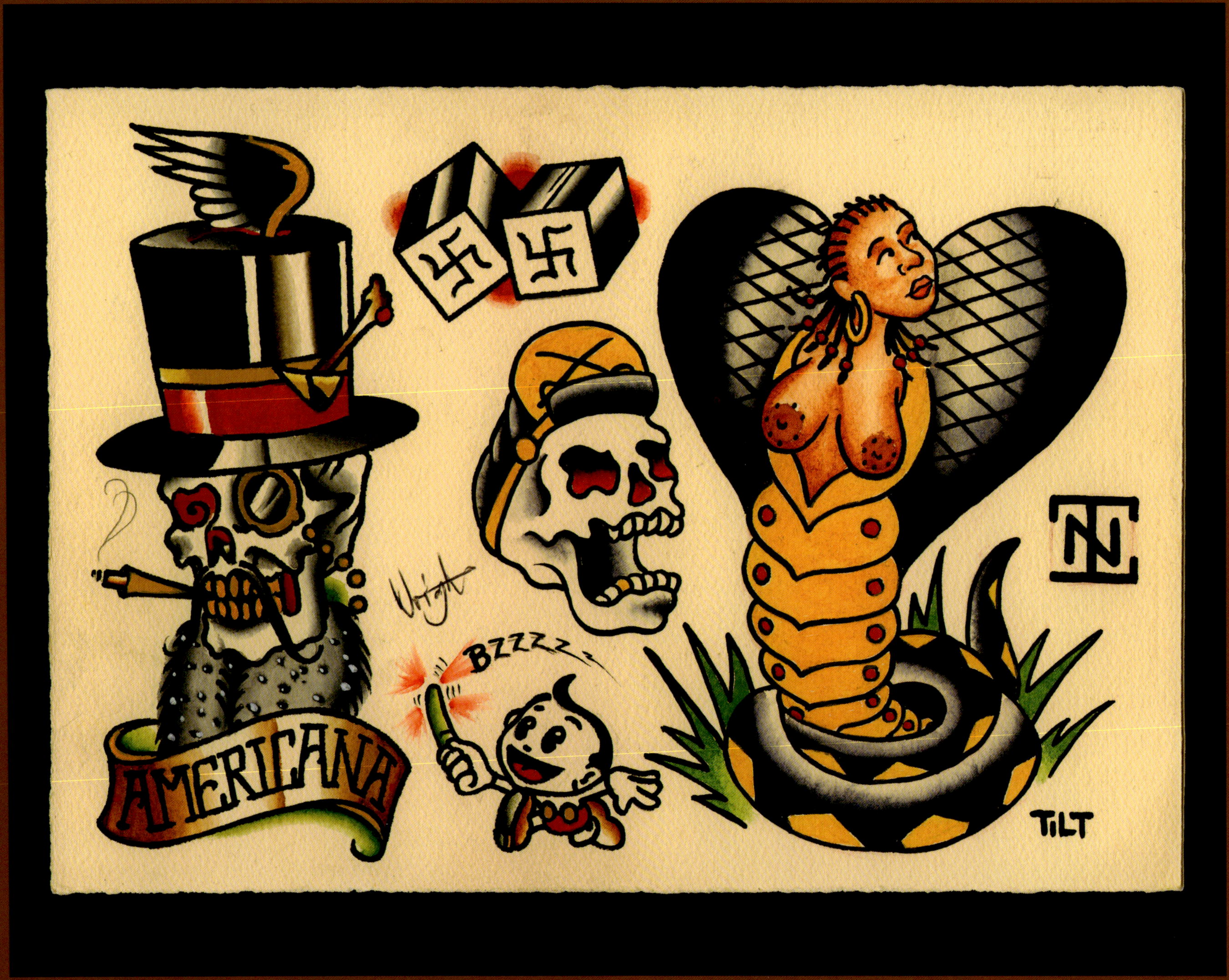

Jef Wright & Tilt

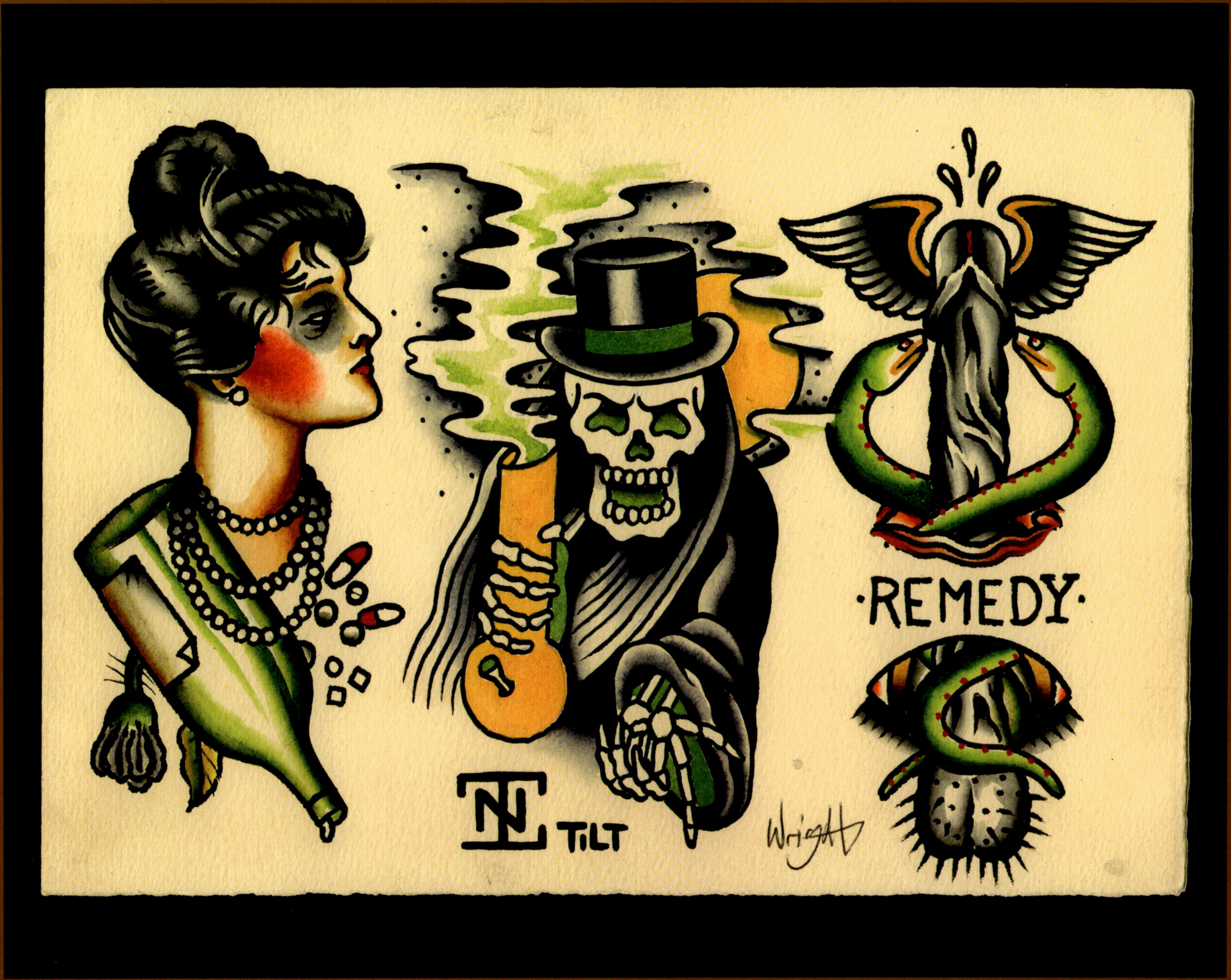

Jef Wright & Tilt

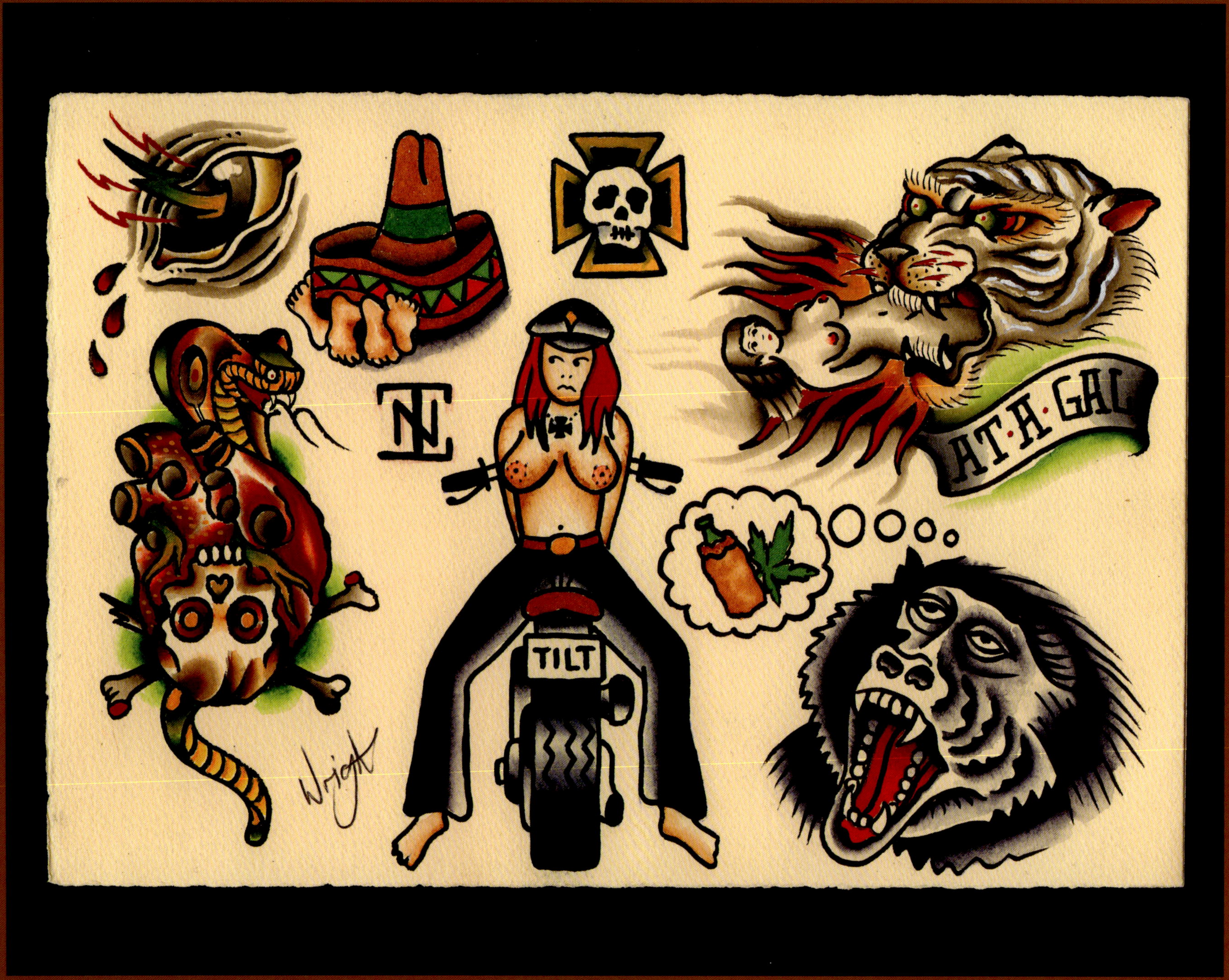

Jef Wright & Tilt

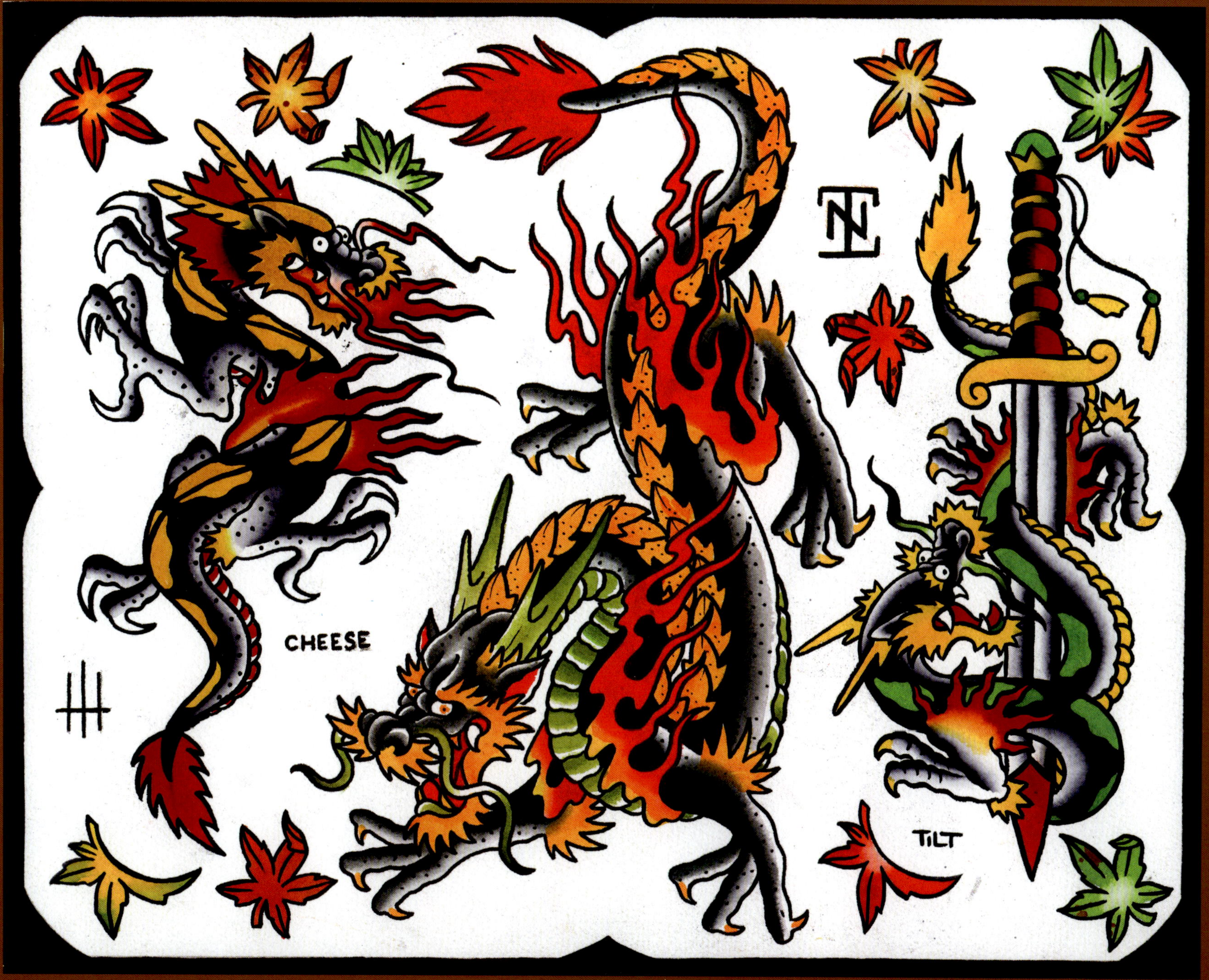

Ben Cheése & Tilt

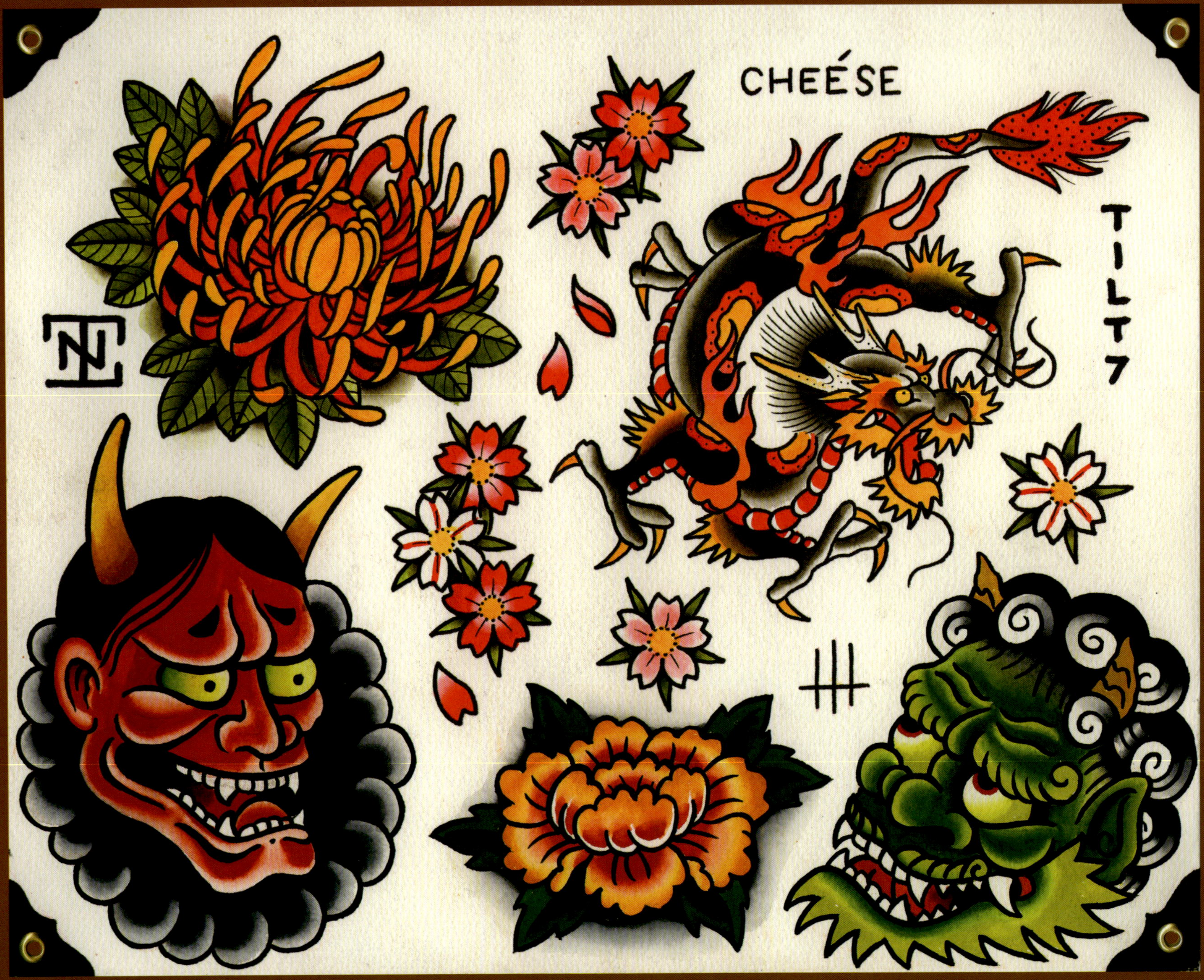

Ben Cheése & Tilt

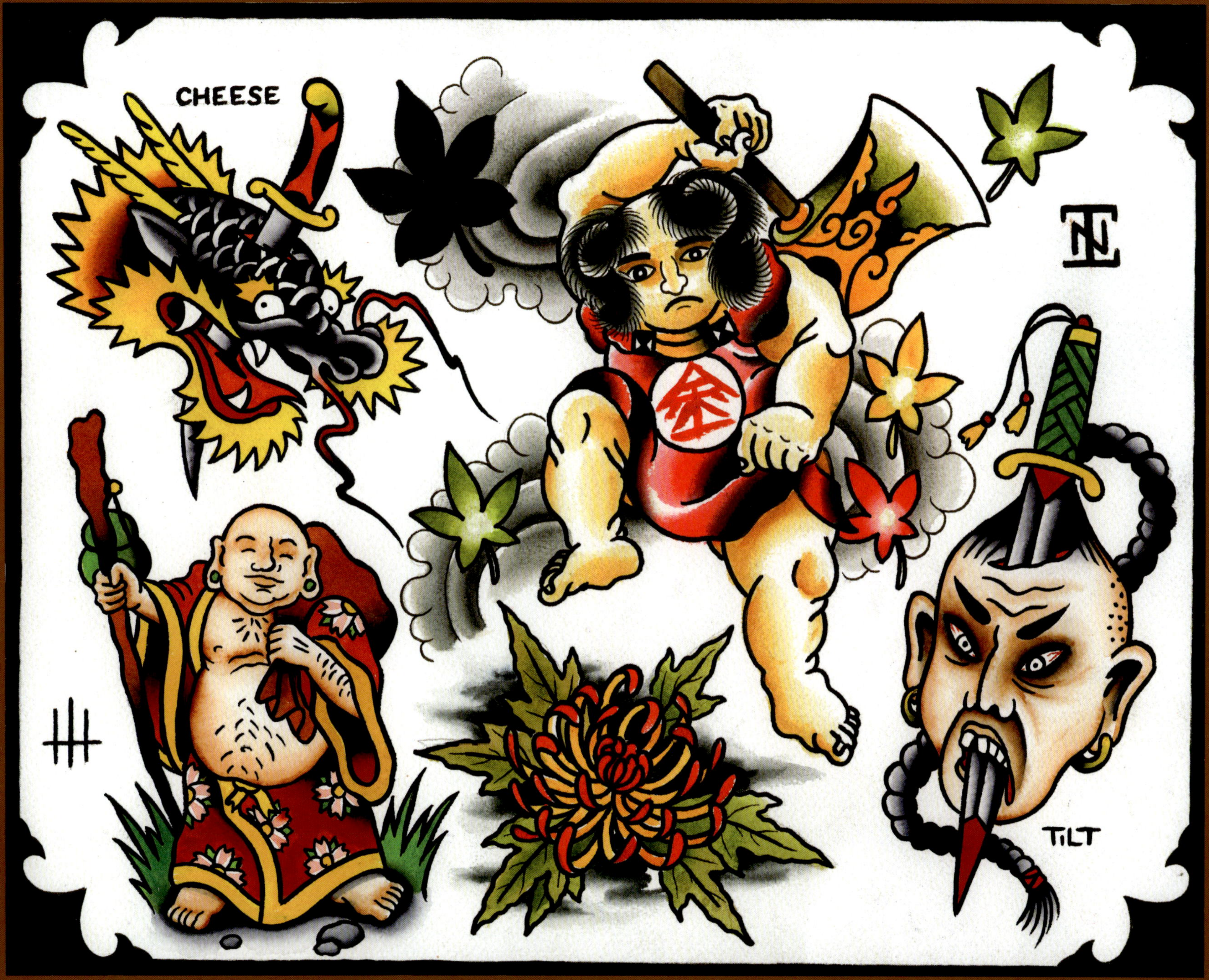

Ben Cheése & Tilt

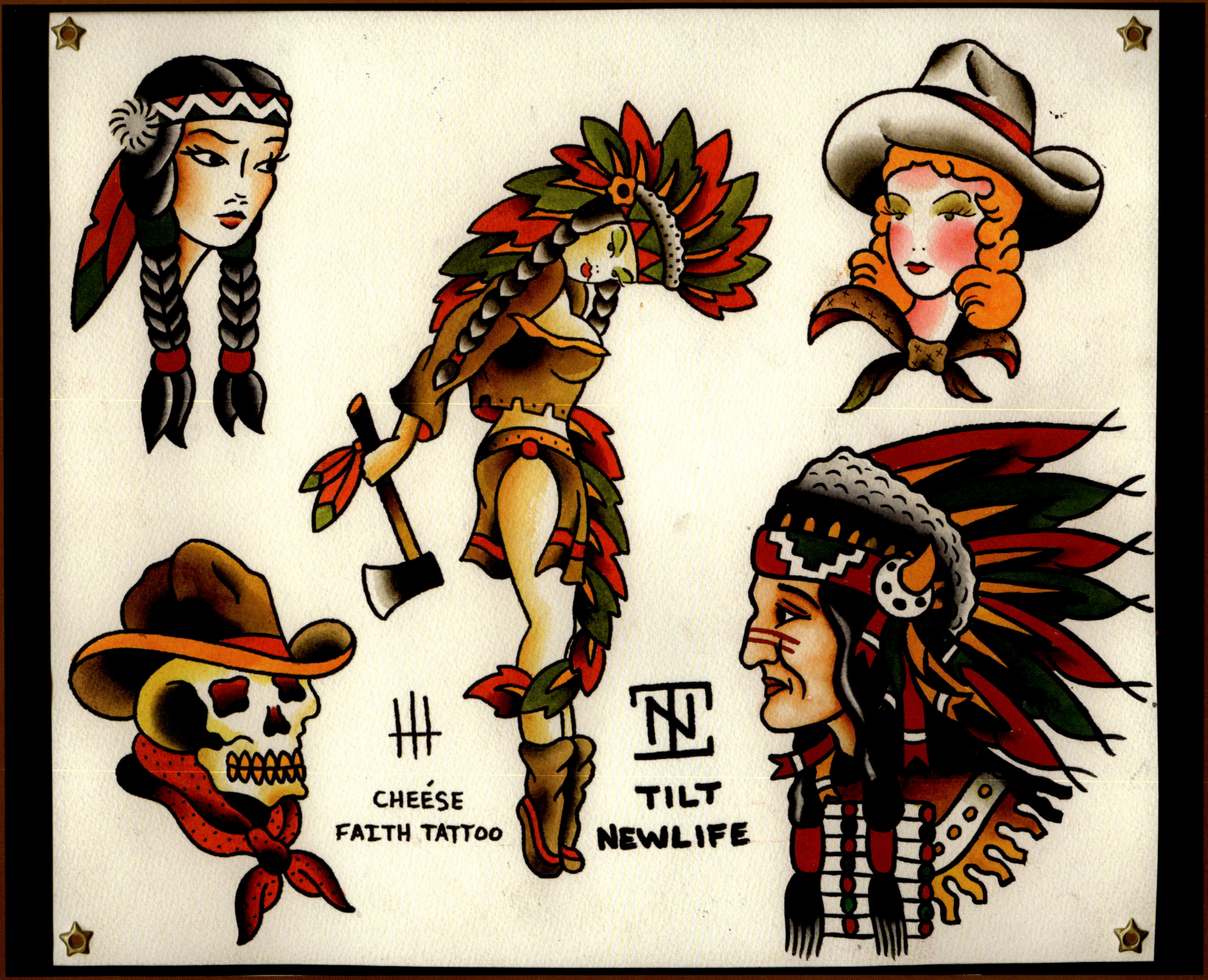

Ben Cheése & Tilt

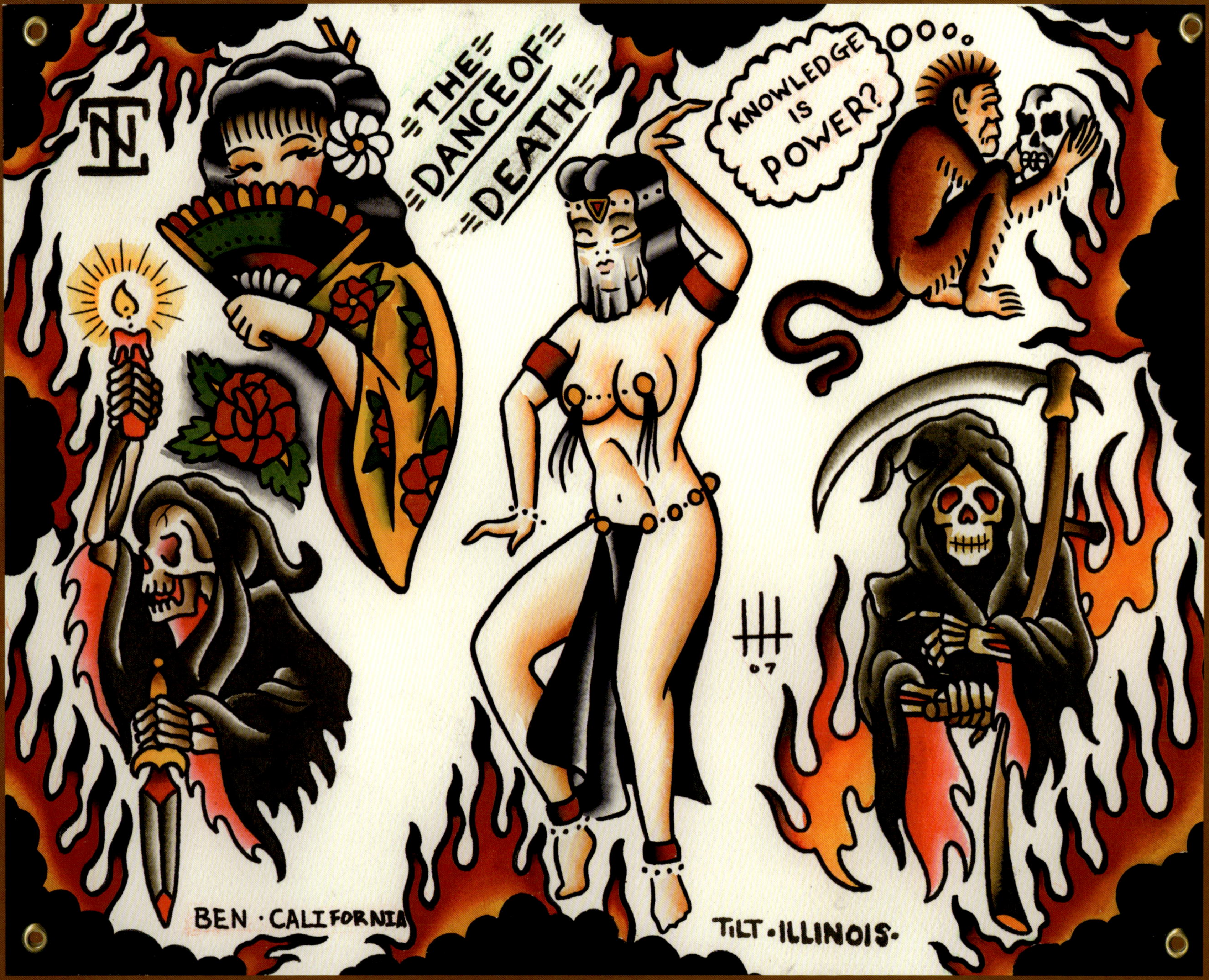

Ben Cheése & Tilt

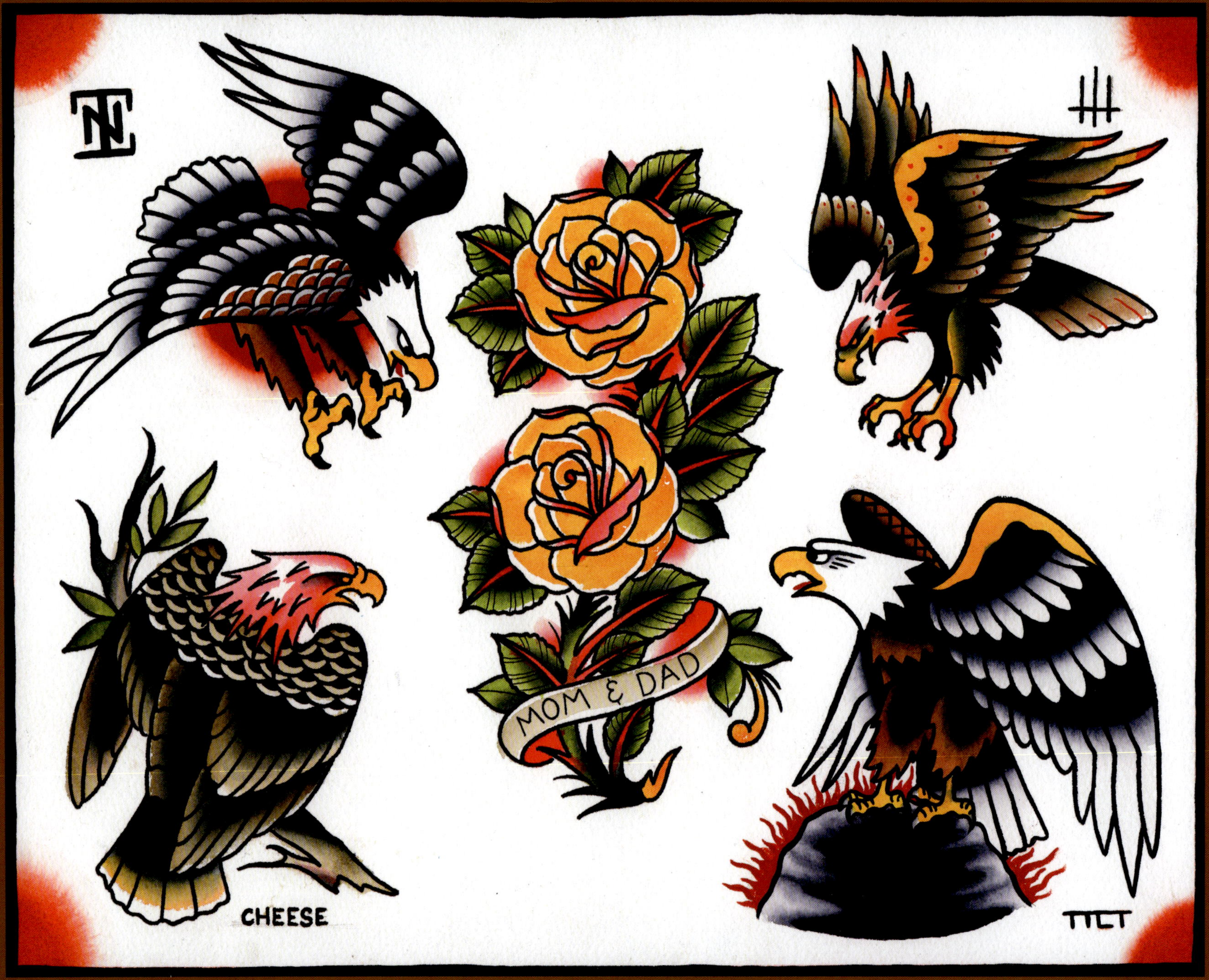

Ben Cheése & Tilt

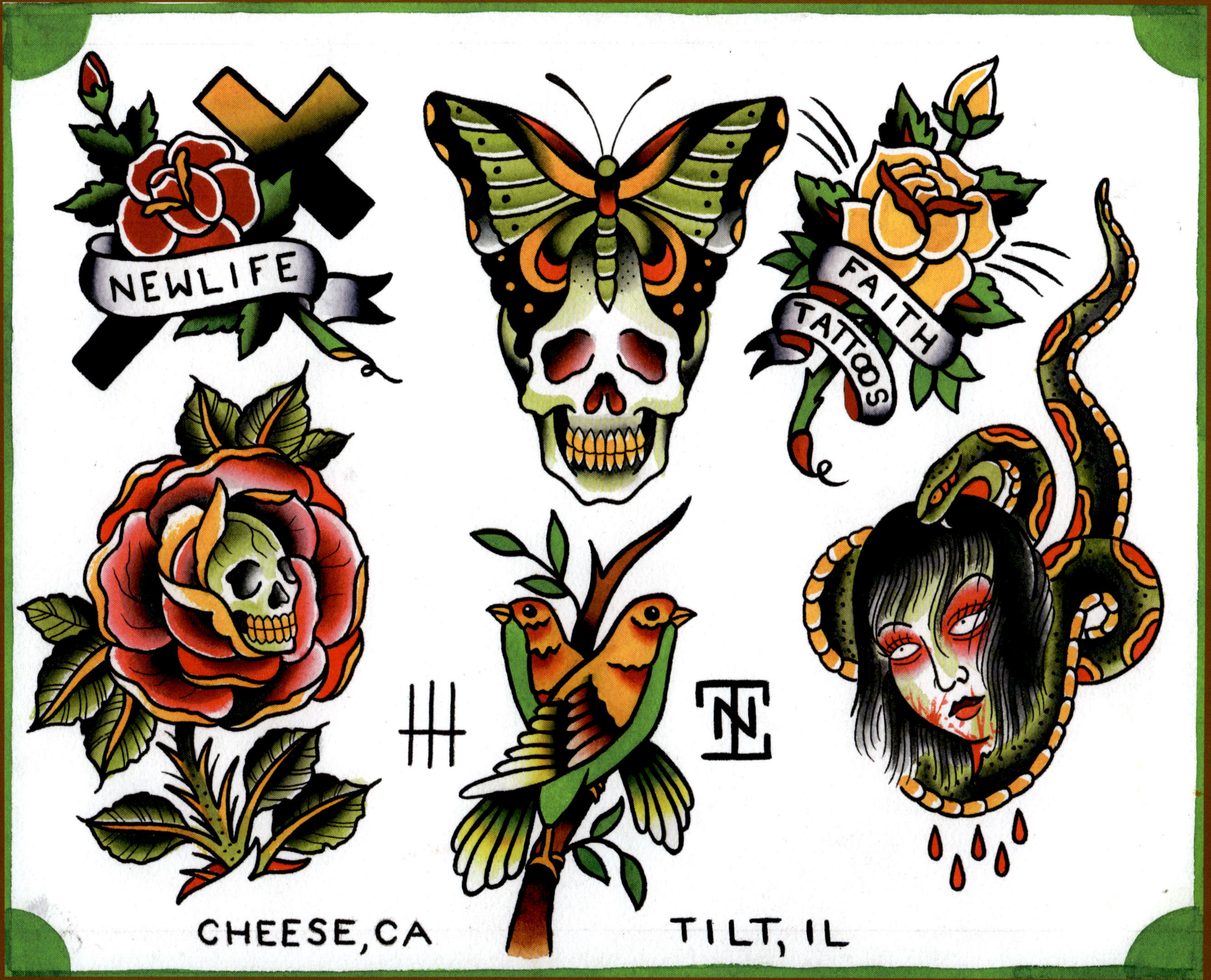

Ben Cheése & Tilt

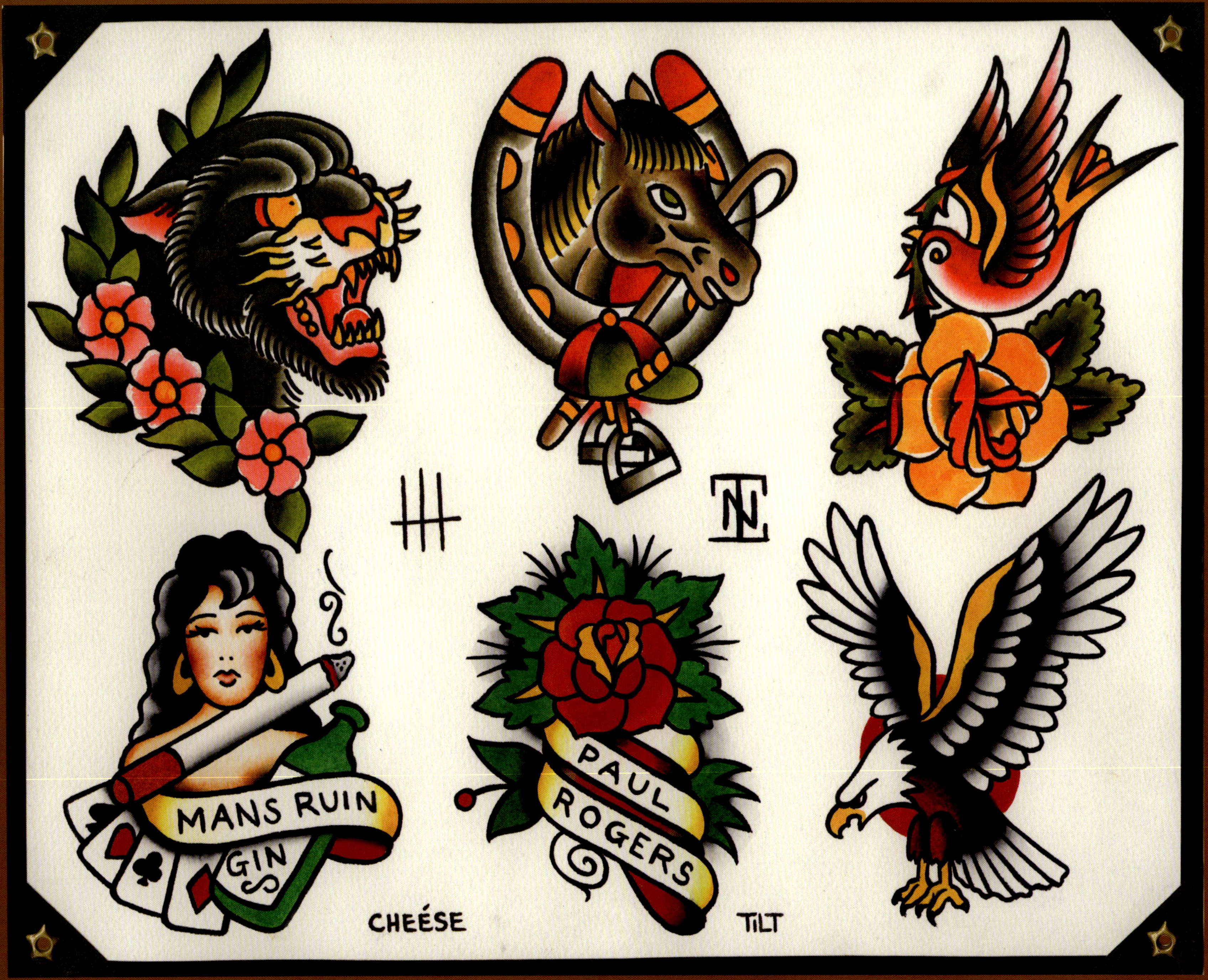

Ben Cheése & Tilt

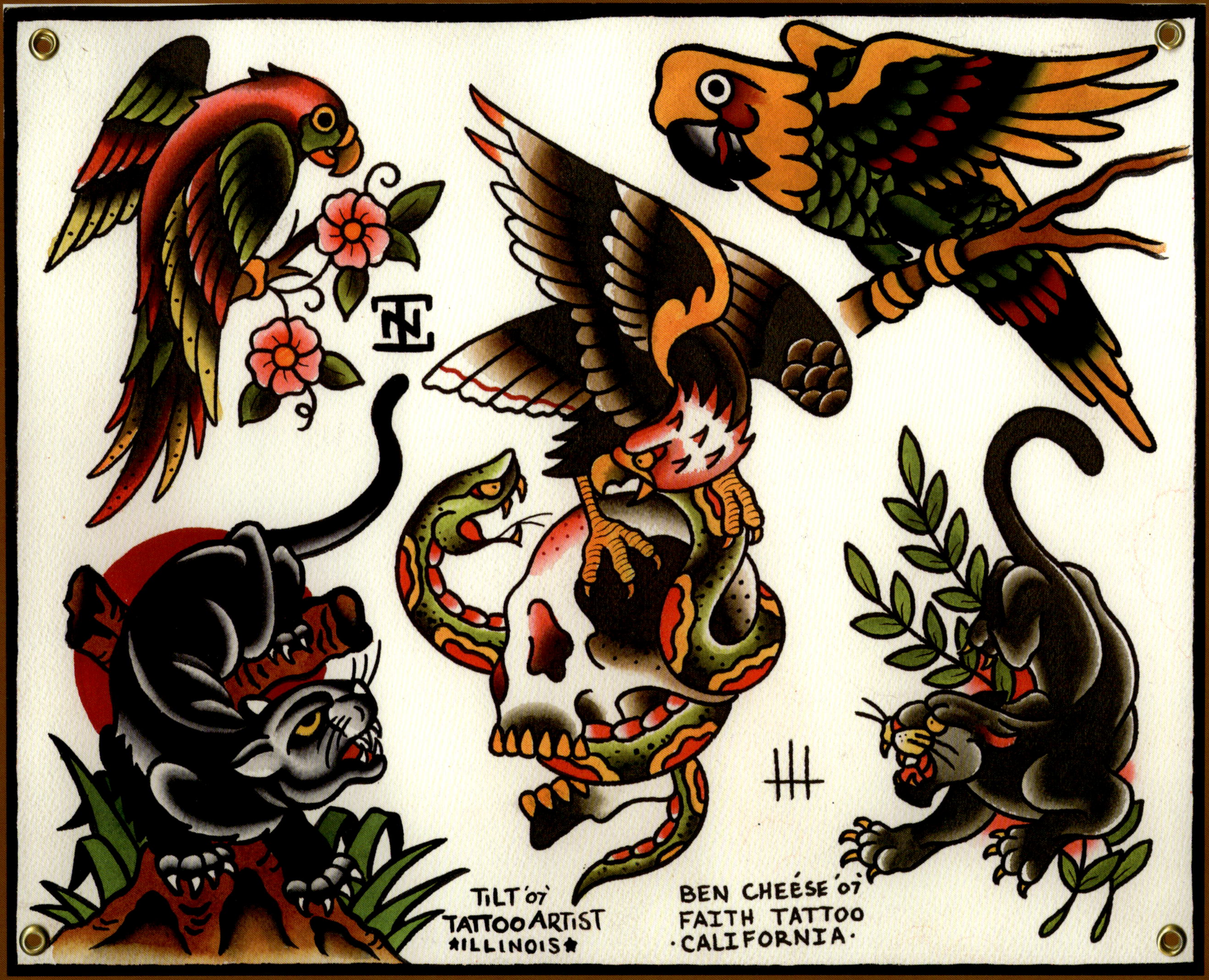

Ben Cheése & Tilt

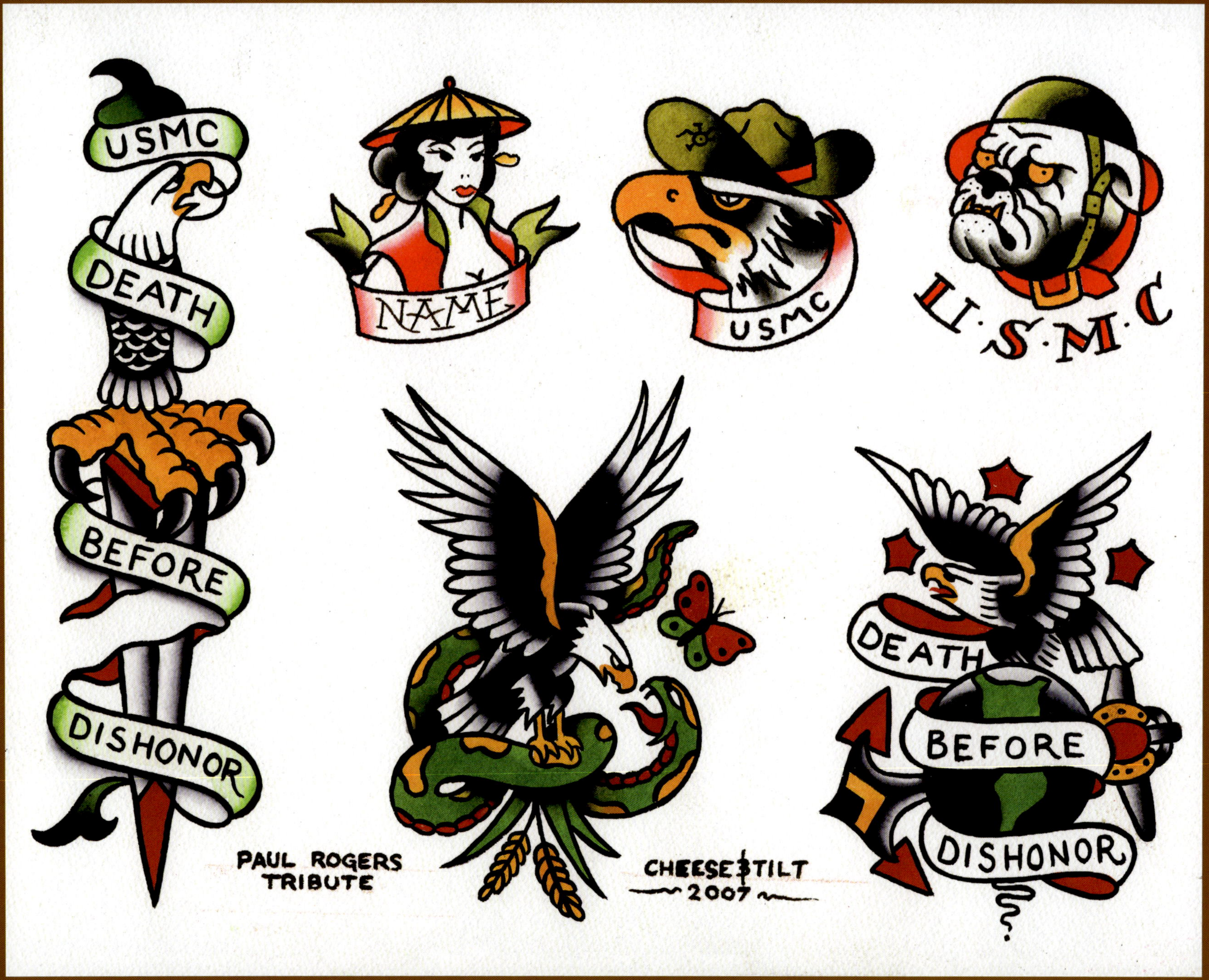

Ben Cheése & Tilt

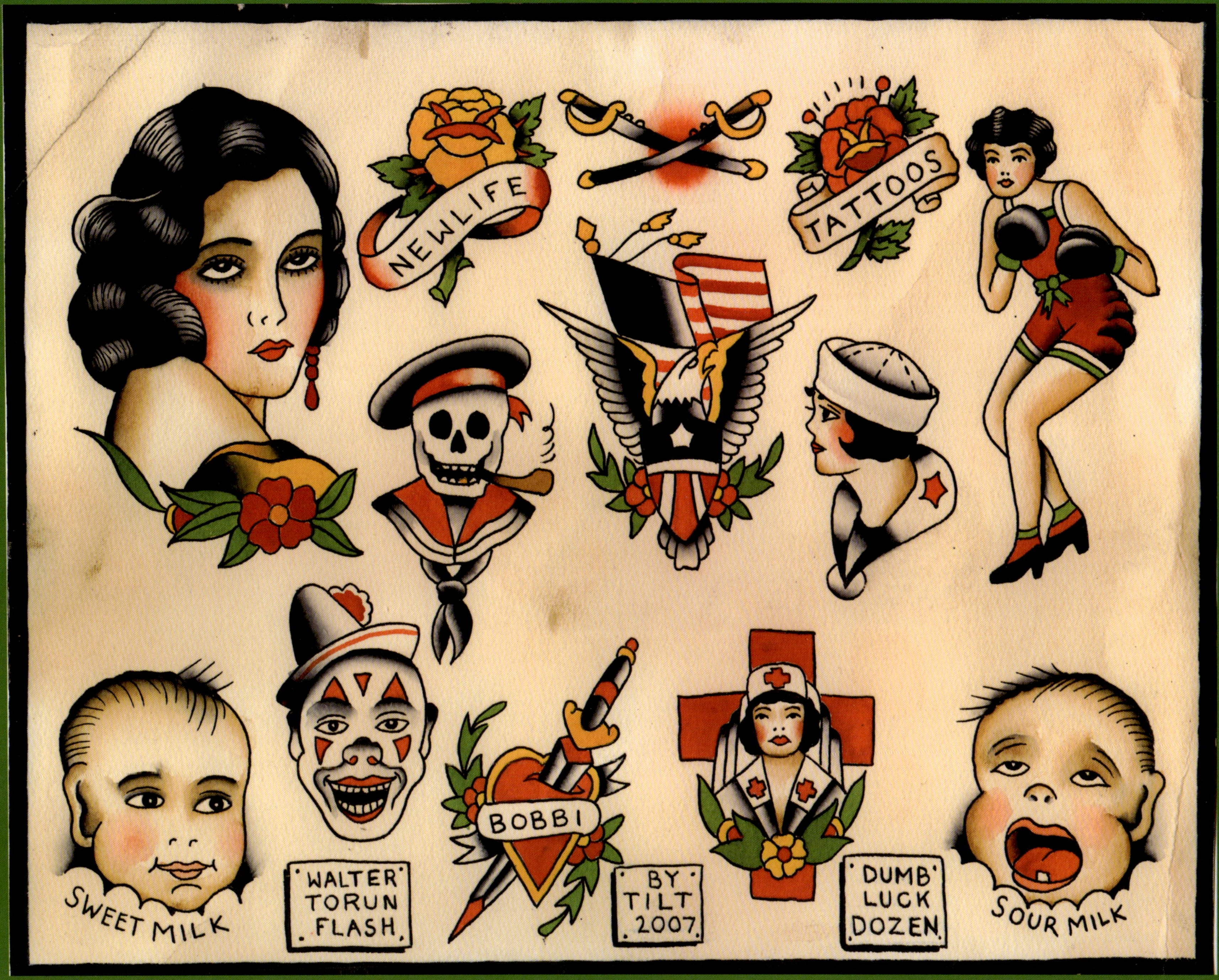
NEWLIFE
TATTOOS
BOBBI
SWEET MILK
WALTER TORUN FLASH
BY TILT 2007
DUMB LUCK DOZEN
SOUR MILK

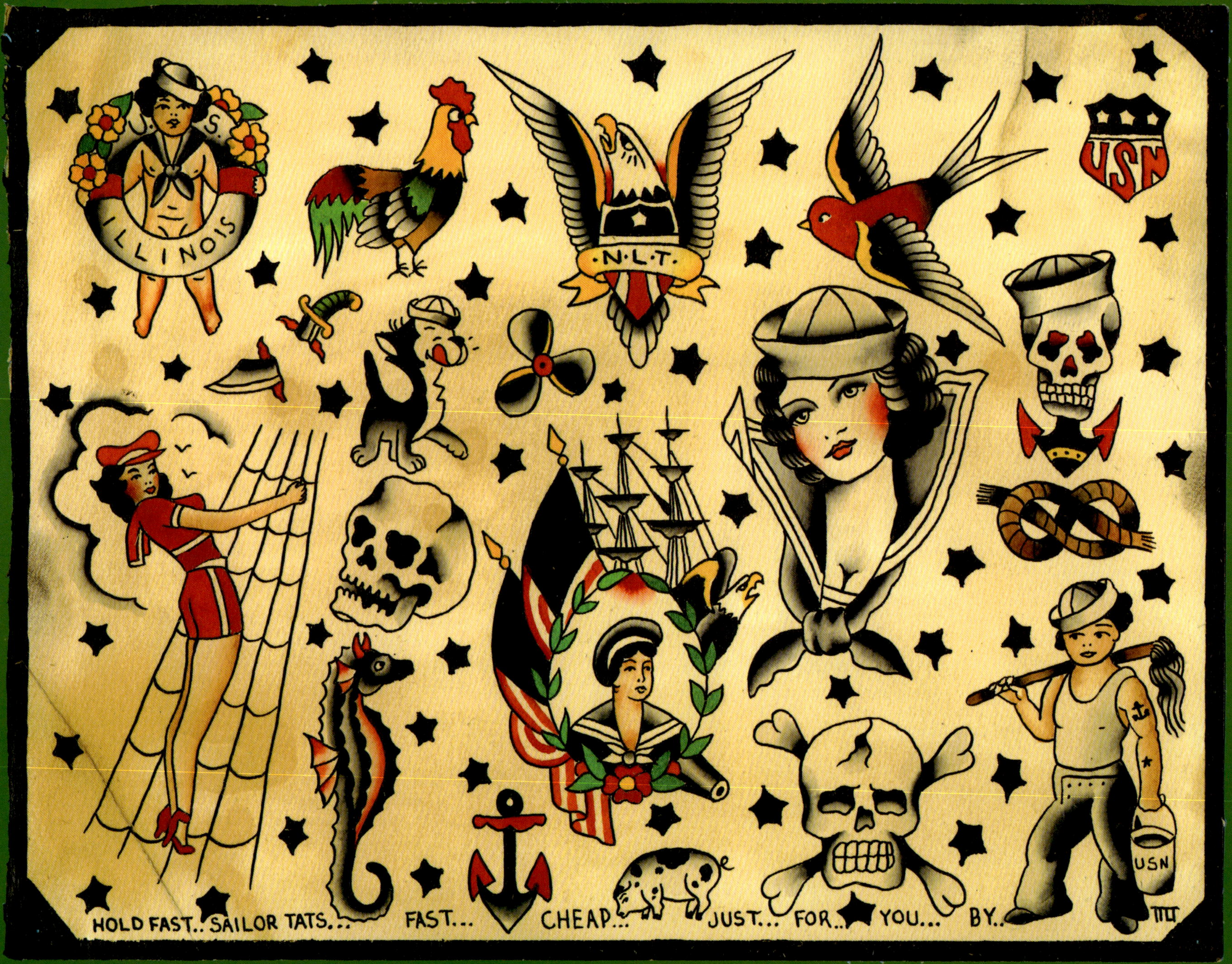
U.S.
ILLINOIS
N.L.T.
USN
USN
HOLD FAST.. SAILOR TATS... FAST... CHEAP... JUST... FOR.. YOU... BY..

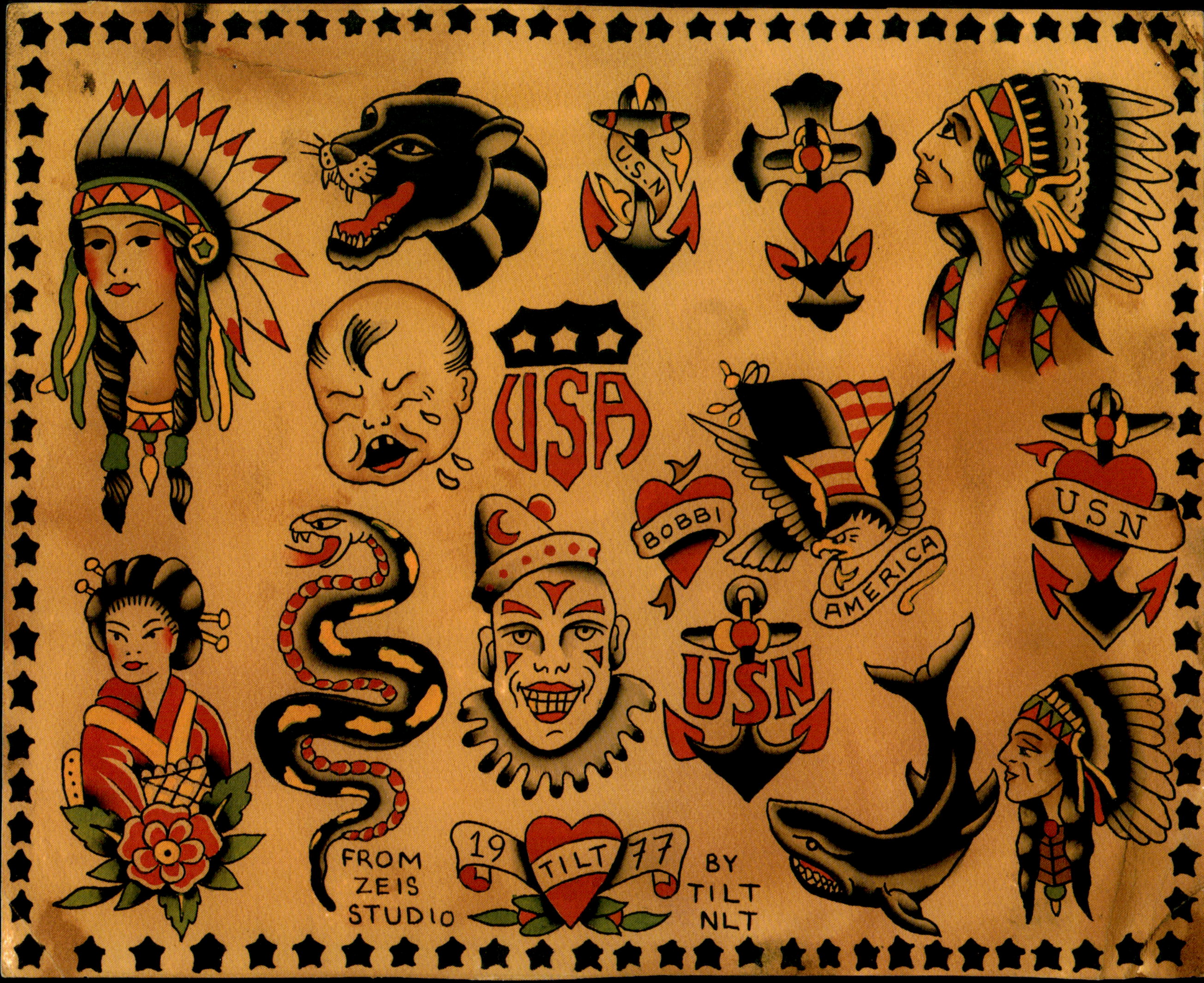
U.S.N
USA
BOBBI
AMERICA
USN
USN
FROM
ZEIS
STUDIO
19
TILT
77
BY
TILT
NLT

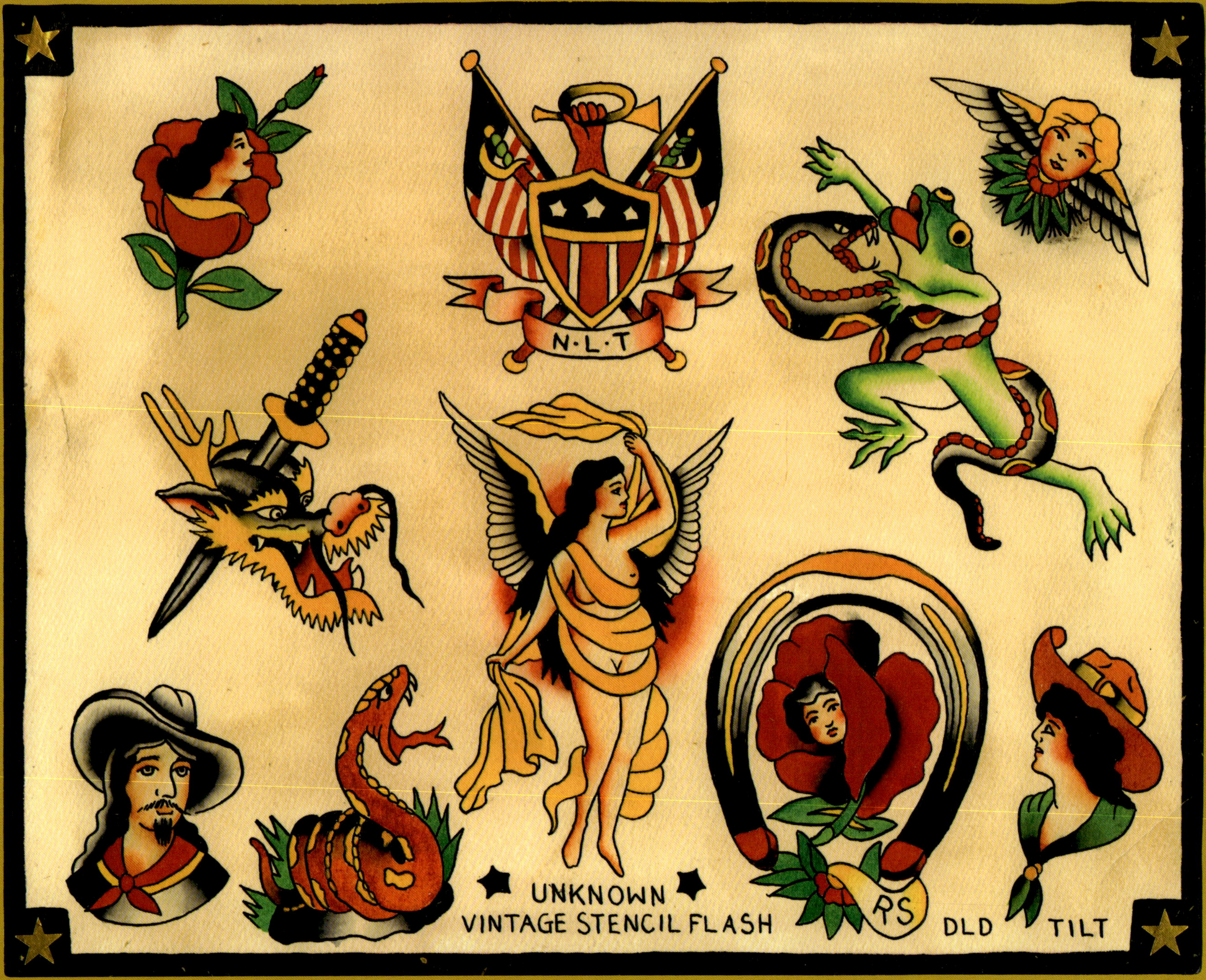
N·L·T
RS
UNKNOWN
VINTAGE STENCIL FLASH
DLD
TILT

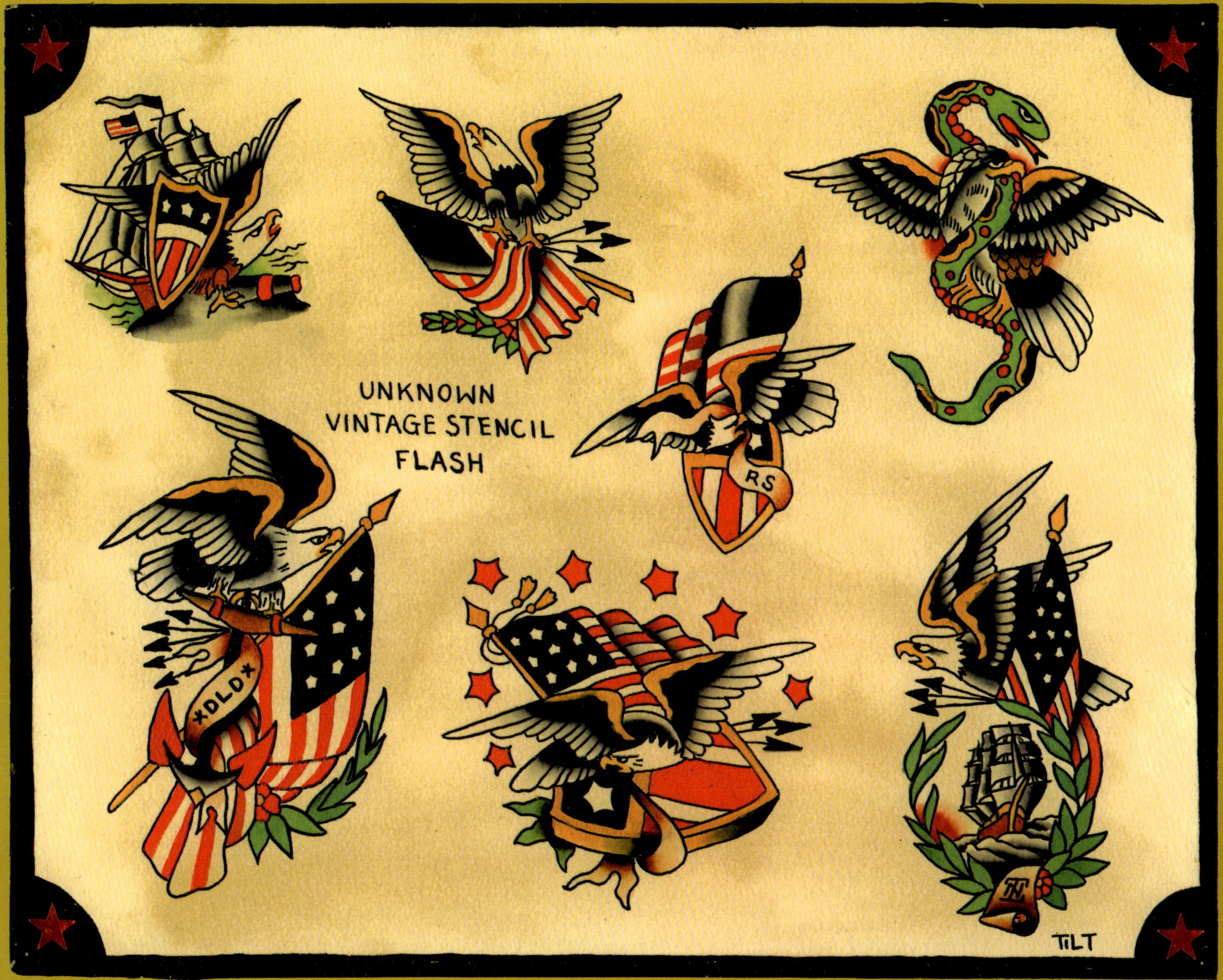
UNKNOWN
VINTAGE STENCIL
FLASH
RS
XDLDX
TILT

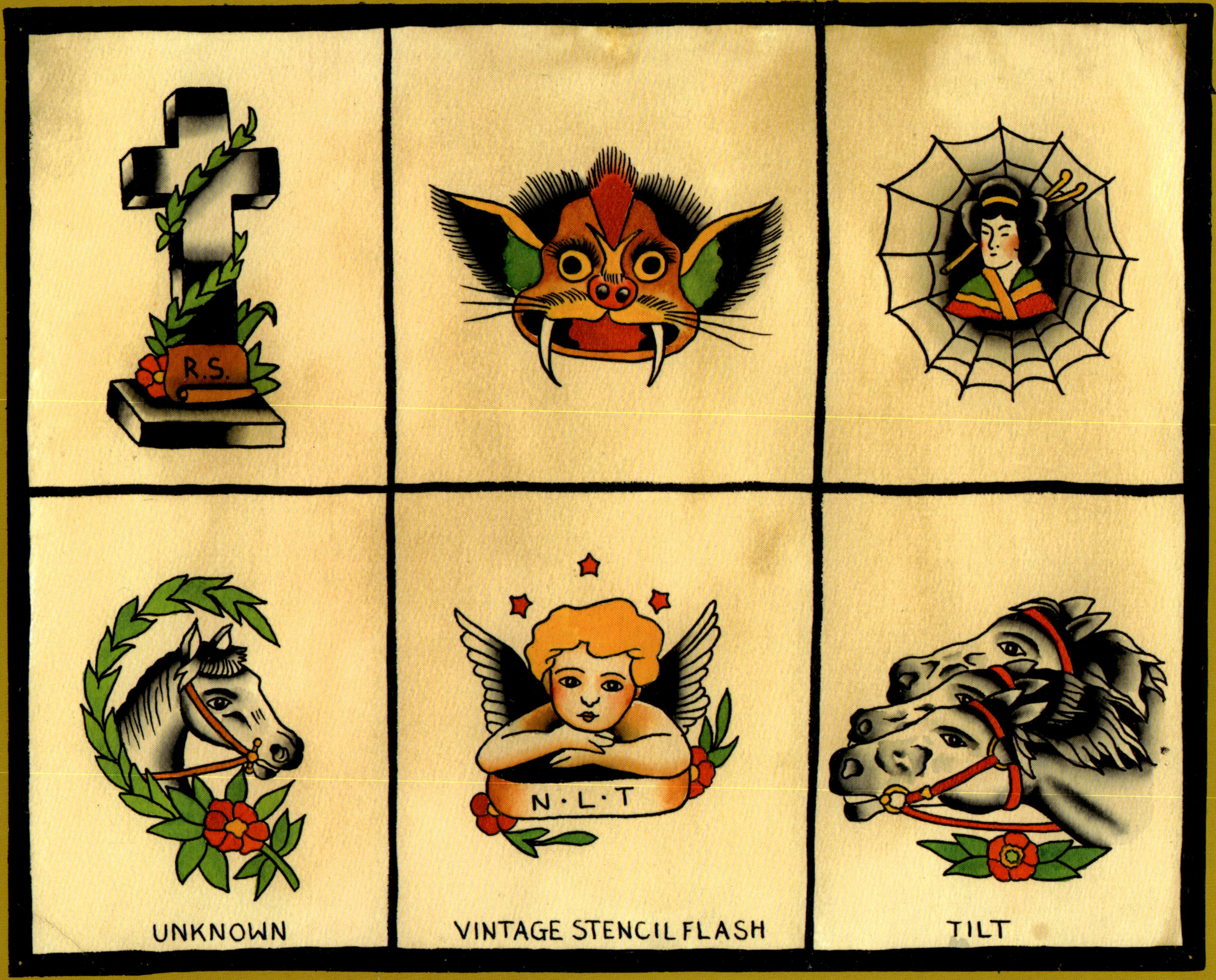
R.S.
N·L·T
UNKNOWN
VINTAGE STENCIL FLASH
TILT

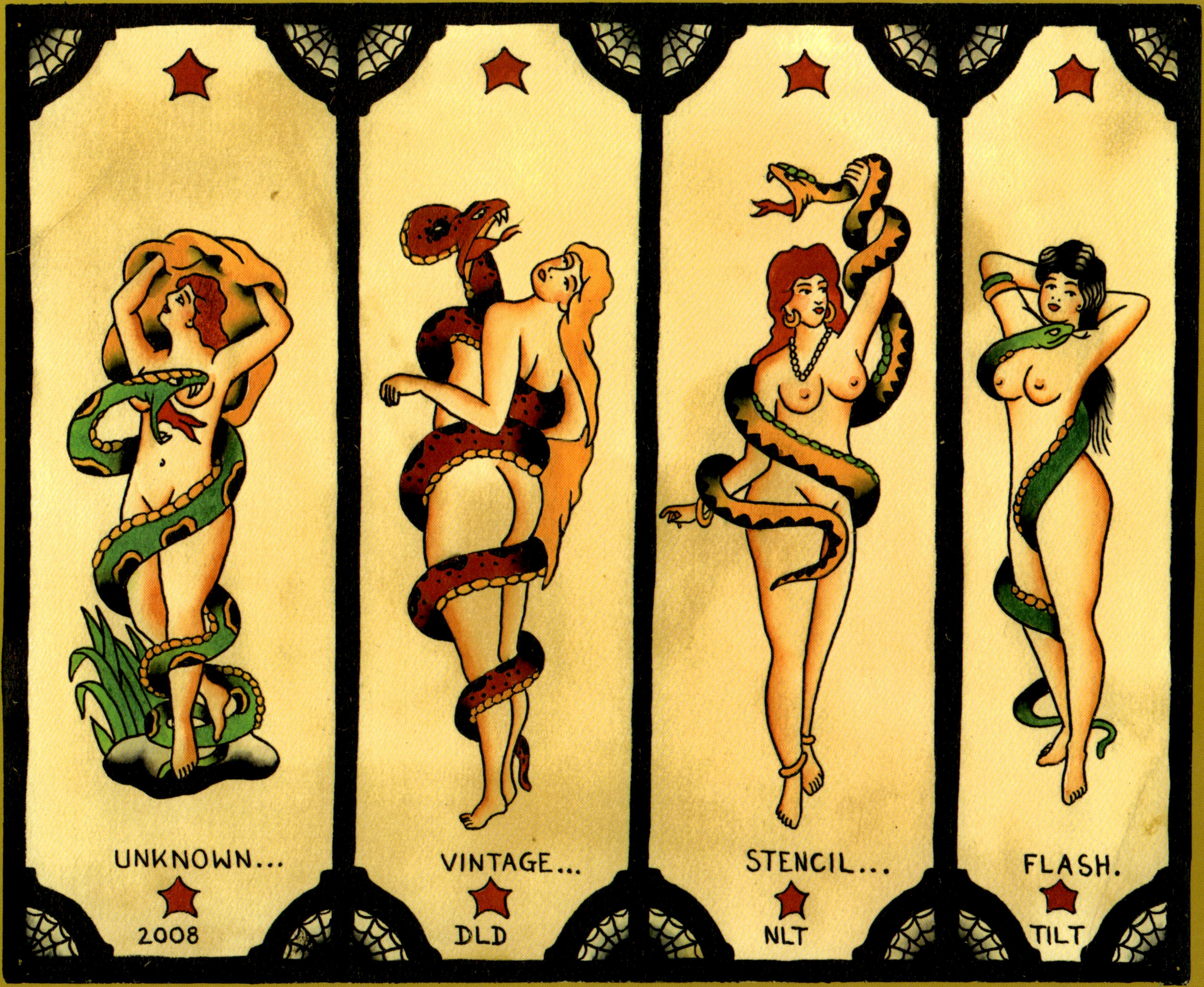
UNKNOWN...
2008
VINTAGE...
DLD
STENCIL...
NLT
FLASH.
TILT

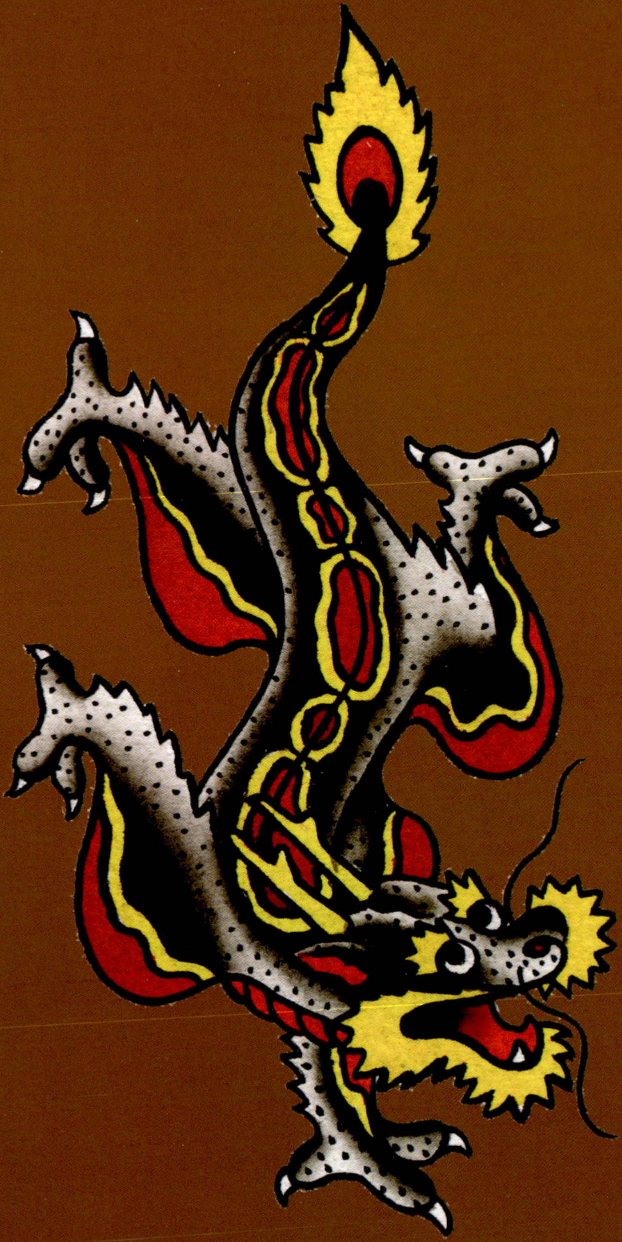